Star Civilizations 101

To Charisse,
Blessings to you
beautiful Soul!
Barbara Stone, PhD

Barbara Stone, PhD

Star Civilizations 101

First edition June 2021
Second edition March 2023

The names and identifying details of case histories included in this book have been changed to protect client identity. The information on Star Civilizations is presented as food for thought for the reader to evaluate whether or not it resonates as truth. The content is for general informational purposes only and is not a complete listing of all Star Civilizations in relationship to our planet. No warranties are implied about the reliability of the authors mentioned. If you apply any of the information in this book, you do so at your own risk. While overwhelming evidence of the presence of Star Civilizations is available, many people still ridicule anyone who believes this evidence is true.

"Soul Detective" is a registered trademark for Dr. Stone's work. For the ease of the reader, the ® symbol will not be used throughout the book.

Stonepower Publishing
1817 State Route 83, Unit 513
Millersburg, OH 44654

Print book ISBN: 978-0-578-24783-0

e-book ISBN 978-1-893129-10-8

Cover image Circinus galaxy. Image credit: images-assets.nasa.gov/image/PIA13942/PIA13942~orig.jpg
Secondary Creator Credit: NASA/JPL-Caltech/UCLA 3-24-2011

Printed in the United States of America

Other Books by this author

Invisible Roots: How Healing Past Life Trauma Can Liberate Your Present (2008)

Case histories of clients whose emotional and mental disturbances originated in Past Life Trauma and Earthbound Spirit Attachments, plus the Soul Detective Protocols Dr. Stone developed to safely and gently resolve these problems.

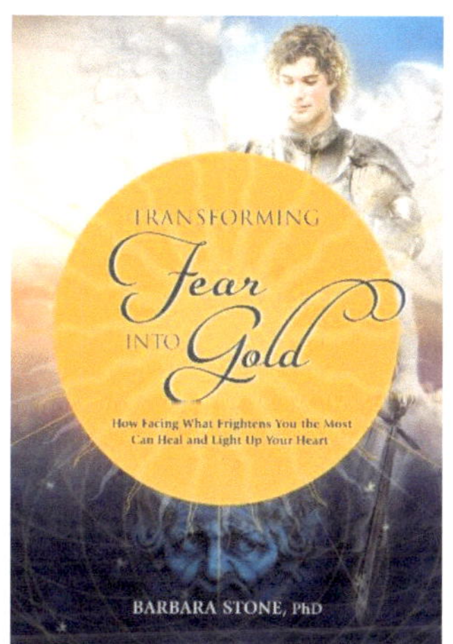

Transforming Fear into Gold: How Facing What Frightens You the Most Can Heal and Light Up Your Heart

Section 1: "Transforming the Dark Side"

Section 2: "I Want This Nightmare to End"

Section 3: "Hope for Humanity"

Cancer As Initiation: Surviving the Fire (1991)

The personal, inspiring story of Dr. Stone's diagnosis of breast cancer in 1991 and the complementary treatment plan she used to survive, including Western treatments of surgery, radiation, and chemotherapy and Eastern practices of yoga, meditation, herbs, and acupuncture.

Dedication

This book is dedicated to Commander Valiant Thor and all the other Star People who have dared come to Earth to help us evolve, and to all the humans who have listened to them!

Table of Contents

Foreword

I feel honored to write the foreword to *Star Civilizations 101* by Barbara Stone, PhD. Her excellent book is a valuable gift to people interested in extraterrestrial life as well as those who are only curious about whether life might exist on other planets. Dr. Stone presents material about various and unique extraterrestrials, their origins, reasons for contacting humans, their histories, and their interactions with our species. An open mind is necessary when reading her very carefully researched book. Concepts are presented for the first time, and some are almost beyond belief. Her book is beautifully illustrated with photographs and artwork.

Carl Sagan, the late famed and extremely well-respected astronomer, considered one of the best-known scientists of the 20th century, said before his death in 1996, "Surely there may be other inhabited planets." Although, at another time he added, "No definitive, unambiguous evidence for extraterrestrial life has been found, much to our ignorance." He also said, "There are more stars in our Universe than there are grains of sand on all the beaches on Earth."

The Hubble Ultra Deep Field exploration in 2018 estimated that there are about 200 billion galaxies in the observable universe—and even more impressive, suggested that there are more than two trillion galaxies, many beyond detection. To make it more personal, scientists from the Kepler and Gaia explorations say our own galaxy, the Milky Way, has a billion stars and 100 billion planets, 300 million of which are habitable. Just from these huge numbers, some would speculate that we on Earth are not alone in the universe.

The subject of extraterrestrial life is one that has been of immense interest to me since I was 20 years old. A friend of the family gave me Retired Major Donald Keyhoe's fascinating book, *The Flying Saucers are Real.* Major Keyhoe was an American Marine Naval aviator who wrote about the experiences of United States Air Force fighters, personnel, and other aviators with unidentified aircraft, and the government cover-up of these encounters. In the years that followed, I have read numerous books on the subject, including Timothy Good's 1987, *Above Top Secret: The Worldwide U.F.O. Cover-up*, which is about many countries' dealings with the subject. A few countries have revealed the existence of UFOs to their people. Only recently, our own government has admitted that UFOs have been seen by some naval and air force pilots.

Before I retired, in my work as a clinical psychologist, I used hypnosis to successfully relieve symptoms and problems. Over the years of my practice, quite a few of the patients I regressed remembered CE4's, close encounters of the fourth kind, which means abduction by or contact with one or more aliens. Fortunately, in about half of my abduction cases, the Star People performed a physical healing on my patients. Most of the aliens were described as what is widely known as a grey: a short being, with huge eyes, no ears, and bald.

For many years, I have been a member of MUFON, the mutual UFO network, which carefully researches sightings from around the world. Each month MUFON publishes its findings: the number of sightings from various countries, from our states, the size and shape of the crafts, the distance from the observers, and often the number of entities seen, as well as personal accounts of sightings and/or encounters. For example, in the December 2020 edition, 493 sightings from 28 countries were reported, 20 entities observed, and 13 landings, hoverings, or take offs.

According to a 1987 Gallup poll, almost half of U. S. citizens believed in UFOs, and one out of eleven reported having seen them. All these years later, it is probable that even more than one half believe in UFOs, especially with the success of movies such as *ET, Close Encounters of the Third Kind,* the *Star Wars* series, and other media soft disclosures which present truth as if it is fiction. I feel frustrated that I have never seen a UFO.

After reading *Star Civilizations*, I have learned of star citizens I never knew of, but now acknowledge are credible. UFOs exist and are piloted by technologically-advanced intelligent beings from other planets, and this ground-breaking book describes some of the passengers in those spacecraft.

Edith Fiore, Ph. D. (retired Clinical Psychologist)

Preface

When I was 42 years old, I found a lump in my breast that was malignant. The night before my surgery to remove the tumor, I was praying for help to get through whatever was ahead. In my mind's eye, I saw Jesus come and stand before me. Having been raised in the Christian tradition, Jesus was the face that spoke the most love to my soul. Others raised in different traditions might have seen Krishna, Quan Yin, Mother Mary, or White Buffalo Calf Woman as the face radiating Divine Love. Jesus tapped on my sternum and communicated a complete telepathic thought, "I now heal your soul." With that touch of the master, a deep wound in my soul healed, and I absolutely knew I would survive the cancer. I was filled with joy! That day happened in 1991, and now 30 years later, I am in radiant health.

Whatever Is Most Needed

After I recovered, I felt so grateful to be alive and to have a chance to meet my grandchildren that I dedicated my life to serving God in whatever way was most needed for the collective good. Shortly after that prayer, the woman I call Paula in my book *Transforming Fear into Gold* (2012) walked into my office. She said she was a survivor of Ritual Abuse from a group that worshipped Satan. She told me unspeakable horrors of torture and human sacrifice and then asked me to write her story. That book took me 20 years to get into print. Working with Paula is the reason I started to learn energy therapies, to cope with my vicarious traumatization just from hearing what had happened to her. Along the way, I sometimes wished I had not given my consent for “whatever is most needed,” because the journey was difficult. But now, Paula is doing well, and light is revealing the abuses done in the name of darkness on this planet. As Paula said, “I want this nightmare to end!” The work with Paula turned into a great blessing in my life, as working with energy therapies transformed me and my practice.

What Next?

Several years ago, I asked Spirit what I most needed to focus on next. What I heard from my intuitive guidance was a call to work with ETs. I responded, "Wow, that is way out of my comfort zone! Will they come to my front door?" I was imagining flying purple people eaters on my doorstep! Spirit just communicated telepathically, "You will know, and they will know." From that point on, I started noticing things that came up about Extraterrestrials in my Soul Detective work. This book is the result of my research on the topic. I have no memory of ever being personally abducted, but I have talked with people who say they have had that experience.

Angelic Help

I believe that I saw a Star Person in the third dimension once. On my way to the airport for my older sister’s memorial service, I got stuck in a snowbank in a remote area. I prayed for help, and a minute later, an incredibly handsome man showed up in an SUV. He did not say anything, but he got out a yellow tow belt, hooked my car up to his, and pulled me out of the snowbank. I watched in awe, especially since I had never seen a yellow tow belt before. I wondered whether I should offer him $20 for pulling me out, but I was pretty sure he was an angel, so I asked him, “What is your name?”

He responded, "My name is Justin, and this is what I do for fun." I thought, "Justin—he came just-in time so I could catch my plane!" I thanked him warmly for helping me. I watched as he left, going around a bend in the road, but his car never reappeared at the next bend in the road. Then I knew from his disappearance that he really was an angel!

I believe that many of the spiritual helpers that show up in my Soul Detective work are higher dimensional beings from the Stars. These helpers are available to all of us, but because of the law of free will, they are not allowed to intervene unless we ask for help. I asked Jesus if it was safe for me to publish this book, as some people disclosing information about extraterrestrials have been killed or have disappeared. Jesus sent me the telepathic thought, "It is not safe to not publish it!" People need to know this information, as the future of our planet and our whole galaxy is at stake.

Gratitude List

I thank all my clients, Soul Detective students, Soul Detective teachers, colleagues, friends, family, and most of all, my husband, Robert Alcorn, MD, for their presence and contributions to this spiritual journey!

I also thank my daughter, Sarah Courtemanche, for editing this book.

I am enormously grateful to all the Beings of Light from higher realms who are helping our planet to raise our vibration out of fear and war into love, peace, and joy!

"Get rid of the fear. You have nothing to fear. You are an immortal, timeless being who has an infinite future in a glorious universe that is so filled with beauty and life that we on this little tiny planet couldn't begin to grasp."

--Robert Dean, Retired US Army Command Sergeant Major[1]

Introduction

This book brings insight into how our souls got so deeply wounded from events in the ancient history of our race and offers guidance to heal those wounds and step into the fullness of our True Selves. This material grew out of the experiences of my clients having past lives and parallel lives on other planets and their interactions with Star Civilizations. My own inner work has also presented peek holes into other worlds and telepathic communication with some of the Creator Gods spoken of in ancient texts. Through this work, I developed a Soul Detective protocol to remove extra-terrestrial interference patterns, including implants. This book is my truth, what makes sense in my innermost wisdom. If this material resonates as truth in your soul and heals your heart, wonderful! If it does not resonate as truth for you, feel

---

[1] Cassidy, K. (2008, October 21). *Video interview of Bob Dean: "The Coming of Nibiru."* United States: Project Camelot. https://www.youtube.com/watch?v=sFxB4mdUNxI

free to lay it aside and find your own truth and the healing path that is right for your soul.

Many Star Civilizations have been interacting with humans for thousands of years. Most of them are humanoid, looking a lot like us, and are benevolent. Some sightings of angels that people have reported down through the centuries may be helpful Star Beings in higher dimensions, where they do not have physical bodies, just bodies made of brilliant light.

"Angel of Global Peace"
Original Visionary Artwork by Eva M. Sakmar-Sullivan
www.stardolphin.com

Some Star Civilizations are neutral, observing us from their spaceships and studying our physiology and culture for their university term projects. A few of them are detrimental, mostly Reptilians and some types of Greys, but insiders from the US Military claim that our Space Force now has technology superior to theirs, and an Alliance is working to overcome their interference in our lives.

Med Beds

As we put fear aside and disclosure of the presence of Star Civilizations becomes more prevalent, we open the way to receive the profound benefits our Star Friends can bring to humanity in helping us raise our spiritual vibration to be ready for ascension, technology to bring us anti-gravity and free energy devices, and health care technology that can eradicate disease, regenerate organs, reverse the aging process, and extend the lifespan. We have seen this alien healing technology called Medical Beds, Med Beds for short, in movies such as *Star Trek* and this five-minute clip from the movie *Passengers* where Aurora saves Jim by putting him in a tube-shaped Med Bed which scans his body and repairs it: https://youtu.be/7-2Z8Re7qV0

According to Michael Salla's inside information, we already have this healing technology in the secret space programs, and it will be released to the public soon, transforming the health care system.[2] Another YouTube describing the Med

---

[2] Salla, M. (2021, March 27). Webinar "Great Awakening vs. Global Reset: How Full Disclosure Trumps Transhumanism & Artificial Intelligence." www.exopolitics.org

Beds in more detail is from Canadian psychic Tracey Milne at https://www.youtube.com/watch?v=H5aKTsI1NFU.

Superman

Superman is a fictitious Star Being who captured the imagination of the American people when his story was first published in comic books in 1938. Many TV shows and movies have been made of this superhero who came from the planet Krypton, the source of his superpowers. As a baby, named Kal-El at birth, Superman was sent to Earth in a space capsule by his parents just before a natural disaster destroyed their planet. Superman could see better, with his x-ray vision; he could hear better; and he could levitate, flying through the air. He tirelessly worked for justice and prevention of evil takeovers. While Superman is fiction, some of the helpful Star Civilizations in contact with Earth at present also have what we would consider superpowers and have been helping us fend off nefarious ET activity for centuries.

Galactic War between the Nordics and Reptilians

A Galactic War has been going on for a long time between the beneficial Nordic Star Civilization and the detrimental Reptilians, but this conflict is not just among different Star Civilizations: this war rages within each of us between the reptilian part of our brain that has ruthless survival programming, hoarding a huge stash of toilet paper in the COVID-19 crisis, and the limbic brain and neo-cortex, which is programmed to value interpersonal relationships.

The goal of this book is to present a cosmic view of the interaction of conscious beings from other planets with humans on Earth, so we understand the bigger picture of the political situation with Extra Terrestrials, called "Exopolitics" by author Dr. Michael Salla. This insight can help us overcome our fear of lack and bring internal peace by integrating our shadow reptilian parts, to bring balance to the dark and light within our own hearts. This integration creates a powerful energy vortex within the soul and empowers a person to stand in the fullness of one's direct connection to Divinity, one's True Self/Higher Self, which is a direct connection to Source. Each person who does this work for inner peace and chooses to stand in the fullness of human potential improves our chances of collectively electing a path of global peace, sustainability, and harmony.

Galactic History

Studying galactic history helps us understand how other civilizations that came from the stars have impacted the genetic development of Homo sapiens, why they genetically engineered our species, and how we can transcend the challenges resulting from their design for the human race.

I believe the great Creator of All infinitely and unconditionally loves everyone and everything in all of creation, and that when we attune to and align with this energy, we can develop into magnificent, empowered, radiant beings. To get from the fear programs predominant in the consciousness of most of humanity into that wondrous vision of our future, we need to heal the deep wounds we have as a species.

Ascending from Third Dimensional Duality and Scarcity

Most of society has been locked into a worldview where resources are insufficient for everyone, where the ones who have the most military power or the most money set the rules, and where war tears up families and countries. In a multi-dimensional model of consciousness, this situation is classified as third dimensional duality, which splits good and evil, assigning good to ourselves and evil to those not of our religion, race, culture, or political party. The emotions predominant in the heart of many on our planet at the present time are the lower fourth dimensional feelings of fear, rage, hate, shame, and terror. For our planet and our species to survive, we need to radically change this perspective and ascend into the upper part of the fourth dimension, where love, peace, forgiveness, joy, and unity consciousness rule. When we realize we are all passengers on the spaceship Earth, all connected in the web of life here, and then make decisions from the heart about what is in the highest good of everyone, peace will come to this planet.

NASA's famous "Blue Marble" image
Credit: NASA, Rob Simmons

Webster's definition of Extra-terrestrial:
originating, existing, or occurring outside the earth or its atmosphere

From the upper fourth dimension, we can further ascend into the fifth dimensional state of being in which we are able to create and manifest with thought alone, being conscious co-creators of our lives. If people are locked into negative thinking about our enemies defeating us and global catastrophes striking, we would not want these thoughts to manifest! Our hearts need to be pure and centered in love before we get this kind of power and ability to create with thought alone in the 5th dimension.

The theory of evolution says that all creatures on this planet developed over time from other creatures, starting with single-celled organisms and then evolving into more complex forms. While evolution does happen, slowly over time, sometimes quantum shifts have happened in human development, like the sudden jump from *Homo sapiens,* who could not talk, to *Homo sapiens sapiens,* who had speech, without intermediate evolutionary steps. A possible explanation for rapid leaps would be that Star Civilizations have helped our development as a species. Crick and Watson, the scientists who discovered the double-helix form of DNA, came to the conclusion in their 1981 book *Life Itself* that due to the way life forms begin, the origins of our species had to come from somewhere off of this planet.

Starseeds

Perhaps some people whose home culture is in the Stars may have incarnated into human bodies, bringing the soul values of their home worlds to Earth to help raise the vibration of this planet. Some people reading this book may identify with one Star Civilization or another as being their true home. We call these people "Starseeds," here to help with the ascension process for Earth.

Altair
NASA ID: PIA04204
Secondary Creator Credit:
NASA/JPL/Caltech/Steve Golden
Altair, a star spinning so fast its mid-section is stretched out has been directly measured by an ultra-high-resolution NASA telescope system on Palomar Mountain near San Diego.

Chapter 1: Whales and Dolphins

Whales and dolphins, collectively called cetaceans, have been swimming in the waters of this planet for over 50 million years.[3] On the other hand, most scientists estimate that Homo sapiens have been on this planet for approximately 200,000 years. Authors of the book *Forbidden Archeology* cite evidence of human remains that are five million years old. With careful scholarly research, they document the cover-up in the scientific community of evidence that does not fit mainstream scientific theories.[4] Whichever timeline is more accurate about how long humans have been on Earth, the whales have been here much longer!

All whale photos in this chapter are by Vicki Bosler-Kilmer

[3] Foer, J. (2015, May). "It's Time for a Conversation: Breaking the Communication Barrier Between Dolphins and Humans." *National Geographic*, p. 47.

[4] Cremo, M. & Thompson, R. (1998). *Forbidden Archeology: The Hidden History of the Human Race.* Bhaktivedanta Book Publishing.

Scientists who believe in the theory of evolution say that whales evolved from land mammals and adapted to life in the ocean. Science has not found a clear evolutionary path to explain the highly developed intelligence of whales. Whale evolution lacks intermediate steps in a similar way that human evolution has some missing links. Some authors say that cetaceans came here from the stars. As a group, cetaceans are superior to humans in their linguistic abilities, complex associative capacities, and their ability to survive.[5] For example, Dr. John Ford has monitored the speech of orcas off British Columbia. He found speech patterns so distinctive that he can identify dialects between orca populations and link a captive orca of unknown origin with its lost family in the wild.[6] As a calf, each dolphin invents a unique signature whistle to call itself and keeps that name for life. Dolphins remember the signature whistles of other dolphins for decades.[7] To discipline their young and chase off sharks, dolphins emit loud burst pulses of broadband packets of sound.

Dolphins sleep with one half of their brain resting and the other half alert for sharks and other danger. Then the sides of the brain trade, and the other half of the brain rests. What a system! Also, their eyes operate independently of each other. *National Geographic* says, “They’re a kind of alien intelligence sharing our planet—watching them may be the closest we’ll come to encountering ET.”[8]

---

[5] Watson, P. (2014, August 28). “The Cetacean Brain and Hominid Perceptions of Cetacean Intelligence.” https://knowledgeutopia.

[6] Ibid.

[7] Foer, 2015.

[8] Ibid, p. 36.

They also have strong social bonds and ingenious cooperative feeding strategies. Dolphins will support a group member in distress. In Australia in 2013, a large group of dolphins followed a sick dolphin into shallow water, where the whole group was at risk of becoming stranded. Humans intervened by capturing a juvenile in the group and carrying her out into the open ocean. Her cries of distress at being separated from her family drew the group back out to the safety of the sea.

Through the ability of cetaceans to echo-locate, they can see inside the bodies of others. Dolphins produce clicks which they focus and amplify to bounce off a target which can be up to half a mile away. They can also instantly detect emotional states.[9]

Rescuing a Human

One day as a team of researchers were studying a group of dolphins feeding in a circle off the shore of Los Angeles, one dolphin suddenly left the pod and headed out into the ocean. Then the whole school followed. The researchers decided to track the group to see why they suddenly had disrupted their feeding and raced away from shore full speed. Three miles out, the dolphins circled around something in the water which turned out to be a young woman from Germany who had been vacationing in LA. In a plastic bag around her neck was her passport and a note explaining that she was attempting suicide. Barely alive and suffering from hypothermia, the

[9] Ibid, p. 37.

researchers pulled her on board and took her to the lifeguard rescue boat. The dolphins saved her life.[10]

Cetaceans as ETs

Patricia Cori, a gifted clairvoyant, teaches that whales and dolphins come from a planet called Oceana, which is mostly water, a planet revolving around the Sirian star known as Sirius B, also called Satais.[11]

"Coming to Earth" Original Visionary Artwork by Eva M. Sakmar-Sullivan www.stardolphin.com

---

[10] Bearzi, M. (2012). *Dolphin Confidential: Confessions of a Field Biologist.* University of Chicago Press.

[11] Cori, 2011, *Before We Leave You: Messages from the Great Whales and the Dolphin Beings.* North Atlantic Books, p. 60.

Alex Collier says Cetaceans came from Cygnus Alpha to migrate and explore other worlds and that their songs carry the history not only of their home planet, but of the history on this planet too.[12] Most people think that humans are the most intelligent species on this planet, but let's compare a human brain with the cetacean brain.

An Extra Lobe

Humans have a three-part brain:

A. The reptilian complex which includes the brainstem and the cerebellum

B. The limbic brain

C. The supralimbic, with the neocortex covering its surface

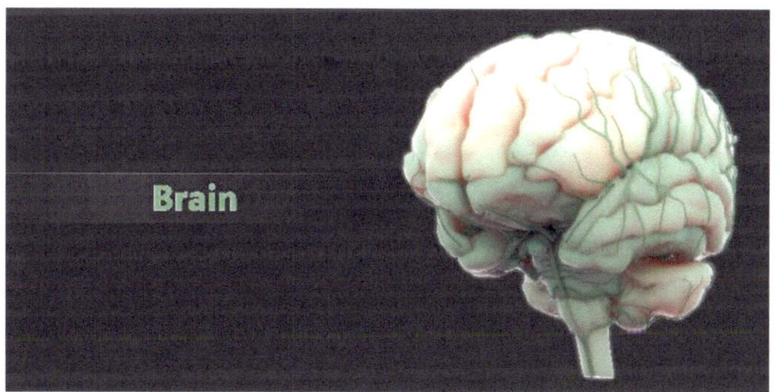

[12]Collier, A. "Alex Collier on Whales and Dolphins." Golden Age of Gaia. http://goldenageofgaia.com/disclosure/who-are-the-extraterrestrials/alex-collier-on-whales-and-dolphins/

Cetaceans have a fourth segment in their brain between the limbic and supralimbic that is called the paralimbic. This extra lobe integrates sensory and motor functions much more rapidly than is possible in the human supralimbic lobe, where sensory information travels through long fiber tracts losing a lot of time and information. Thus, the Cetaceans have at their fin tips a wealth of information and perception that we cannot possibly imagine.

Improved Problem-Solving Ratio

A rat's brain uses 90% of its space to take in sensory information with just 10% left for problem solving, resulting in a 9 to 1 ratio. A cat's brain has a 1:1 ratio, a chimpanzee 1:3, and a human 1:9. Humans need to use only 10% of their brains to interpret sensory stimuli, leaving 90% for problem solving. Are we the smartest creatures on this planet? Maybe not. Whales and dolphins have a brain ratio that ranges from 1:25 to 1:40.[13]

---

[13]Watson, 2014.

When compared to the human brain, cetaceans are superior in several measures of how the nerve cells connect to each other through their system of dendrites, the long tendrils which project out of the nerve cell, and the synapses where they connect to other cells. Cetaceans are superior in "synaptic geometry, dendritic field density, and neural connectivity.... In addition, the centralization and differentiation of the individual cerebral areas are levels higher than the human brain."[14]

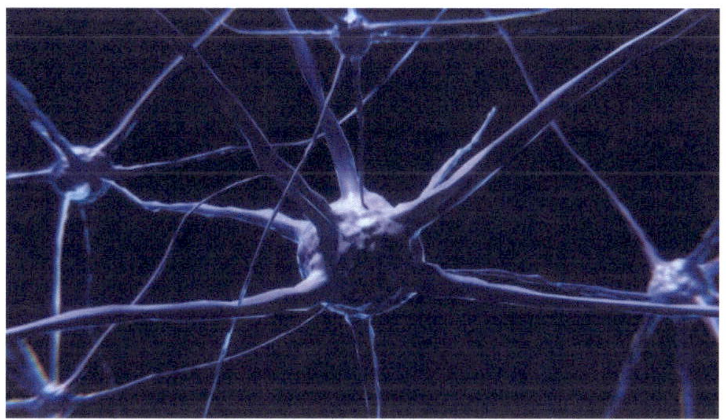

Nerve Cell Image by Colin Behrens from Pixabay

Average IQ

The average human has an IQ of 100, a dog has an IQ of about 15, and a chimpanzee an IQ of about 35. In comparison, a sperm whale's IQ is around 2,000![15]

[14]Ibid.
[15]Ibid.

No Need for Technology

We tend to equate intelligence with technological development and think that whales are dumb because not only do they not have technology; they do not even have fingers. We humans evolved as tool-makers and needed to protect our limited food supply on land from others who encroached on our territory. The theory of evolution says that we developed fingers to be able to make the tools we needed. In contrast, the whales developed with ample food supplies and without fear from external dangers. Watson likens a whale to an organic submarine, a submersible ship that contains everything it needs.

Swimming in the Wild with Humpback Whales

In 2001, I first got into the water with wild humpback whales swimming in their mating and birthing grounds in the Silver Banks, off the coast of the Dominican Republic. We took a large boat out 85 miles from shore and anchored for a week, going out in smaller boats twice a day to look for whales. We had a long encounter with a mother whale and her baby, which the group named Pearl. During the time in the water with this mother-calf combination, I opened up my heart to the mother whale in appreciation for her letting us watch her and her precious little calf all day long. I called the mother Minerva. Watching a baby 24-7 is hard work, and with our snorkel group interacting with the calf, Minerva could get some 20-minute naps between needing to come up for a breath of air. The babies need to come up around every 5 minutes, and Pearl was fascinated with us funny looking humans with our fins and snorkel masks. With glee, she entertained us.

Tail Slap

When a mother whale slaps her tail on the surface of the water, it is generally a call for the calf, who may have wandered off, to come back right away. Pearl was trying to master the tail slap technique. She would lift her tail and bring it down slightly on one side or the other, so it only made a gentle splash. She finally got her tail centered, but when it landed on the water, it was bent up, so it did not make much sound. At last, Pearl finally got her tail just right and made a loud noise with her tail slap. Pearl was so exuberant that she did about 50 more tail slaps, showing off her new skill. We all cheered each time!

Be All You Can Be!

As I was meditating on my appreciation for Minerva and the magnificence of the whale kingdom, suddenly, I felt a bubble of limitation pop from around my energy field. Simultaneously, Minerva sent me a telepathic message, "Be all you can be!" This message is for all humans. May we all release the limitations around us and step into who we truly are!

I fell in love with these gentle giants and went back many times to swim with them. When I made the 9th visit in 2020, while we were out on the boat, a mother whale surfaced near us and started slapping her pectoral fin, as if she were waving hello to us.

Then she and her calf swam right under our boat. I sensed this whale was Baby Pearl, all grown up now with a calf of her own. I think she sensed my vibration and came to greet me, because my heart was moved to tears, sensing the love and recognition her soul had for mine.

Spy Hop

One of my favorite whale behaviors is the "Spy Hop," where the head comes up out of the water to see a clearer view of what is going on at the surface.

Fluke

When a whale wants to go down to the bottom of the ocean for a rest, it may go straight down vertically, with the tail going into the water last—called a fluke.

Each fluke print is different, ranging from almost pure black to almost pure white. Scientists record photos of fluke prints to recognize and track individual whales.

The whale in the photo below has a fluke print that is almost pure white. In addition, she is performing an acrobatic feat of diving down with her belly side up!

In conclusion, with all the evidence of these creatures being so different and more advanced than us, the theory that they came here from outer space long ago and are much more highly developed makes more sense to me than the theory that they evolved from ancient animals on earth. I think they arrived with a very different kind of Star Civilization presence—non-threatening, non-aggressive, great ability to perceive, and hearts filled with unconditional love.

Mating Practices

The one exception to the peaceful, loving nature of humpback whales is that when the topic of mating comes up, they are very serious about keeping their genetic pool the strongest possible. A female whale chooses her mate, and the males in the area compete with each other, slugging it out in what is called a "rowdy group" to prove their strength and to try to be chosen to sire the new calf.

During one of my trips, we observed a male whale, called an escort, with a female who had two tiny scratches on her dorsal fin that looked like the word "it." While we were watching, another male called a challenger came in to pick a fight with the escort in hopes he could mate with the female. However, the female rolled over on her side and started slapping her 15-foot-long fin, making a very loud noise.

Our guide said the whale did not like either one of the males and was soliciting others to let them know she wanted to mate. A couple hours later, we observed a rowdy group of five whales chasing a female and discovered when she came up that she was the same one we had observed before, with the scratches on her dorsal fin. She was having a grand time with the males chasing her to see who was the strongest.

Rowdy Group Video

In the YouTube video below that I made of my trip in 2015 with my husband Robert Alcorn, MD, we were right in the middle of a rowdy group of eight males pursuing one female, vigorously fighting with each other. Our 20-foot boat was surrounded by 40-foot whales! Also included in this video is footage of being in the water with a singer whale. Only the males sing. See if the theory that these songs carry the records not only of the history of their own species, but of the history of this planet makes any sense to you.

Swimming with Humpback Whales 2015

https://www.youtube.com/watch?v=2DgLy2bWoOM&feature=youtu.be

Photo Credit:

All whale photos in this chapter are by Vicki Bosler-Kilmer

Used with permission

Chapter 2: Andromedans

The closest galaxy to ours is the spiral Andromeda Galaxy, which is approximately 2.5 million light years away.

The Andromeda Galaxy
photo from NASA Galaxy Evolution Explorer[16]

According to the Spitzer Space Telescope, an infrared space observatory launched by NASA in 2003, the Andromeda galaxy has a trillion stars, more than double the number of stars in our galaxy. The width of its disc is 260,000 light years, whereas the width of the Milky Way galaxy is 100,000 light years.[17] A slight cosmic problem is that Andromeda is heading toward our galaxy at the rate of 110 kilometers per second and will collide with the Milky Way in about four billion years.[18] For people who want to worry

---

[16] https://images.nasa.gov/details-PIA15416

[17] "Amazing Andromeda Galaxy." NASA Jet Propulsion Laboratory: California Institute of Technology. http://www.spitzer.caltech.edu/images/2216-sig06-024-Amazing-Andromeda-Galaxy

[18] Cowan, R. (2012, May 31). "Andromeda on a Collision Course with the Milky Way." *Nature: International weekly journal of science*.

about the future, they can put this on their list, as many orbits of planets will shift when the two galaxies merge.

A Galactic Waterfall

In this spectacular photograph from NASA/ESA Hubble Space Telescope, the galaxy NGC 2799 on the left appears as if it is being pulled into the center of galaxy NGC2798 on the right.

Alex Collier

Author and public speaker Alex Collier claims that two Andromedans named Moraney and Vasais have been in contact with him with messages to help our civilization.

> **Note:** these visitors were from a star in the Andromeda Constellation in our Milky Way Galaxy. The Andromeda Constellation includes the Andromeda Galaxy, visible to the naked eye only on a clear night with a very dark sky.

As with most people who have been contacted by Star Civilizations, some people think Collier made up the whole

---

http://www.nature.com/news/andromeda-on-collision-course-with-the-milky-way-1.10765#

story and is a fake. Collier, in conjunction with Jon Robinson, published a newsletter titled "Letters from Andromeda" from November 1995 through February 1997, available online.[19] To know more about Collier's messages, you can read these letters and evaluate them for yourself.

Collier's First Contact

According to Collier, these Andromedans first contacted him when he was eight years old, in August of 1964. Alex was at a family gathering at his grandparents' cabin in Woodstock, Michigan. Alex went out to play and lay down in tall grass. He fell asleep, and when he woke up, it was almost 9 pm. He ran back to where his family was having their picnic and found a police car and the whole family alarmed. Collier got whipped for disappearing. He told his family where he had been, and they claimed they had searched that whole area. He took them to where he had made his bed in the grass, and his body imprint was still there. Collier did not understand at the time what had happened to him, that the reason his family could not find him at that place was because the Andromedans had taken him somewhere else. After the abduction, they wiped his memory of the event, so Collier had no memory of what happened to him that day.

When he was 14, one night in October, he went to bed and awakened to find two men looking down at him. They were human beings from Andromeda, but they had no hair. The larger one, Moraney, had blue skin, and the skin of the

---

[19] Letters from Andromeda newsletter http://www.bibliotecapleyades.net/andromeda/lfa/lfa.html#contents

elderly one, Vasais, had turned white because of his advanced age. The Andromedans told Collier that all human life originally came from the constellation Lyra and that they were genetic cousins to us. They came to help because humans were in trouble with extraterrestrials interested in Earth because of our solar system and the minerals we have here. Collier reports multiple abductions where he was taken out of bed and given information, physicals, and brain scans. He says they put a cap on his head that showed him who he was in past lives and his direct connection to them and to the earth. He reports the contacts are both physical and telepathic. [20]

In his book *Defending Sacred Ground,* Collier reports that the Andromedan council saw tyranny in our galaxy 357 years in the future. Through time travel, they traced the origin to Earth and also Mars, and the Moon, locations where Collier says humans have bases.[21] He reports the Andromedan council came here to help us evolve to avert a dystopian nightmare in the future of slavery and total control, like in the book and movie *Hunger Games*. Earth problems affect the whole galaxy, so what we do with our future is very important!

Case Example: 135,375 Year Life Span

A woman I will call Maryann came to a Soul Detective workshop I was teaching where people were finding

[20] Collier, A. (2013, February 27). "Alien kinds or races and presence on Earth, bases on Mars and the Moon." YouTube lecture: https://www.youtube.com/watch?v=OTZJrHJNWlk

[21] Collier, A. (1997). *Defending Sacred Ground: The Andromedan Compendium Volume One.*

positive past lives to download talents and abilities their souls had developed in previous incarnations into their current lives.[22] Maryann set the intention to find a past life where she had been connected to higher dimensional energies to use for healing. Readings with astrologers, healers, and teachers had told her she was from another world and that this incarnation was a "vacation lifetime," but she had no direct experience of the things these intuitives had been telling her.

We used muscle testing to identify a lifetime that was connected to higher dimensions. Maryann found a lifetime where her soul incarnated somewhere in the Andromedan Galaxy in the year 7,667 BCE (Before the Common Era) in Earth time. That society did not have gender. The name this incarnation wanted to be called was Ariel. Naturally, we assumed this was a past life since it started more than 9,000 years ago. We tested how many earth years it took Ariel's planet to orbit their sun and got 361 years. We also tested that the average lifespan of people on Ariel's planet was 375 orbits around their star. That meant that the average Andromedan on Ariel's planet lived the equivalent of 135,375 earth years!

Suddenly, 9,000 years did not seem like such a long time, and we discovered that Ariel was still living—a parallel life. Maryann connected with the happiest time in Ariel's life and found a transcendent connection beyond words. The ecstatic connection Ariel has to Divine Source is

[22] Soul Detective is the name I have trademarked for the system I developed to find and resolve the hidden origins of emotional and mental problems. For course descriptions, see www.souldetective.net.

filled with joy and bliss, a heart-expanding, positive energy. Maryann asked Ariel how she can download this divine connection into her current life. Ariel said to meditate. Then Maryann asked Ariel how to keep the connection even when she is not sitting in meditation. Ariel communicated,

Each person has a divine spark in the center of one's being which radiates outward. When we consciously connect with this spark, it grows into a blissful expansion of the heart energy that goes up to entangle with Divine Source.

This work put all the puzzle pieces together for Maryann, as she now has a direct experience of her Andromedan parallel life. One of her teachers had admonished her, "You need to take care, Maryann, for you are not of this world." During an Energy Medicine chakra clearing session, another practitioner found Maryann's heart chakra to be a radiance beyond human heart energy. She told Maryann, "You have never been a human before. You live in pure joy and balance." The color of new growth was around Maryann's throat chakra, because her incarnation as Ariel had never used words before or directly interacted with people. The practitioner found an extra layer around each of her chakras that is not found in humans and a parallel universe glowing in her third eye like a serene, tranquil drop of water. As the practitioner grounded her session through Maryann's left foot, she saw divine parallel universes and higher frequency beings, which brought tears of joy to her eyes.

Maryann's soul, which has a parallel life as Ariel in the Andromeda Galaxy, took a short human incarnation to bring these higher vibrational frequencies of pure love, peace, and joy to Planet Earth to help with our shift into a higher dimension.

Andromeda in Colors

Image Credit: NASA/JPL-Caltech/K. Gordon (Univ. of Arizona) & GALEX Science Team

Stargate to Andromeda?

The documentary movie *Above Majestic* reports that the United States secret space program has been traveling outside of our solar system for decades. One of the most unusual reports in this movie is from witnesses who were taken through some kind of Stargate to the Andromeda galaxy in the warp speed of just 20 minutes. They reported seeing eight planets in Andromeda which were like Earth and had humans on them. On two of these planets, the people spoke English and had cars, roads, and cities.[23] If inter-galactic travel ever becomes an affordable vacation plan, one could go to Andromeda for a huge get-away and still speak English!

---

[23] Goode, C. & Sather, J. (Producers). Richards, R.R. (Director). (2018). *Above Majestic.* [Film]. U.S.A. SBA Media.

Chapter 3: Greys

According to William Tompkins, who worked in Secret Space Programs, there are eleven types of Greys interacting with our planet, and all of them have different agendas.[24] Elena Danaan presents very specific information on variations of many Greys and Grey hybrids in her 2020 book *A Gift from the Stars: Extraterrestrial Contacts and Guide of Alien Races.*

Representation of a Grey Alien and Spaceship

The largest number of people who report abduction experiences talk about interactions with short, bald aliens with gray skin, large almond-shaped eyes, small chins, and a tiny mouth, who appear to be wearing a tight-fitting body suit. Sometimes they are called Zeta Reticulans, Greys, or Grays. I admit that I get a creepy feeling whenever I see representations of these life forms which look so different from humans.

[24] Tompkins, W. M. (2020). *Selected by Extraterrestrials Volume 2,* p. 139.

The Honorable Paul Hellyer

The Honorable Paul Hellyer, former Minister of National Defence in Canada, has revealed what he knows about the interaction of Star Civilizations with humans. Hellyer is one of the most credible sources of ET information because of his former position having access to classified information and his international reputation for credibility and integrity. In 2005, he came out publicly to say that at least four different species of aliens have been visiting Earth for thousands of years, with different agendas. The four groups he mentions are the following:

1. The Greys
2. The Insectoids (Chapter 8)
3. The Tall Whites (Chapter 9)
4. The Nordics (Chapter 10)

Hybridization

One of the main agendas of the Greys seems to be to hybridize with humans. When I first heard about the idea of an ET-human hybrid, I thought it was totally ridiculous. Yet, the topic comes up over and over in the UFO information. I started to think about all the hybridization programs we have

on Earth today.

Mixed Breed Puppy

Hybridization programs abound in animal breeding and agriculture. I once had a precious puppy that was a cross of a Terrier and a poodle, a Terripoo. We named her Terri. Poodles are intelligent and do not shed their hair, but they have weak eyes. Poodles are crossed with many other breeds to create "designer dogs" incorporating the strengths of other types of dogs like the Schnoodle (Schnauzer-poodle cross), Yorkipoo, Westiepoo, and the Labradoodle.

Most commercial seeds are hybrids of two genetic strains, like beans bred for not having strings in them, producing greater yield, and increasing resistance to common bean diseases.

Genetic Experimentation

Most documentaries and disclosures of "hidden information" tell stories of aliens abducting humans and doing genetic experimentation with the goal of creating an alien-human hybrid. In physical experiences, the abductee is put on an examination table. Body samples are taken, including sperm from the men and eggs from the women. "Abductees experience being impregnated by the alien beings and later having an alien-human or human-human pregnancy removed. They see the little fetuses being put into containers on the ships, and during subsequent abductions may see incubators where the hybrid babies are being raised…."[25]

According to researcher John Mack, these hybrid babies in general do very poorly. The Greys have no emotion, so they cannot give the babies the love they need. Sometimes women report they are abducted just to hold the hybrid babies, so they get some human love. In informational abductions, the Greys stare at the humans with their huge eyes, and the

[25] Mack, J. (1994). *Abduction: Human Encounters with Aliens,* p. 38.

humans "may feel as if the contents of their minds have been totally known, even, in a sense, taken over."[26]

Bud Hopkins: *Intruders*

A UFO researcher named Bud Hopkins researched in detail the case of a woman named Kathie Davis who wrote to him in 1983. Kathie was abducted by short aliens with large heads and gray skin in 1977 and became pregnant. When the fetus was several months old, the aliens returned and removed it. Her abductors were caught by surprise when Kathy had an "outburst of pain and anguish when her abductors removed the fetus she was carrying…."[27] These abductors seemed to have no emotional understanding of how devastating the theft of her baby was to Kathie. Lacking an understanding of human bonding, they did not know why one of their test subjects would object to having her baby removed from her body.

In 1983, Kathie was again abducted, and the short grey aliens presented her with a little girl who looked like a cross between their race and humans. Kathie reported, "She didn't look like them, but she didn't look like us, either. She was real pretty. She looked like an elf, or an…angel. She had really big blue eyes and a little teeny-weeny nose, just so perfect."[28]

Her tiny mouth was also perfect and her skin pale, except for pink lips. Her thin hair was white and wispy, and Kathie

---

[26]Ibid.

[27] Hopkins, B. (1987). *Intruders: The Incredible Visitations at Copley Woods*, p. 193.

[28] Ibid, p. 155.

thought the aliens did not know what to do with it—because none of them had any hair! Kathie wanted to hold her, but she could not because the child was afraid of Kathie. The aliens seemed very pleased with the child's development and promised Kathie she would see her again. In 1986, they showed her this child again along with a baby boy. They told Kathie the baby boy was also her child and that Kathie had a total of nine hybrid children, meaning they had fertilized and grown nine of her ova. They let her name them all. She named the little girl she had seen before Emily and the little boy Andrew.[29]

Hopkins was unable at first to believe that these stories had any basis in reality. But after hearing many reports of females abducted, becoming pregnant, and then suddenly not being pregnant anymore with no signs of miscarriage, he came to believe in the reality of a hybridization program. Another clue bringing this shocking phenomenon into reality was seeing the scars from incisions that had been made into their bodies. "A central goal of UFO abductions, I now believe, is the apparent interbreeding of an alien species with our own. And that process, it would seem, is both covert and very widespread."[30]

Hopkins makes a point that these ETs are physically very frail and fighting for the survival of their species. They never try to do deliberate harm, and they carry out the abductions like a well-run dental office, picking people up, doing a procedure, and dropping them back off. But the Greys have

---

[29] Ibid, p. 180-181.

[30] Ibid, p. 179.

no grasp of the psychological trauma to a woman who has been carrying a child when the fetus suddenly disappears from her womb.[31]

Case Example

One woman I worked with reported that she was pregnant and then at 3-4 months of gestation was suddenly not pregnant anymore. She had no bleeding and no miscarriage. Twenty years later, she got a telepathic message from her son that he and other "Earth Boys" who were ET-human hybrids had taken control of the spaceship they were on and defeated the ET scientists. He had died in the battle, but he wanted his mother to know of his existence and what he had done with his life.

Soft Disclosure

Just who is doing all this hybridization, and why? We can find clues in science fiction movies and TV series such as *Stargate: SG1*, a popular American-Canadian series that ran for 10 years from 1997 to 2007. While these stories are presented as fiction, their scenarios may be closer to truth than consensus reality!

According to Michael Salla, one of the ways the government is getting people ready for disclosure of the amazing technologies the military has developed through contact with Star Civilizations is through this "soft disclosure," putting out information about what is currently happening in the secret space program as if it were fiction. The US Air Force let the *Stargate: SG1* producers film their secret underground

[31] Hopkins, 1987.

facility near Colorado Springs at Cheyenne Mountain. Air Force personnel read every script, removed mistakes, and approved airing of the show. A standout vote of confidence for the show was the appearance of two serving Air Force Chiefs of Staff, General Michael E. Ryan in the Season 4 episode "Prodigy," and General John P. Jumper in the Season 7 episode "Lost City, Part 2."[32]

Cloning

In the *Stargate SG-1 series*, a highly intelligent, benevolent race of beings called the Asgard looked like greys and wanted to extend their lifespans. When an Asgard was ill or injured, they transferred that person's consciousness into a crystal, cloned a new body for the Asgard, then downloaded the consciousness from the crystal into the clone. Over time, copies of copies of copies degenerate, leading to death of the Asgard race. In the Stargate series, the Asgard protected the Milky Way Galaxy, but they had an enemy called "The Replicators," which were ferocious Artificial Intelligence adversaries. In the TV show, the Asgard became extinct, but before their Star Civilization ended, they transferred their secrets of technology, which included being able to beam people from one location to another, to humans on Earth.

Barbara Streisand Has Her Dog Cloned

When Barbara Streisand's beloved dog Samantha died at age 14, Streisand paid $50,000 to have two clones made from cells of Samantha's mouth and stomach. She named the two clones "Miss Violet" and "Miss Scarlet." She reports they

---

[32] Salla, M. (2019). *US Air Force Secret Space Program: Shifting Extraterrestrial Alliances & Space Force,* p. 278.

have different personalities, though their DNA is identical.[33] South Korean researchers at Sooam Biotech were the first to clone a dog in 2005, and by 2015, they had cloned over 600 dogs.[34]

J-Type Omega Human Clone

Dr. Michael Kruvant Wolf worked in The Sentinel Project, a top-secret military program which grew the first human clone in the 1970's and named him "J-Type Omega." They worked in collaboration with the Greys, who had vast genetic knowledge. Some of Wolf's genetic material was used to make the clone, which was grown in a water tank from an embryo. Wolf reports that J-Type Omega had to be terminated because the clone refused orders to kill a dog. The clone saw no reason to kill the dog and so refused. Evidently, the researchers wanted a clone who would simply take orders, even immoral ones. Another project that Wolf worked on was using advanced techniques to increase the potential of the human brain to create super-strong super-soldiers.[35]

According to Secret Space Whistleblower Corey Goode, "Clones are widely used, and they have been for a while."[36] Goode reports cloning of humans is done extensively, and clones are employed in warfare and in off planet programs. These clones have some severe psychological issues. When

---

[33] Salla, M. (2018, March 1). "Human Cloning About to Be Unleashed Upon the World." Exopolitics.org. https://exopolitics.org/human-cloning-about-to-be-unleashed-upon-the-world/.

[34] Ibid.

[35] Wolf, M., 1996, *The Catchers of Heaven: A Trilogy.*

[36] Sphere Being Alliance Episode 83 Journey to Truth: https://www.youtube.com/watch?v=DK7SQA6vJrs&feature=youtu.be (clone topic from 1:19:25 to 1:21:50).

a clone experiences torture, abuse, or a traumatic death, some of that trauma is fed back through consciousness to the human whose DNA was cloned, and the human DNA donor may experience severe PTSD and suicidal impulses.[37] Another reference to cloning from author William Tompkins comes from a list of problems the Reptilians have caused on our planet, including trafficking humans to other planets and cloning us.[38]

When I first watched the YouTube with Corey Goode talking about clones, the concept was so far outside my comfort zone that I did not want to believe it was true. However, I added "Clone Trauma" to the checklist of interference patterns I use in my work to see if the subject came up for anyone. To my great surprise, clone trauma came up quite often, and people got emotional and physical relief from treating the topic as if it were true.

Clone Case Example #1

Francesca had been working on her right knee in physical therapy for months, and it was almost completely recovered. Then suddenly, with no physical injury, Francesca felt a sharp pain in the back of her left knee. The pain went down her leg and scared her, as she had a big trip planned in two days. Francesca's goal for her Soul Detective session was having more confidence in her physical body. The interference pattern we discovered that was disrupting her body's ability to heal was clone trauma.

---

[37]Ibid.

[38] Tompkins, 2020, p. 157.

Two Clones

Francesca had two clones. One was on another planet, raising flowers, and she loved her job. This clone was treated well and had no trauma. But the second clone was underground in a lab on Earth, and her physiology was being studied. She felt imprisoned, and the physical procedures they did to her were painful.

We telepathically reported this clone abuse to the Galactic Federation, a coalition of many different Star People and their Planets, to their Clone Abuse division. We asked higher Beings of Light who had the technology to beam this clone out of the research facility to a place where she would be safe. Francesca felt the extraction happen, and she felt the clone was surrounded by loving, caring beings. Then, from her True Self connection with Divinity, Francesca commanded that no more clones of her DNA be made unless with written consent!

Outcome

Immediately after this intervention, the leg pain disappeared. The pain returned later, but it was not as severe and decreased each day, with the help of Arnica Cream. The following day, Francesca tripped over a bale of hay and landed face first in a hay pile, but miraculously, she did not injure herself. Her daughter, who witnessed the fall, could not believe she was not hurt. Even with this fall, her left leg had no increase in pain. Francesca feels that because her clone who had been underground is now in a safe place, her leg went into healing mode. The recovery path continued to have challenges, as twinges of pain would bring up fear that her body was falling into disrepair. Fortunately, Francesca knew how to treat negative thought patterns with energy work. Clearing the Clone Trauma was just one step in her recovery process.

Clone Case Example #2, from Robert Alcorn, MD
A young mother I will call Maria was suffering uncharacteristic episodes of rage in response to dealing with the stresses of becoming a mother for the first time and caring for her three-week-old infant, named Angel. Maria would have feelings of overwhelm which would instantly turn into rage. She would scream and yell and even do physical damage, such as ripping down the curtains or throwing things.

Mind Control Super Soldier Experiment
When our dowsing indicated the problem was coming from a living clone of Maria, we asked to tune into the clone to get a sense of her situation and the nature of her trauma. The Guides immediately instructed us to ask to beam the clone out of her underground military base to a place of safety. The military was experimenting on the clone to induce mind control and to make her able to function as an enhanced soldier. For example, they were taking the sadness she felt and causing it to transform into rage, so she could use the rage energy as a super soldier.

At this point in the inquiry, Maria reported that her partner said he had seen a clone of her walking behind her into the bathroom! The clone had a distorted face, but clearly looked like a double of Maria. It seemed to us that the energies of Maria and her clone were in two places at once, both in Maria's home and in the deep underground military base.

Tissue Sample

We inquired how these military people obtained her DNA for cloning purposes. The Guides showed Maria that it happened in childhood, from a blood test taken during a visit to a doctor's office. But because Maria also had memories of having an alien child when she was a child, we questioned whether she might have had a military abduction, called a MILABS. The tissue sample taken for cloning could also have come during this event.

Healing Changes

After the session, Maria reported several improvements in her functioning. Most notably, the rages were gone. When she became overwhelmed with caring for baby Angel, instead of instantly flying into a destructive rage, she recognized that she was feeling overwhelmed, that she should set Angel down in the crib for a short time, have a good cry, and then carry on. This change has endured ever since the healing session.

From these improvements, it appears that the feelings of a traumatized clone of a client can "bleed through" to the original person and have an effect on the client's inner states and behavior. Taking steps to rescue the clone from the trauma has a beneficial effect on the client.

President Truman's Contact with UFOs

Leaders of our country have had both direct and indirect contact with Star People. From July 12 to July 29 of 1952,

Washington DC was flooded with UFOs flying over the Capitol. The most intense sightings were on the weekends, and thousands of people saw these UFOs and their bright lights. President Truman ordered the US Air Force to defend against them, but our advanced jet fighters could not match the speed or maneuverability of these craft. Some of the UFOs had swastikas on them, and some the German cross. Michael Salla reports these craft had been produced in Antarctica by the collusion of the Germans with the Reptilians (Chapter 11). No shots were fired in the Washington DC Flyover, and no blood was shed, but the event demonstrated that this German-Reptilian alliance had technology far greater than that of the US, forcing the United States into a one-down position.[39]

President Eisenhower's Contact with ETs

According to Michael Salla, from Feb. 20-21, 1954, President Eisenhower was secretly taken to what is now called Edwards Air Force Base for a meeting with a benevolent Star Civilization who called themselves Nordics (Chapter 10). According to whistleblower William Cooper, astronomers had detected a fleet of alien aircraft in 1953 which went into orbit around our equator. Two human-looking white-haired Nordics with pale blue eyes warned Eisenhower that these aliens could not to be trusted and offered to help the United States with our spiritual development on the condition of nuclear disarmament. Some accounts say they offered to help us with our technology, and others say they were unwilling to trade any technology

[39] Salla, M. (2018). *Antarctica's Hidden History: Corporate Foundations of Secret Space Programs,* p. 109-110.

because they feared we would use it for destruction of human life. They warned us we had to stop polluting the earth and raping her resources and learn to live in harmony with our planet.[40] This offer did not appeal to U.S. military commanders. They felt that dismantling our nuclear weapons would leave us vulnerable to attack and refused their terms.

Eisenhower's Meeting with the Greys

Later in 1954, Eisenhower met with the group of large-nosed Grey aliens who had been orbiting the earth. They said they were from the belt of Orion from a planet called Betelgeuse, and that their planet was dying.[41]

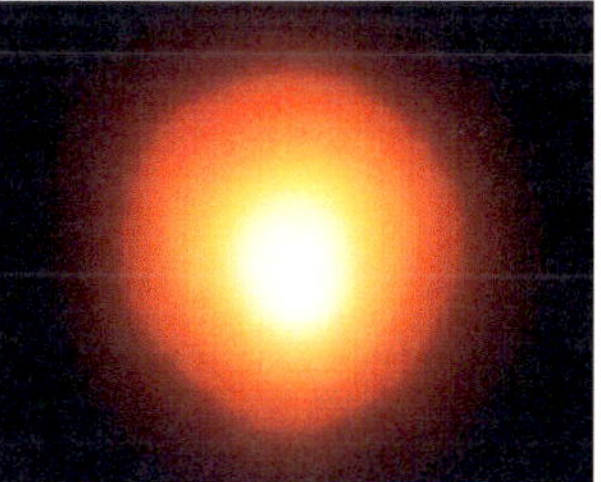

Betelgeuse Credit: A. Dupree (CfA), R. Gilliland (STScI), FOC, HST, NASA

With a demonstration of the superior technology and military power the Greys possessed, Majestic 12 went behind the back of President Eisenhower and made a treaty with these Greys that circumvented the U.S. Constitution by not going through Congress. The conditions in the treaty were the following:

1. Non-interference in each other's affairs.
2. We would keep their presence here secret.
3. They would provide us with secrets of advanced technology.

---

[40] Salla, M. "Eisenhower's 1954 Meeting with Extraterrestrials: The 50th Anniversary of Contact?" Research Study #8. February 12, 2004. www.exopolitics.org

[41] Salla, M. (2004). *Exopolitics: Political Implications of Extraterrestrial Presence*.

4. They would not make a treaty with any other nation on this planet.
5. They could take a few cows and some humans to experiment with their implantation devices but would give details about everyone involved.
6. They could abduct humans for medical examination and monitoring, but they would not harm them and would return them to the place of abduction, having wiped out their memory of the event.
7. The Aliens would furnish a list of everyone abducted to Majestic Twelve, a group reported to have been organized by President Harry Truman to deal with UFO affairs and cover-ups.

Cattle Mutilations

Since the 1960's, cattle ranchers worldwide have lost cattle in mysterious deaths in which specific organs or tissues are removed from the animal and bloodless incisions have been made, all without sign of attack by wild animals. So many cattle were found dead or missing that ranchers were terrorized. A 1979 FBI report estimated that Colorado alone had 8,000 cattle deaths, a loss worth a million dollars.[42] David Perkins, an Investigative Journalist who wrote a pamphlet titled *Altered Steaks*, reports, "Aliens have been a prime suspect in the cattle mutilation phenomena. The blood is removed, the rectum is cored out, the sex organs are missing, having been done with incredible surgical

[42] "Operation Cattle Mutilation," section 4, FBI report on cattle mutilations.

precision."[43] Sentries trying to stop destruction of their livestock would see strange lights appear in the sky before a cow was mutilated.

In 1979, Linda Moulton Howe began investigating the torrent of reports coming in about strange animal deaths and wrote about her findings in *An Alien Harvest: Further Evidence Linking Animal Mutilations and Human Abductions to Alien Life Forms.*[44] One eyewitness reported seeing a cow being levitated onto a spaceship, legs flailing, and then later on, the dead carcass of the cow being dropped out of the spaceship.

Why would large-nosed Grey aliens want blood and body parts from cows? Human and Bovine DNA are similar in large sections of the human chromosome, though cows have 30 pairs of chromosomes, while humans have only 23. "Cow hemoglobin can be used in an emergency transfusion for humans because it so closely matches hemoglobin in human

[43] Clare, C. (Producer & Director). (2016). *ETs Among Us: UFO Witnesses and Whistleblowers. Part 1.* [Documentary Film.] U.S.A. Prism Pictures.

[44] Howe, L. M. (1989). *An Alien Harvest: Further Evidence Linking Animal Mutilations and Human Abductions to Alien Life Forms.*

blood."[45] Howe reports the speculation that the cattle mutilators may be harvesting bovine DNA "to create biological clones, androids, hybrids, or something unimaginable."[46]

Grey Aliens Prove Untrustworthy

By the year after signing the treaty with Majestic 12, the US government found the aliens did not deliver as much technology as they had been expecting. They also did not give Majestic Twelve complete lists of abductees, and some people were not returned. Just as the Nordics had warned, these Grey aliens did not prove trustworthy. The government decided not to disclose what happened. Perhaps one factor was that they were embarrassed by the results of what happened when they broke Constitutional Law. The Majestic 12 Special Operations manual outlined government policy for the interaction with this Star Civilization:

> Any encounter with entities known to be of extraterrestrial origin is to be considered to be a matter of national security and therefore classified TOP SECRET. Under no circumstances is the general public or the public press to learn of the existence of these entities. The official government policy is that such creatures do not exist, and that no agency of the federal government is now engaged in any study of extraterrestrials or their artifacts. Any

[45] Ibid, p. 115.
[46] Ibid, p. 114.

> deviation from this stated policy is absolutely forbidden.[47]

Many years later, we found out that this same group of extraterrestrials had made treaties with Russia, Germany, China, and many other countries, each time saying the agreement was only with that country and demanding secrecy. Now we know why they wanted their agreements kept Top Secret!

1955 Eisenhower Meeting with the Greys

A number of military personnel witnessed President Eisenhower land in Air Force One at Holloman Air Force Base in New Mexico in early February of 1955. They reported seeing two saucer-shaped metallic aircraft 25' to 30' wide. One landed right in front of Air Force One, and the other one hovered above the one on the ground. President Eisenhower got out of Air Force One and entered the alien spacecraft for a meeting that lasted about 45 minutes. The cover story was that Eisenhower went hunting in Georgia, got a cold, and was missing from Georgia for over 30 hours while he flew to New Mexico for the meeting and back, which included an overnight stay. Many of the men on the base heard President Eisenhower talk in the Base Theater after the meeting, but they had to take an oath not to disclose what Eisenhower said.[48]

---

[47] Majestic 12 Group "Special Operations Manual SOM1-01 – Extraterrestrial Entities and Technology, Recovery and Disposal," April, 1954 Part 2.

[48]Campbell, A. & Kirkland, A. (2010, Nov. 29). "President Eisenhower's Secret Meeting with ETs in 1955—the Real Story." X-Conference Live Speaker Presentations. [YouTube]. UFOTV.com https://www.youtube.com/watch?v=iv1ZCEiVrgg

Central Intelligence Agency (CIA) Collusion with the Nazis

The CIA was originally formed by President Truman in 1947. Michael Salla says the CIA was given the task of dealing with exopolitics, meaning political agendas with extraterrestrials. The CIA is supposed to report all their expenditures for congressional approval, but in reality, they do not list their black budget activities. Allen Dulles, head of the CIA from 1953 to 1961, was the person who forged the agreements between Eisenhower and the Nazi Germans who escaped to Antarctica during and after World War II with advanced technology that included antigravity flying aircraft of ET origin. During WWII, Dulles had been in the Office of Strategic Services (foreign intelligence during the war) and forged agreements with the Nazis. Dulles was a very powerful man and was comfortable with the Nazi elite. "He in fact was part of a group of American industrialists and corporate lawyers that actually facilitated Hitler's rise to power."[49]

Ford Motor Company's Involvement

Before World War II, the German auto industry was a lucrative market. Being an industrialist, Henry Ford had automobile plants in Germany. "Hitler was an admirer of American mass production techniques and an avid reader of the antisemitic tracts penned by Henry Ford. 'I regard Henry Ford as my inspiration,' Hitler told a Detroit News reporter two years before becoming the German chancellor in 1933,

---

[49] Salla, M. (2018, October 4.) "Dr. Michael Salla- Exopolitics and Extraterrestrial Life Civilizations." [YouTube interview]. Conscious Spirit Media. https://www.youtube.com/watch?v=TYTR6gatZZE.

explaining why he kept a life-size portrait of the American automaker next to his desk."[50]

In 1938, German diplomats awarded Henry Ford with the highest honor they could give to a foreigner, the Grand Cross of the German Eagle. For the record, Henry Ford later retracted his antisemitic tracts.

When the United States entered WWII after the bombing of Pearl Harbor in December of 1941, US corporations in Germany were supposed to divest themselves of their German assets. Ford did not do that, because he did not want to lose the income from his German investments. He valued money over loyalty to his country. The German Ford auto factories were converted to making war machinery for the Germans and used forced labor.

German Panzer Tank

Slave Labor

To put a face on forced labor, Elsa Iwanowa brought a class-action suit against Ford in March of 1998. Back in 1942, German soldiers abducted Elsa, age 16, and hundreds of

[50] Dobbs, M. (1998, November 30). "Ford and GM Scrutinized for Alleged Nazi Collaboration," *Washington Post*. https://www.washingtonpost.com/wp-srv/national/daily/nov98/nazicars30.htm#TOP.

other Russian women from their homes in southern Russia to work at the Ford plant at Cologne. Elsa reported,

> The conditions were terrible. They put us in barracks, on three-tier bunks. It was very cold; they did not pay us at all and scarcely fed us. The only reason that we survived was that we were young and fit.[51]

The Ford company profited from this unethical use of slave labor in the German Ford companies making German war machinery. After the war, Henry Ford sought compensation from the United States for the bombing of his German Ford plants.[52] The image of Henry Ford as an ethical, apple-pie-eating American Citizen is an illusion.

Upsetting Religions

Another reason why the government does not want to disclose the presence of Star Civilizations is that people will be shocked to realize that many of their religious teachings are not entirely true. Salla's research shows that Star Civilizations came to planet Earth half a million years ago and started to do genetic manipulation with indigenous humanoid species here. The belief in Homo sapiens sapiens being created exactly as they are by a Supreme Being is not totally accurate. I do believe that all life comes from the One True Creator of All. However, the indigenous humanoid species on earth were gene spliced with other life forms. If the Sumerian story of creation that will be presented in the next chapter on the Anunnaki is true, then the Anunnaki

---

[51] Ibid.
[52] Ibid.

spliced some of their intelligence into an indigenous humanoid species, likely Homo erectus, making Homo sapiens. The Anunnaki then said they had created the humans, which is only partly true. They did not create themselves, and they did not create the indigenous species, they just hybridized these two life forms into a new species. According to Michael Salla, the genetic experimenters from Star Civilizations created different races on this planet—red, white, brown, black, and yellow, to see how they would interact in Earth's environment. They wanted to know which races had aptitude for advanced technologies and which ones would evolve more quickly. These secret programs are required to "hide in plain sight," so one of their favorite tactics is to tell a person known as a con man something that is true with instructions to tell everyone else. But because the spokesperson is known as a con artist, nobody believes the story. Movies such as *Jupiter Ascending* and *Men in Black* portray as fiction things that may be true about our interaction with Star Civilizations.[53]

According to Salla, forty to sixty ET races are on the planet and are involved in genetic experimentation. He says the Star Civilizations want to learn about themselves, and the best way is doing these genetic experiments. They want to see "if the humans in the experiment are able to handle the infusion of galactic energies in a certain way, then maybe we in the galaxy can handle the infusion of galactic energies in a way that is more conducive to our long-term survival and growth."[54]

---

[53] Salla, M. (2018, October 4). Conscious Spirit Media interview.
[54] Ibid.

Salla's Recommendations

Salla recommends that people start to read the information on Star Civilizations to discover what the witnesses and the insiders say. Salla's books on the secret space programs have testimony from these insider witnesses.[55] He recommends that people take to heart the significance of the phenomenon and reflect on how it impacts us. He warns that we cannot understand these events with just the intellectual process alone. Salla encourages heart awareness to "feel the sincerity of people, who is doing what and why, and to kind of feel things. We have to develop emotional intelligence, not just IQ."[56]

The Serpo Project

Paul Hellyer, former Canadian Minister of Defence, reports a friendlier encounter with a group of Grey aliens.[57] Hellyer claims that under the auspices of the United States Defense Intelligence Agency (DIA), in July of 1965, twelve U.S. astronauts were transported to the planet Serpo in the binary star system Zeta Reticuli. The mission was an ambassadorial exchange, and the program was referred to as "Operation Crystal Night" or "The Serpo Project." The website www.serpo.org has extensive information on this event from a source who needs to remain anonymous.

---

[55] Salla, M. (2017). *The US Navy's Secret Space Program and Nordic Extraterrestrial Alliance. (Secret Space Programs Book 2)*, and Salla, 2019.

[56] Salla, M. (2018, October 4). Conscious Spirit Media interview.

[57] Hellyer, P. (2018, February 3). "Paul Hellyer Earthshaking Confession 'Four Races of Aliens Are Here on Earth.'" [YouTube]. https://www.youtube.com/watch?v=EgrCQpWz6iI

According to this source, the civilization on Serpo was 10,000 years old. They had originated on another planet but were forced to leave 5,000 years ago due to volcanic destruction. Their population was only around 650,000, much smaller than our seven billion. If any other Star Civilization wants to live on our planet, they would benefit from hybridizing with people already living here who would be adjusted to the atmosphere, gravity, and food available on this planet. Star People with dwindling populations could look at our planet and our race as a resource to save their species from extinction.

Close Encounters of the Third Kind

The 1977 movie *Close Encounters of the Third Kind*, written and directed by Steven Spielberg, while presented as fiction, very closely parallels the account of what transpired in the Serpo Project. The story begins at Roswell.

Some Highlights from the book *The Day After Roswell*

Fifty years after the Roswell crash, the Freedom of Information Act has allowed people to write about the events they witnessed. Retired Former Pentagon official Col. Philip J. Corso reveals the shocking cover-up of the truth about Roswell in his book *The Day After Roswell*, published in 1997 when the 50 years of non-disclosure were over. The story is so amazing that I will present some of Col. Corso's major themes and the motives he assigns to the actions taken.

In Roswell, New Mexico, on July 4, 1947, radar operators were seeing pulsing blips of a craft they could not identify. These images were darting across the radar screen at speeds more than a thousand miles per hour. Military personnel did not know whether this craft was Russians spying on our rocket test site at Roswell, whether the craft was from the Germans, who had developed ET technology during World War II and had a hovercraft flying saucer, or whether the occupants riding around in that fierce thunderstorm were from a Star Civilization. Then with a lightning strike, the unidentified craft crashed. The military personnel who arrived at the crash scene saw a small scout ship with its nose in a hill and two delta wings sticking up. It did not look like an ordinary plane crash, because the hull was largely intact, with a split down the middle. Strewn around the opening were little dark gray figures about 4 ½ feet tall with large bald heads, almond-shaped eyes, a tiny mouth and ears, and appearing to wear a bodysuit of a metallic cloth. Some were dead, and others were still alive.

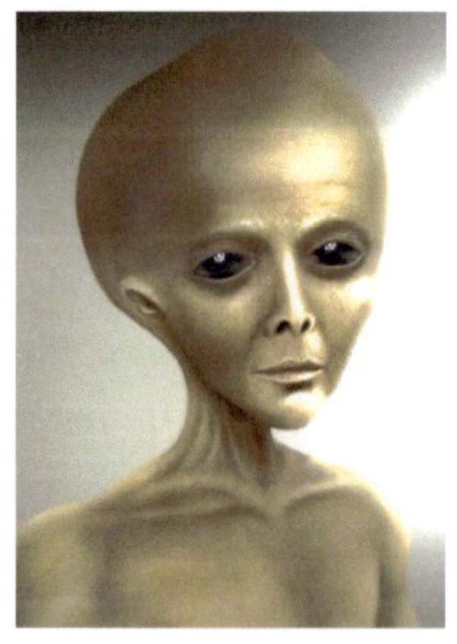

Little People

The craft was unlike anything they had ever seen. It had no kitchen, bathroom, or sleeping facilities, and even more astounding, it had no engine or power generation apparatus. The craft had no steering controls, only an indentation for a handprint. Some of the little people were wearing a headband with electrodes on it connecting to four sections of their brain, but the headband had no batteries or diagrams. Later, we would figure out that the ship was controlled with the thoughts of the pilot through the headband's brain-ship interface. The military personnel put the bodies on stretchers, cleaned up the debris, and loaded the spacecraft onto a truck and took it to an air force base for analysis. They told the local people who had witnessed the crash not to tell anyone about what happened there. The captain threatened, "We'll know if you talk; we'll know who you talk to and all of you will simply disappear."[58]

Corso was stationed at Fort Riley in 1947 when a convoy of trucks from Fort Bliss in Texas stopped there on their way to Wright Field in Ohio. As a post duty officer, he had to inspect each building at night. One of the enlisted men told him the guys driving the trucks said they were loaded with things from a crash out in the desert in New Mexico. The men had looked inside the boxes and were shaken by what they saw. Corso had security clearance to also look, and he saw a deceased Grey suspended in thick blue liquid inside a glass container. It had four fingers, no thumb, a tiny slit for a mouth, and no apparent damage to the body. The invoice said it was an inhabitant of the craft that had crashed at Roswell, and it was on its way to Walter Reed Army Hospital for autopsy. Corso felt a combination of fascination and horror and tried to bury the memory of that night.

New Technology

Years later, in 1961, Corso was recruited to the Pentagon's Research and Development agency to monitor what other countries were developing and to liaison between scientists working on new projects and the defense contracts with industry. Corso got a Top-Secret file of debris from Roswell and the assignment to figure out what the aliens used these pieces of technology for and to get them into the hands of

---

[58] Corso, P.J. (1997). *The Day After Roswell*, p. 21.

corporations working for the military, all without revealing that any of the objects came from an extraterrestrial source. In particular, Corso did not want any information leaked to the CIA. His viewpoint was that the CIA and the KGB (Russia's intelligence agency) collaborated with each other, and both spy agencies cared more about maintaining their organizations than about protecting the countries they were supposed to serve. He had no respect for the CIA.

Reverse Engineered ET Technology

Some of the ET debris Corso placed for product development were the following:

1. **Night Vision Goggles.** The first project Corso worked on was the lenses over the eyes of the ETs, which gave them the capacity for night vision. The military had already been trying to develop night vision goggles to be able to see the enemy in the dark. Corso took these lenses to companies already involved in the project. calling them foreign technology as if they were something the military had procured from the French or the Germans.
2. **Bullet-proof vests.** The fabric of the ET body suits was extremely strong. When bent, it would pop right back into shape. It was so strong it could not be punctured or cut by scissors. Analysis showed the fibers were extremely condensed. Corso farmed samples of this fabric to manufacturers who eventually came up with the Kevlar bullet-proof vest.
3. **Transistors.** Corso had stacks of plastic wafers with little wires going through them. Some of these had been given to Bell Labs right after the crash, and they

aided them in developing transistor and solid-state technology. Formerly, a computer was so large it took up a whole room and was clumsy and unreliable. Now our computers have chips in them that make them much smaller and more efficient.

4. **Brain-wave-controlled helmets.** The headbands the ETs wore somehow interfaced with the system of the craft and made an interface between the pilot and the ship. One commercial application of this technology is in video games with a headband interface.
5. **Fiber optics.** Corso had long strands of thin glass that conducted and bent light. These fiber optics were wrapped all around the craft, and nobody had ever seen anything like that before. Now, fiber optics are in common usage in our technology.
6. **Lasers.** The scientists could not figure out what a tiny pencil-sized device they found in the ship was for. It projected a tiny red light on a wall, which heated up whatever it shined on, plus it could cut through metal. They had never seen a laser before. Now we have microwave and laser technology which came from reverse engineering Roswell debris.

Why All the Secrecy?

Corso reports several reasons that the military did not divulge the truth about our government's contact with this Star Civilization.

1. First, they did not want the Russians to know that we had an ET craft in our possession, for fear that they would try to steal the secrets of our technology. The Cold War was

in full swing, and the two countries were competing for military superiority.

2. Second, they assumed that the intention of the Star Civilization was hostile. They did not have the concept portrayed in the 1951 movie *The Day the Earth Stood Still* of a peaceful alien coming to our planet, the flying saucer landing on the lawn by the White House, and a benevolent ET warning the nations of the world that we must unilaterally disarm from nuclear weapons. The human-like alien in the movie, portrayed by actor Michael Rennie, warned that if we persist in warlike mentality, nuclear weapons could eliminate all life on our planet.

   Furthermore, nuclear use on Earth also threatens other planets. Although he did not say why, the theory is that just as all the cells of the body are part of one organism and influence each other, so all the planets in our solar system affect our lives. The study of astrology delineates the current influence of each planet, both individually and as a group, as in when Mercury goes retrograde, mechanical things tend to not work as well.

   So too, what we do on Earth affects our solar system and our galaxy and other galaxies in the web of life. One theory I have heard is that an atomic blast rips a hole through the dimensions, upsetting other worlds. I realize that in 1947, the military had not seen this movie yet, since it did not come out until 1951, and military policy was to shoot down and destroy anything in the skies they could not identify. Friendly Star Civilizations coming to try to help us needed to be very careful about how to manifest safely.

3. Third, Corso also explained that the military decision makers were worried that if the general public knew of a threat to our civilization that our armed forces had no way to defend against, mass hysteria could result. They were concerned that the public would react in the same way they did to the Orson Welles broadcast on October 30, 1938, part of a "War of the Worlds" series, where a radio broadcast said that ETs had invaded New Jersey. Some people thought the invasion was real, and they panicked.

According to Corso, the military needed to develop a missile capable of taking out an ET ship, but they could not go to Congress and ask for a budget to develop an anti-ET spacecraft missile—because officially, ETs did not exist, so their spacecraft also did not exist. Instead, army Research and Development cloaked the budget request as an anti-missile missile project. Supposedly, they wanted to be able to blow up any Soviet missile aimed at us. The military did get the anti-missile missile project funded after Corso disclosed to Secretary of State Robert Kennedy the true nature of the threat, and a Secret Space Program was developed. Corso says the United States now has technology we can use in space to defend ourselves against nefarious ET ships. He claims they used it to blow up an ET craft threatening one of our sites.

One Grey Survivor from Roswell

Moving back to Paul Hellyer's information, he reports that an informant who needs to remain anonymous says that one survivor of the crash at Roswell in 1947 was found hiding behind a rock. This survivor, called an EBEN (military abbreviation for extraterrestrial biological entity), made tonal sounds, just like the ETs in the Spielberg movie. The scientists at Los Alamos where he was taken were able to establish communication with him. The EBEN/Grey pointed to a star map to indicate he was from the planet Serpo in the binary star system of Zeta Reticuli—binary meaning their solar system has two suns bound by gravity to rotate around each other.

Two Suns Image Credit: NASA/JPL-Caltech/T. Pyle

The Zeta Reticuli star system is about 39 light years away from Earth. The EBEN also showed them how to operate the devices found in the crashed spacecraft, including a communication system with his home planet. The EBEN sent six messages which were not answered, and then he died later that summer.

Eventually Los Alamos was able to contact Serpo in December of 1952. They began communication that resulted in plans for an ambassadorial exchange of sending 12 United States astronauts to Serpo, with the Greys leaving one EBEN here with the US government. The movie *Close Encounters of the Third Kind* shows only one American going aboard the spaceship, with 11 more in gear ready to go. The movie also shows the one EBEN who stayed here.

Choosing the Astronauts

The government screened 56,000 files to pick the astronaut ambassadors based on the criteria of being career military, single, with no children, preferably orphans themselves, and having multiple skills. Ten men and two women were chosen based on complex tests. All IDs were purged, and all were listed as missing and discharged from the military. They went through difficult training for 6 months. Four pilots were trained to fly a Grey craft in case they had to escape from Serpo. Other team members included two linguists, one biologist, two doctors, two scientists, and one security agent. The mission was approved by President Kennedy.[59]

Serpo

The alien craft landed in 1964 as scheduled. They picked up the bodies of the 9 EBENS who had died in the Roswell crash, but the EBENs decided to wait another year for the exchange. In July of 1965, the alien craft returned to the pre-arranged test site in Nevada about 95 miles north of Las Vegas. The twelve courageous astronauts boarded along with 45 tons of supplies for an intended stay of 10 years. Serpo is 39 light years away from earth, and the journey to Serpo on the antigravity alien craft took 10 months.[60] They travelled

---

[59] Kasten, L. (2013). *Secret Journey to Planet Serpo.*

[60] Kasten, L. "Secret Journey to Planet Serpo." [YouTube Video]. Beyond 50 Radio. https://www.beyond50radio.com/Article-Secret_Journey_To_Planet_Serpo.html.

around 40 times the speed of light and used an anti-matter device to flow more smoothly through space with no friction from the atmosphere. The Serpo pilots used a series of traversable wormholes to go great distances almost instantaneously. Getting from one wormhole to the next one required ten months of stellar navigation.[61]

Cloning

Seven of the original 12 astronauts returned. One died of respiratory problems during the 10-month journey to Serpo. Two died while on Serpo, one from an accident and the other from pneumonia. Two chose to remain on Serpo because they fell in love with the culture.

A diplomatic problem arose when the EBENs took the body of the astronaut who died on the journey to Serpo and refused to return it to the Americans. The American team considered this body to be the property of the United States government and demanded to have it returned. The EBENs told them that very little was left of the body, as they had used the blood and organs to clone other creatures. The American team was extremely upset over the body being used for cloning without permission. The EBENs could not understand why the Americans would not want to let them use this prize tissue sample for their genetic research, a top priority for the EBENs. They could not understand why the Americans were attached to the corpse of their colleague.

As the Americans pressed the EBENs to find out what had happened to their friend's body, the team commander's diary

---

[61] Ibid.

reports they were shown the EBEN clone research facility. They saw beings that mostly looked human, but two of them looked like humans with dog heads, like the Egyptian god Anubis.

Egyptian God Anubis

The EBEN guide explained that "the growing process involved cells taken from other beings, grown and mixed with chemicals and then inserted into the bodies of other beings."[62] The Americans asked to see the being the EBENs had cloned from their teammate's blood and cells. They were horrified when they saw what looked like a like a large EBEN with human hands and legs. They were horrified at what had been done and amazed that the clone could have been grown so quickly.[63]

Death Ray

The EBENs had prevailed in a hundred-year war with an enemy civilization, where both sides used particle-beam weapons like the directed energy weapon developed by Nikola Tesla. The EBEN weapons "project a stream of ions or electrons at tremendous velocity approaching the speed of light, with each individual ion packing up to a billion volts of power."[64] The press called Tesla's teleforce ray a "death ray." The Sumerian tablets report that the Anunnaki (Chapter 4) had a weapon they called the Death Ray, which could

---

[62] Kasten, 2013, pp. 156-157.

[63] Ibid, p. 157.

[64] Ibid, p. 209.

produce death instantly. Perhaps it also used some kind of particle-beam.

The Return

Because the team lost track of Earth time when the batteries powering their Earth clocks wore out, they shifted over to Serpo time and wound up staying 13 years instead of ten, returning on August 18, 1978. They were debriefed for one year, resulting in a classified 3,000-page book which the anonymous source had in his possession. The last astronaut died in 2002. Their lives were shortened by the massive amounts of radiation they had absorbed on Serpo.

What did President John F. Kennedy Know?

President Kennedy died five months before the first landing in 1964. He knew about the project, and Paul Hellyer believes that Kennedy may have been planning to televise the landing to disclose to the public the presence of Star Civilizations. Kennedy's knowledge of ET activity started with his position in Naval Intelligence during World War II. After the war, his father's friend James Forrestal, Secretary of the Navy from 1944-1947, recruited JFK to accompany him on a tour of the devastation in Europe in the summer of 1945. Forrestal and Kennedy likely saw firsthand some of the flying saucers the Nazis had developed.[65] JFK met General Eisenhower on that tour and was briefed on the covert program called "Operation Paperclip" to import German scientists who had been working with Nazi advanced technologies.

---

[65] Salla, M. (2013). *Kennedy's Last Stand: Eisenhower UFOs, MJ-12 & JFK' Assasination*, p. 22.

Forrestal's "Suicide"

Forrestal and JFK became fast friends, and Forrestal was a mentor to Kennedy. Forrestal was also a member of the Majestic 12 committee to oversee ET interactions and wanted to disclose to the American public the presence of Star Civilizations. "As a former journalist dedicated to the principles of a free press and open society, the indefinite coverup of such a momentous event as the discovery of extraterrestrial life was anathema to Forrestal's convictions."[66]

Forrestal became the first Secretary of the Department of Defense in 1947. His desire to get the truth out about UFOs was overruled by Majestic 12, and President Truman forced him to resign in 1949. The official story is that Forrestal suffered a nervous breakdown, was hospitalized, and committed suicide by jumping out a window two months later. However, Forrestal was denied normal visitation rights during his seven weeks at the Bethseda Naval Hospital. One visitor who came to see him was someone Forrestal did not want to see, Congressman Lyndon Baines Johnson, who was likely "part of a group of public officials pressuring Forrestal to remain silent about something."[67] As part of Majestic 12, Forrestal had to abide by majority decisions. If he did not, he would be considered a threat to national security, and any means necessary could be used to silence him.

Forrestal's brother Henry finally got to visit him four times, after threatening to go to the press and sue the hospital. Henry reported that James was doing well and planning the things

[66] Ibid, p. 27.

[67] Ibid, p. 25

he would do after his discharge. He was in no way suicidal. Just a few hours before Henry was to pick up James, he supposedly jumped out of a window and fell to his death. Given the circumstances, suicide makes no sense. More likely, James was strangled and then thrown out the window to silence him from telling the public what he knew about the interaction of our government with Star Civilizations.

Majestic 12's Mandate

President Truman set up Majestic 12 (MJ-12) in 1947 after the Roswell crash to deal with UFO issues. The Joint Chiefs of Staff approved the mandate of Majestic 12 to include the following points:

a. A psychological warfare plan.
b. An unconventional warfare plan.
c. Cover and deception plans.
d. A civil affairs/military government plan.
e. A command plan.
f. A logistic plan.
g. Transportation guidance, to be included in the logistic plan.
h. A map and chart plan.
i. A communication plan.[68]

When Eisenhower was elected president in 1953, he appointed Nelson Rockefeller to head his committee to reorganize the government. Rockefeller, as Special Assistant for Cold War Planning, argued to move covert CIA operations out of the view of the President so that if the public

[68]http://www.majesticdocuments.com/pdf/jointlogisticplan_majestic.pdf

found out about an assassination or other Black Ops activity, the President could deny US involvement in an international incident. Also, Rockefeller argued that MJ-12 needed autonomy from the president so they would not have to depend on the politics of someone needing re-election. To his later deep regret, Eisenhower agreed to remove MJ-12 from direct oversight by the president and therefore lost control and information about what was happening with Star Civilizations. The CIA acquired Area 51 from the Department of Energy, out in the Nevada desert far away from the eyes of the President.[69]

Control of Area 51 and S-4

In 1958, Eisenhower became very frustrated by not knowing what Area 51 was doing. He summoned a CIA operative and his boss and told them to take the message to Area 51 that they had a week to get to Washington and let him know what was going on there, or he would take the First Army from Colorado, invade the base, and take it over.[70] Reluctantly, Area 51 leaders complied. A dying CIA agent reports that he and his boss were taken to the S-4 area and saw different saucer crafts. The first one was from Roswell, and the saucer was all crashed up. It looked strange, like heavy aluminum foil that could be rocked, weighing only around 150-300 pounds. At S-4 they also viewed an alien autopsy film. Then the Colonel said, "What we have in here is that we are interviewing a Grey alien."[71] The CIA agent and his boss

---

[69] Salla, 2013, p. 72.

[70] "A Dying CIA Agent reveals the truth about the US Government and Alien Life." https://www.youtube.com/watch?v=GX0FaindPPo&feature=youtu.be.

[71] Ibid.

were surprised that they were going to see an actual alien. They described it as looking non-human, with a large brain, ears like holes, and a very small nose and mouth. Then they were taken to Area 51 and saw two black ops programs: a Lockheed U-2 spy plane, which they did not know existed, and a model of the SR-71 Blackbird. The CIA agent and his boss flew back to Washington and reported what they had seen to Eisenhower, Nixon, and Hoover. Eisenhower looked totally shocked, and worried. He told them to keep this information Top Secret.[72]

Eisenhower's Warning

On January 17, 1961, in his farewell speech, President Eisenhower warned of the power that the military-industrial complex had gained:

> In the councils of government, we must guard against the acquisition of unwarranted influence, whether sought or unsought, by the military-industrial complex. The potential for the disastrous rise of misplaced power exists and will persist. We must never let the weight of this combination endanger our liberties or democratic processes. We should take nothing for granted. Only an alert and knowledgeable citizenry can compel the proper meshing of the huge industrial and military machinery of

---

[72] Ibid.

> defense with our peaceful methods and goals, so that security and liberty may prosper together. [73]

One day before JFK's inauguration, Eisenhower privately explained to him the depth of the UFO coverup problem. The secret Majestic-12 group Truman had set up to deal with the UFO situation was refusing to give him, even as head of the executive branch of the government, any further information on what was happening in the top-secret research facilities.

Peace with the Russians

In addition to what Forrestal had disclosed to Kennedy, JFK had learned of alien threats from his brother Bobby's briefing from Col. Philip Corso. From his heart, knowing the extent of the threat nefarious alien technology presented against our world, Kennedy wanted world peace and made overtures to the Russians to work collaboratively. He met with Khrushchev in Vienna on June 4, 1961. But the CIA was refusing to release classified information on UFOs even to the President. In an end-run around the CIA, Kennedy visited military facilities at three locations where he knew Operation Paperclip scientists were working on advanced extraterrestrial technology—White Sands Missile Range, Holloman Air Force Base, and Fort Bliss. Vice-President Johnson joined him on the tour, likely to keep tabs on what he was shown.

---

[73]Eisenhower, D. (1961, January 17). "Eisenhower's Farewell Address." [YouTube]. https://www.c-span.org/video/?c4455718/user-clip-military-industrial-complex.

Author Michael Salla makes a case in his book *Kennedy's Last Stand* that the CIA orchestrated Kennedy's death to stop him from the reforms he was making in government, including trying to get the CIA under the control of the President and for Congress to establish a joint space and lunar mission with Russia to end the Cold War and work together on the UFO problem.[74]

In a move to disclose secret UFO information, "Kennedy instructed the CIA to release classified UFO files to NASA as part of the cooperative space effort with the Soviet Union."[75] Kennedy's death stopped him from broadcasting the Serpo landing on world-wide TV, as powerful people did not want this disclosure to happen.

Those with economic ties to the oil industry did not want competition with the free energy from Star Civilizations that would ruin the oil business, even though it would decrease pollution of our environment and reduce our planet's global warming. Those in the pharmaceutical industry did not want disclosure of the advanced medical technology Star Civilizations have developed. James Jesus Angleton was the CIA's Chief of Counterintelligence from 1954 through 1975.

---

[74] Salla, 2013.
[75] Ibid, p. 196.

Angleton especially hated Kennedy because JFK wanted to reduce the power of the CIA. Kennedy's assassination on November 22, 1963 silenced any disclosure plans he might have had and stopped his planned governmental reforms.

Kennedy and Marilyn Monroe

According to multiple sources, Kennedy was having an affair with Marilyn Monroe and told her in a huge breach of national security "that he had personally witnessed extraterrestrial artifacts at one or more classified military facilities."[76] Monroe had unrealistic dreams that JFK would divorce Jackie and marry her, making her become the First Lady. FBI chief J. Edgar Hoover laid down the law to JFK about the security risk Monroe held because of her connections with left wing people, and Kennedy immediately disconnected her private line to the White House.[77] JFK sent his brother Bobby, the Attorney General, to try to smooth things over with the breakup. Monroe became enraged with both brothers for their distancing from her. "Monroe was planning a 'tell all' press conference using notes from her red diary to spite the Kennedy's for their treatment of her."[78]

Photo Credit: Bert Parry - Page 39, Public Domain, https://commons.wikimedia.org/w/index.php?curid=49950311

[76] Ibid, p. 183.

[77] Ibid, p. 163.

[78] Ibid, p. 174.

The testimony of Monroe's housekeeper, Eunice Murray, and Norman Jeffries, son-in-law of Eunice, who worked for Monroe as a handyman, placed Bobby Kennedy at her home on the day of Monroe's death. Bobby went to her in the afternoon to dissuade her from doing the press conference. When she refused, Bobby came back later with a doctor who injected her "with enough barbiturate to kill 15 people."[79]

Mary's Mosaic

Mary Pinchot Meyer was another paramour of JFK after she divorced from her husband Cord Meyer, a prominent CIA agent. Mary was haunted by JFK's assassination. She read the Warren Commission's report on the JFK assassination and started to piece together the trail that led to the CIA being responsible for killing JFK. An example of the fox guarding the hen house is that Allen Dulles, Director of the CIA from 1953 to 1961, was a member of the Warren Commission's investigation.

Mary was murdered on October 12, 1964, just three weeks after the Warren Commission's report came out. Author Peter Janney knew Mary personally and investigated her death. The results in his 2012 book *Mary's Mosaic* are shocking, showing that the CIA was responsible for Mary's murder and set up the scene to blame an innocent person, Ray Crump Jr., for her death. Peter was horrified to find out that his own father, Wistar Janney, a career CIA agent and close friend of James Jesus Angleton, was involved in the planning for Mary's murder.

Evidence uncovered points to Angleton as being the one who issued the directive for Kennedy's assassination since the

[79] Wolfe, D. (2012). *The Last Days of Marilyn Monroe,* p. 462-463.

CIA considered JFK a threat to national security.[80] Had Kennedy revealed the presence of Star Civilizations and their free energy systems, the oil industry would have been put out of business. The oil industry security would have been compromised, not the security of the country or the planet. Howard Hunt's dying confession to his son of his involvement in Kennedy's assassination points to the order coming down through vice-President Lyndon Johnson,[81] who as a Texan was a strong advocate of the oil industry. The CIA coined the term "conspiracy theory" to apply to anyone looking beyond their explanation of Lee Harvey Oswald killing JFK.

Abduction Researchers

After examining the connections between disclosing the presence of Star Civilizations and the murders of JFK, Marilyn Monroe, and Mary Pinchot Meyer, we return to the topic of abductions with summaries of the work of several abduction researchers. Open-minded researchers who look at the evidence of first-hand reports of contact with Star Civilizations have found strikingly similar accounts, ranging from short Greys doing hybridization experiments to taller Grey beings helping the evolution of our species.

Edith Fiore, PhD

Psychologist Edith Fiore has written books about topics very close to my heart, including spirit possession,[82] abductions

---

[80] Salla, 2013, p. 210.

[81] Hunt, S.J. (2012). *Bond of Secrecy: My Life with CIA Spy and Watergate Conspirator E. Howard Hunt.*

[82] Fiore, E. (1987). *The Unquiet Dead: A Psychologist Treats Spirit Possession.*

by extraterrestrials,[83] and past lives in her book *You Have Been Here Before: A Psychologist Looks at Past Lives.*[84]

Spirit Trapped Between Worlds

My mother gave me Dr. Fiore's book *The Unquiet Dead* when I first started my clinical work. This precious little book helped me understand the paranormal activities that were happening with the people in my caseload. Some people die without realizing that the spirit has left the physical body. These earthbound spirits may need help to get to the world of light, a subject I also wrote about in my book *Invisible Roots* (2008).

In her book titled *Encounters* (1989), Dr. Fiore presents 14 case histories of people who have had encounters with Star Civilizations. Using hypnosis, she was able to help her

---

[83] Fiore, E. (1989). *Encounters: A Psychologist Reveals Case Studies of Abductions by Extraterrestrials.*
[84] Fiore, E. (2005).

subjects through the initial terror of being abducted against their will and having very uncomfortable physical examinations done to them, including extraction of sperm and eggs. She helped them find meaning in their abduction experiences and to overcome their panic attacks, anxieties, and fears.

One Contactee named Linda came from a psychic family who often did healings together. Linda reported to Dr. Fiore that she had been abducted by small people with pointed heads, big eyes, and greenish, knobby-looking skin. They opened up her stomach and cleaned out black junk, telling her she had cancer and that they were trying to help her.[85] In future regressions, she learned that many of her family members were abducted together and taken aboard the spaceships, where the Star People's medical teams worked on humans to heal many different medical problems. They said they were helping people be healthier. They taught Linda how to scan a body with her hands, moving energy around, and to channel healing energy through her hands. The Star People had Linda and many others gather around a large crystal which emanated beautiful, healing energy that raised their vibration. They told Linda they had come to help our world make the changes we need to keep Earth from disaster. The Star Beings said, "There will be changes so powerful that only the strong will survive. We are here to give knowledge and understanding to the world of light and the world of children of God. We are here to change the world for a better development in the universe."[86]

---

[85] Fiore, 1989, p. 90.

[86] Ibid, p. 109.

In the memory of her very first contact with Star People, Linda was four years old. Beings came into her room and talked as if they had known her for a long time. A being named Revance felt like a father to Linda and told her about another place, a city with lots of blue, brilliant lights, that was her true home. Revance said Linda had to be on Earth for the present time, but when she was finished here, she would be going back to this beautiful place. "They say that I'm in a different body this time, but we'll continue working together. This will be an exciting time. Wonderful things will be happening."[87] After this encounter, Linda told her mother an angel came to visit her!

Dr. Leo Sprinkle

Another of the first modern researchers to publish accounts of abduction phenomenon is Dr. Leo Sprinkle, of the University of Wyoming, who began studying ET material in 1960. His 1999 book *Soul Samples* recounts his personal experience of interactions with Star Civilizations plus other case reports he studied. Dr. Sprinkle was ridiculed by his peers, who considered his interest in extraterrestrial phenomenon unworthy of scientific study. He was ostracized by his peers, which was hurtful both personally and professionally.

The discipline of psychiatry has drawn a line in the sand and decided that UFO and ET phenomenon are fantasies. Psychiatry labels anyone who believes in those things to be a quack. This prejudice is still present today, and I too have been personally ridiculed for taking the possibility of

[87] Ibid, p. 112-113.

interaction with Star Civilizations seriously. As a species, we need to put aside our pre-conceived notions of the nature of reality and find out what is true, because this knowledge is vital for the survival of life on planet Earth.

Psychiatrist John Mack

In the early 1990's, a respected Harvard professor named John Mack was commissioned to study 200 men and women who reported alien abduction experiences. In Mack's research,[88] most abduction encounters with the Greys reported extraction of genetic samples, especially sperm and eggs, genital examination, and attempts at hybridization. The ones who commissioned Mack suspected that the Contactees were suffering from mental illness; however, his study disproved that theory. He did not find emotional pathology in them, but he did find that as a group, their sense of spirituality was heightened, and their concern for the environment increased. Mack wrote two books, *Abduction: Human Encounters with Aliens* (1994) and *Passport to the Cosmos* (2002). Mack was killed by a drunk driver in London in 2004.

Contacted but Not Chosen

Sometimes the Greys check out people but decide they are not right for their experiments. I met a woman in her 30's I will call Ronnie at a UFO conference. She told me the following story directly:

---

[88] Mack, J. (1994). *Abduction: Human Encounters with Aliens.*

Bright Lights

I was awakened in the middle of the night by an intensely bright white light. The head of my bed was against a wall, and I had a bank of windows six feet tall, going 15 feet across the room facing the woods. When I looked out, I couldn't see the woods, only the bright, bright light. My husband was asleep beside me. I looked over at the doorway, and three figures entered the room: a tall one in the middle with a shorter one at each side. They did not touch the ground, but rather floated just above it. I was trying to awaken my husband, but I couldn't speak or move. They float-walked over to the bed. Their faces were silhouetted so I couldn't see them clearly, but I wish I could have. I was levitated 3-4 feet above the bed and was still trying to yell to wake my husband, but I could not make a sound. I wondered what was happening to me but couldn't do anything about it.

The next thing I remember is being back down on the bed. It was dark outside. I did not look at the clock as I was in shock from the experience. Now I wish I would have checked to see if I had lost any time. I shook my husband, and asked, "Did you see that?" He was groggy and claimed he didn't see anything.

Incredulous, I asked, "Didn't you see them, the bright lights?" I was in a panic. He told me I must have been dreaming and to go back to sleep. He thought that I did not know what had happened. I laid there, reviewing the event in my mind. Finally, I decided he must have been right, that it was just a very intense dream.

Joking

The next morning, I joked with others saying, "You wouldn't believe what happened to me last night. Have you ever had a dream like that?" Then something happened which confirmed in my mind that the event had been real rather than a dream. That morning, I called a friend and told her what happened. Her husband was a Deputy Sheriff on patrol that night in our small town in the woods. He came home and told my friend that he had noticed the brightest light he had ever seen up towards the mountain that night, in the area where our home was. He got out of his patrol car to look at it but could not tell what it was. He was haunted by the mystery. I discussed the event with my friend, and we agreed that it could have happened, because her husband also saw a very bright light at the same time as my experience. I decided I was not what they were looking for, so they left.

Dr. David Jacobs

I did not talk about my experience directly to anyone else, thinking people would not believe me. But I joked about the subject. Then years later, I heard a lecture by Dr. David Jacobs, a historian who wrote his doctoral dissertation on the UFO controversy and who authored *Secret Life: Firsthand Accounts of UFO Abductions* (1992), *The Threat: Revealing the Secret Alien Agenda* (1999), and *Walking Among Us: The Alien Plan to Control Humanity* (2015). He told a story that sounded exactly like mine and said it was a prevalent example from the people he had interviewed. It brought me to tears, as that was the first time I had ever heard it described that way. I never had another visit from these beings, but having the experience opened my mind to a broader view of reality and to knowing first-hand that other races of beings with technology superior to ours exist. We are definitely not alone on this planet!"

Summary

In summary, some Grey races seem to have lost their ability to reproduce sexually and use cloning and attempts to hybridize with humans to try to avoid extinction of their species. The cover-up of the Greys we found at Roswell and other contacts with Star Civilizations is part of an attempt to keep the American public in ignorance of advanced technology that would give us free energy, greatly improved health, and life extension, because disclosure of Star Civilization technology would ruin the oil and pharmaceutical industries. JFK's plans to reveal the presence of Star Civilizations was an important factor that led to the CIA planning and executing his assassination.

As difficult as it is to imagine at first, in the coming chapter on the Anunnaki, we will see that the ancient records indicate that our Homo sapiens sapiens race may be a hybrid of a Star Civilization called the Anunnaki and a primitive hominoid that once walked the Earth. If this information is true, then the idea that the Greys want to hybridize with us does not seem quite as preposterous, as we have already been hybridized with the Anunnaki Star Civilization.

Chapter 4: Anunnaki

History is always told from the perspective of its authors. Two major theories postulate how our race got to our current state of evolution. Both theories involve a Star Civilization called the Anunnaki altering our DNA.

Humans were Dumbed Down

One theory says that the human template was created on a planet called Lyra, and then human civilizations were seeded on other planets throughout the galaxy.[89] This theory says that developed, very intelligent humans were on planet Earth for millions of years before the Anunnaki arrived, and that the Anunnaki dumbed us down genetically to make us into a slave race to serve them.[90]

The book *Forbidden Archeology* reports scientific findings of bones and artifacts proving that modern humans walked this planet five million years ago, long before the arrival of the Anunnaki.[91] Some theorists believe that early humans were more advanced than we are now, and that rather than making us smarter, the Anunnaki downgraded our DNA so we would be good slaves. Their claim that they upgraded our template may be disinformation.

---

[89] Priest, K., & Royal, L. (2011). *The Prism of Lyra: An Exploration of Human Galactic Heritage.*

[90] Tellinger, M. (2005). *Slave Species of god: Story of humankind from the cradle of humankind.*

[91] Cremo & Thompson, 1998.

Humans were Upgraded

The other story that the Anunnaki tell in the clay tablets found in Iraq, the home of ancient Sumer, say that the Anunnaki genetically altered a primitive hominid race, probably Homo erectus, and made them smarter by hybridizing them with Anunnaki DNA. While most people consider the stories of the Anunnaki to be mythology, our planet shows evidence that at some time in the past, Earth was inhabited by beings with technology that was far superior to ours.

Our civilization does not currently have the technology to build a structure like the Great Pyramids of Giza with their intricate internal passage-ways. Some other Star Civilization did it!

The Great Pyramids of Giza

I took this photo in Cairo, Egypt to show the huge size of the Great Pyramid of Giza. The tiny figure in the blue pants in the center front is my mother.

Full vs. Partial Disclosure

One group of people currently in power wants full disclosure of everything we know about advanced technology from other planets to give us free energy to stop the destruction of our planet through the pollution produced by burning fossil fuels and raping the environment.

An opposing faction wants partial disclosure and says that the Greys are us, what we Homo sapiens sapiens turned into thousands of years into the future. They propose that the Greys have come back from the future to prevent their extinction and correct their mistakes. Perhaps the reason I have so much trouble with the "They Are Us From the Future" theory is that my finite mind does not fully grasp the principles of time travel. In addition, the Greys just do not look like us! This partial disclosure group promotes the Ancient Astronaut theory, that Star People named the Anunnaki came here and were worshiped as gods.

Translation Ambiguity

In their book *The Shining Ones*,[92] authors Christian and Barbara Joy O'Brien point out that the ancient Hebrew texts which were translated into the first book of Genesis had very few vowels, leading to ambiguity. For example, the name of the Hebrew God was made of all consonants and no vowels: YHWH. Two of the many possible interpretations of this name are Yahweh and Jehovah. Early Middle Eastern languages also used a form of punning called paronomasia which allowed different meanings for a single set of

---

[92] O'Brien, B.J. & O'Brien, C. (2001). *The Shining Ones: An Account of the Development of Early Civilizations Through the Direct Assistance of Powers Incarnated on Earth.*

characters. The King James version of the Bible starts with the verse in Genesis 1:1 "In the beginning God created the heaven and the earth." However, the O'Briens postulate that a more accurate alternative translation of this ancient text would be, "In the beginning the Shining Ones cleared the ground (or felled the timber) in the Highlands and the Lowlands."[93]

According to the Sumerian tablets, these "Shining Ones" are a race of beings called the Anunnaki who traveled to Earth from a planet named Nibiru. They came to mine gold and built the pyramids as landing markers for their spaceships. According to these Sumerian texts, the Anunnaki came here from the Sirian star system and were a race of Sirian-Reptilian hybrids.

The Sumerian Tablets

The late author Zecharia Sitchin studied the Sumerian tablets and wrote a series of seven books titled the Earth Chronicles Series. Sitchin presents the story of a star civilization called the Nephilim in the Bible and the Anunnaki in the Sumerian tablets. Sitchin's work has been criticized by scientists and academics for flawed methodology and labeled pseudoscience and pseudohistory. A woman named Arizona Wilder claims she saw Sitchin at Satanic cult gatherings and that his job was to promote the Ancient Astronaut theory.[94]

---

[93] Ibid, p. 58.

[94] Icke, D. "Arizona Wilder and the Shapeshifting Reptilians." [Video]. YouTube. https://duckduckgo.com/?q=arizona+wilder+and+the+shapeshifting+reptilians&va=z&t=hc&iax=videos&ia=videos&iai=https%3A%2F%2Fwww.youtube.com%2Fwatch%3Fv%3DU3LepJjegko.

Still, even with these questions about his methods and his motives, Sitchin's work has been extremely popular with millions of books sold worldwide and translations into 25 different languages. Some disinformation may be mixed with truth. One could read the story with the attitude, "This is what the partial disclosure people want us to think."

Most of the Earth Chronicle books are difficult to read because they are filled with many scholarly details. The Sitchin book that I find flows the best is *The Lost Book of Enki: Memoirs and Prophecies of an Extraterrestrial God* (2002). Here Sitchin pieces together portions of the ancient text to recreate the story from the point of view of the Anunnaki ruler LORD Enki himself, showing what motivated the Anunnaki to come to Earth, the survival dangers they faced, mounting tensions, and their royal succession rivalries. Sitchin shows the influence of Sumerian mythology in the Biblical account of creation. He traces the events from Adam and Eve through the flood to the forming of the Israelite nation as the chosen people of Yahweh.

While initially people considered the content of these tablets to be Sumerian mythology, archeological evidence is being accumulated that points to these tablets being literal recordings of thc events on our planet from olden times, from the view of the Anunnaki themselves.

Sumer was capital of one of the first known civilizations in the ancient world, from approximately 3,500 BCE, and was located in southern Mesopotamia in what is the southern part of the modern-day country of Iraq. The Sumerians wrote their history on clay tablets in a language called cuneiform. In the 1800's, linguists began to decipher ancient tablets in Persian. Then they mastered translation of Accadian and finally of Sumerian, from tablets which had been inscribed in two or three of these languages. Much of the source material for decipherment of the Sumerian tablets came from bricks, tablets, and scrolls excavated at Nineveh from the library of King Ashurbanipal, from the seventh century BCE. Later, Sumer came to be known as Babylonia.

Summary of silver transaction from Shuruppak, Iraq, circa 2500 BCE. British Museum, London

Nibiru

These ancient texts say that Earth has had a longstanding interaction with another planet named Nibiru. When our solar system was first forming about 4.5 billion years ago, a very large planet named Tiamat was orbiting between Mars and Jupiter and destabilizing the orbits of the other planets because of her size and position. Tiamat was the only planet in the system that had a lot of gold, but she did not have the carbon elements necessary for life to form. Tiamat would have forever been a barren planet.

Sitchin's first book in his Earth Chronicles series is titled *The 12th Planet* (1976), which postulates that our solar system has another planet named Nibiru. In his headcount of planets, in addition to the nine planets of Mercury, Venus, Earth, Mars, Jupiter, Saturn, Uranus, Neptune, and Pluto, Sitchin counts the sun and the moon as planets, making Nibiru the 12th planet.[95]

Sitchin points out that a Sumerian Cylinder Seal from at least 4,500 years ago correctly identifies the presence and relative sizes of these eleven bodies orbiting our sun, long before Uranus was discovered in 1781, Neptune in 1846, and Pluto in 1930.

Akkadian Cylinder Seal VA/243.
Housed at the State Museum in East Berlin

Between the two figures on the left an image shows the heavenly bodies with the sun in the center and with Earth above and slightly to the right, with our moon further to the right of Earth. Then going around clockwise, the planets are

[95] Sitchin, Z. (1976). *The Twelfth Planet: Book I of Earth Chronicles.*

Mercury, Venus, Neptune, Uranus, Pluto, Saturn, Jupiter, and one last large planet--Nibiru.

According to Sitchin's translations, a planet from outside of this solar system named Nibiru was passing nearby, having been ejected from its orbit in the star system Sirius and was called into service to deal with the Tiamat problem.

Looking down from the Sun's North Pole, all the planets in our solar system rotate counterclockwise around the sun. Nibiru came into the system moving clockwise around the sun and was set on a collision course with Tiamat. In the first pass through our solar system, one of Nibiru's moons cleaved Tiamat in two, and a large chunk of Tiamat was pulled closer to the sun and went into orbit between Mars and Venus. This chunk is our planet, the Earth. In the Sumerian texts, a god is attributed to each planet, and the actions are attributed to the volition of the gods; however, they seem to describe events that scientists have found concur with the idea that our planet looks like it is cleaved from part of another planet.[96]

A Lopsided Planet

When I first heard this theory, I thought it was ridiculous and sounded like something from Star Trek. What convinced me it might be true was

[96] Ibid.

examining a globe. I saw that almost all the land is on one side of our planet, and the other side is almost all water.

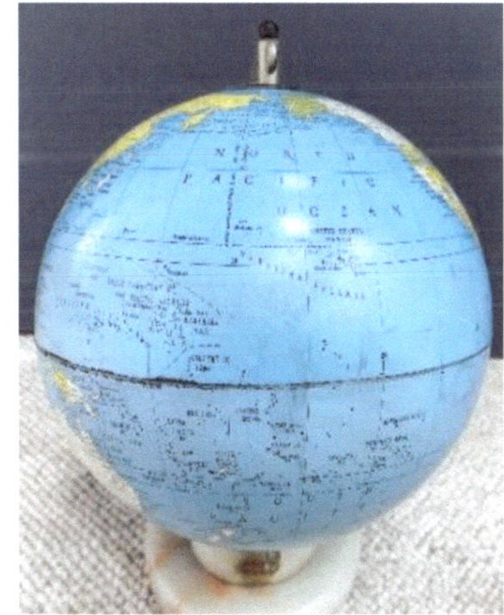

Also, the eastern coast of North and South America fits into the western coast of Europe and Africa, giving rise to the Pangea theory that all the earth present on our planet started out as one land mass, and then the Americas drifted away from the mainland. Earth does look like half of a planet that was cleaved off and then congealed into a ball.

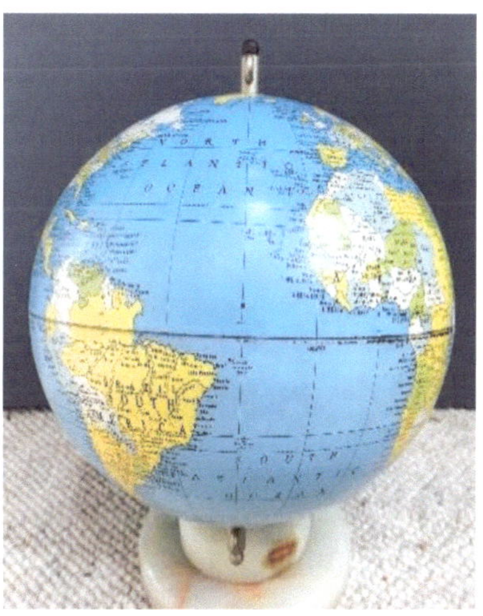

The Moon is Too Big

Another piece of evidence confirming the possibility of this theory is that our moon is disproportionally large in comparison to the size of the Earth. The ancient texts say that our moon had been a satellite orbiting around Tiamat and came with the chunk of Tiamat that became the Earth and got locked into our orbit. The other planets in our solar system have moons that are much smaller relative to the size of their planets. The diameter of our moon is about one quarter the diameter of our planet, and the moon looks as large as the sun in the sky. The laws of physics say that a satellite the size of our moon would never have formed around a planet the size of Earth, but it would have formed around a larger planet the size of Tiamat.

Jupiter with Her Four Main Moons

Jupiter, for example, may have up to 79 moons. The four largest ones are shown in this image:

Io
Europa
Ganymede
Callisto

The diameter of Jupiter is 142,984 km, and the diameter of Ganymede, her largest moon, is only 5,268 km. Ganymede is about 4% the diameter of her planet.

Earth's moon has a diameter of 3,475 km and the diameter of Earth is 12,712, making our moon about 27% the diameter of our planet, much larger than ordinary moons.

Photograph taken by Dr. Stone on 3-22-21 of Earth's moon with a huge ring around it and an orb of light near the bottom of the circle

Going back to the Sitchin story of our origins, the ancient texts say that Nibiru was captured by the Sun's gravitational field and has continued to orbit around our sun in an elliptical orbit that takes about 3,600 years to complete one cycle around our sun and then to travel back deep into space in the direction from where it came. Nibiru's orbit is almost identical to that of the comet Hale-Bopp, whose cycle is 4,000 years. On a subsequent pass between Jupiter and Mars,

Nibiru shattered the other half of Tiamat into the asteroid belt.

One last very important point is that in the collision, elements from Nibiru were transferred to Earth, and over the next four billion years, life forms began to appear on this planet which evolved and reproduced. Without the collision with Nibiru, Earth would never have had the carbon elements necessary for life. She would have remained a barren planet with a lot of gold.

Problems on Nibiru

Scientists estimate that the Universe is about 14 billion years old and that Earth is approximately 4 ½ billion years old, a relative newcomer. Nibiru is billions of years older than Earth, and as life developed on Nibiru, people went to war over resources. The battle grew into a war between the North and the South that escalated into a nuclear war that wreaked great havoc on their planet. A breach developed in their atmosphere so that their summers got hotter, and their winters got colder. Weather patterns were disrupted, winds blew, insects proliferated, and crops failed. Do any of these problems sound familiar?

Nibiru was dying, and the only solution this advanced civilization found to avert this catastrophe was to throw powdered gold up into the sky to fill in the hole in their atmosphere. They needed massive amounts of gold for this repair project and came to Earth because she is the only planet in this solar system with an abundance of this precious mineral. Nibiru's evolution had a huge head start, so when these Ancient Astronauts first came here about half a million years ago, they already knew the secrets of space travel, wormholes, wireless communication, nuclear power, cloning, genetic hybridization, laser weapons, and extremely long life spans that looked like immortality. We can imagine these things now that we also are becoming familiar with some of these secrets, but people in past centuries would have declared these ideas to be myths, as they were not in their belief systems of what was possible.

King Anu

The King on Nibiru was named Anu, and he sent his firstborn son Enki to Earth on a mission to see if gold could be gathered to save Nibiru. Enki came with 50 men and first extracted gold from the seawater. The process proved successful, but it did not provide quantities sufficient for their needs, since Nibiru was about four times larger than Earth. Next King Anu sent a fleet of 600 Anunnaki men to expand the gold mining to splitting open the Earth to get gold. Being from a larger planet, the Anunnaki males were 12-14 feet tall. They brought with them 300 astronauts named Igigi from Nibiru to man a station on Mars used as a holding place for the gold. Since Mars was smaller than Earth, getting in and out of her gravitational field was easier when Nibiru came to pick up all the gold that had been mined in the previous 3,600 years.

Rivalry Between Brothers

Although Enki was the firstborn son of Anu, his mother was not the queen, so Enki was not heir to the throne. Enki's younger brother Enlil was the firstborn by Anu's queen, who was also his half-sister by a different mother, and thus Enlil was the rightful heir to the throne on Nibiru. King Anu made his son Enlil LORD of the Earth, making him commander-in-chief of the Earth mission. Anu gave Enki the title LORD of the Waters and put him in charge of the gold mining operation in South Africa. The mission was successful, and the Anunnaki transported huge quantities of gold to their planet whenever their orbit came close to Earth every 3,600 years.

Gold Miners on Strike

For around 144,000 years, the project went well. Then the gold miners rebelled, saying they were tired of the job, which was getting more difficult for these very tall men as Earth entered a period of global warming. The Anunnaki needed the gold for the survival of all life on their planet, but nobody wanted to do the dirty work of mining it. What were they to do?

According to Sitchin's translation of the Sumerian tablets, LORD Enki suggested to LORD Enlil that they gene splice some of their intelligence into a primitive species of man already walking upright on this planet, possibly Homo erectus, to make a worker willing to mine gold in return for food. LORD Enlil, the top commander of the Earth mission, was a rules-man. He said, "Absolutely not! Galactic Law forbids going to another planet and gene splicing a slave race." We know this as the prime directive from the Star Trek series. However, without gold miners, life on Nibiru would become extinct.

The Anunnaki were faced with a moral choice between the two parts of their hybrid nature. Their Reptilian part was faced with not only personal extinction, but also the death of their whole planet and all life forms on it. Reptiles are programmed to survive, and the Reptilian part of the brain does not consider the impact one's actions have on others. The Sirian part of their nature knew that if they made this choice, it would have far-reaching consequences on the beings they would engineer. The debate in the high council on Nibiru was long and hard. Some said they should just accept their fate, stay in harmony with the higher good, and let themselves all die of starvation. The council finally decided to allow the creation of a slave race. The Reptilian part won, and the council voted for the genetic engineering project because they would all die if they did not.

Genetic Engineering of the Humans

In her book *DNA of the Gods,* author Chris Hardy shows how LORD Enki and his sister Ninmah worked together to create a gold miner template.[97] After much trial and error, Ninmah mapped the whole human genome. She, not Enki, was the master designer of the first human being. After working on their design for a 10,000-year period, they finally created a successful male worker and named him Adamu.

If you would like to see what an ET-human hybrid looks like, take a peek in the mirror!

These Ancient Astronauts told the people they genetically engineered that they had created them. How true was that?

---

[97] Hardy, C. (2014). *DNA of the Gods: The Anunnaki Creation of Eve and the Battle for Humanity.*

The Anunnaki did not create themselves, and they did not create Homo erectus, but their story says they combined the two genetic strains into Homo sapiens, breeding a compliant creature smart enough to take orders. The "Creators" set themselves up as gods and demanded obedience. They established kingship, religion, and the priesthood to manage and govern the workers as they grew in numbers.

Feelings about the humans were divided. LORD Enki loved the humans, as they had been engineered using some of his DNA, and he worked for their betterment. LORD Enlil hated the humans and wanted to wipe them all out in the flood.

The Great Flood

Almost every culture on this planet has in its mythology the presence of a global catastrophe that caused worldwide flooding somewhere around 10,800 BCE.

The account of the flood in Genesis parallels closely the account found in the Sumerian tablets, with a few details omitted. However, the backstory given in the Sumerian account explains why The LORD was so angry with the humans and wanted to kill them all. In the Bible, the Old Testament alternates between the point of view of LORD Enlil hating the humans and LORD Enki being sympathetic to them. Genesis 1:7 presents Enlil's view of intending genocide for not only the humans, but also the animals and other wildlife:

> So the LORD said, "I will wipe from the face of the earth the human race I have created—and with them the animals, the birds and the creatures that move along the ground—for I regret that I have made them."

At the last minute, without any explanation for his change of heart in the Bible, Genesis 1:8 says, "But Noah found favor in the eyes of the LORD." This verse presents LORD Enki's compassion for the humans. The Sumerian tablets report that LORD Enki gave Noah blueprints to build a submersible boat, basically a submarine, to save him and his family and animals to repopulate the Earth. LORD Enki loved the humans and wanted to preserve the species. He and his sister Ninmah collected seeds and plants for agriculture after the flood.

Sitchin's *The Lost Book of Enki* expanded my belief system beyond the literal Bible-based historical worldview taught by the Christian church in which I was raised. I am very grateful for the part of my religious training that connected me to God's love for me and a sense of order in the Universe. The face that speaks the most love to my heart is Jesus. For others raised in different traditions, the face of God might be the Buddha, Quan Yin, Mother Mary, or White Buffalo Calf Woman. I do believe that the Prime Creator is pure love.

When I read the whole Bible as a teenager, I could not figure out why God was so mean in the Old Testament, slaying his people by the thousands, ordering them to commit genocide on others, and wanting to kill them all in the flood. The broader view of the strife between brothers Enlil and Enki explains these conflicts.

Consider for yourself the implications of how the Ancient Astronaut theory might explain much more about who we are and the health challenges we face trying to acclimate to this planet as a hybrid species. The Anunnaki did not give us their perfect DNA, which gave them lifespans of thousands of years. They wanted us to wear out with short lives. This theory also holds the keys to setting us free from 200,000 years of physical, emotional, and spiritual bondage. When we wake up from the slave mentality programmed into our DNA, we can release our fear of the vengeance of the gods. We can reprogram ourselves for health, step into our full human potential, and get ready to shift into a higher frequency of Love and Light.

Biblical Creation Stories

I was raised in a Christian church that took the Bible as literal historical truth. I did not notice that the first three chapters of the book of Genesis have two slightly different versions of the creation story. In one of the versions, an all-powerful God creates the world in six days and then rests on the seventh day. This is how the Biblical God did it:

Days of Creation

Day 1: "In the beginning God created the heavens and the earth. Now the earth was formless and empty, darkness was over the surface of the deep, and the Spirit of God was hovering over the waters." Genesis 1:1-2 NIV
On the first day god created the light and called it day and the darkness and called it night.

Day 2: God created an expanse between the waters to separate the sky above from the waters below.

Day 3: God separated the waters below the sky into one place so dry ground could appear. Then God produced all kinds of land vegetation and trees bearing fruit with seed in it.

Day 4: God created the sun, moon, and the stars.

Day 5: God created living creatures in the water and birds to fly above the earth.

Day 6: God created livestock, creatures that move along the ground, and wild animals. Then God said, "Let us make man in our image, in our likeness, and let them rule over the fish of the sea and the birds of the

> air, over the livestock, over all the earth, and over all the creatures that move along the ground." (Genesis 1:26)

When exactly was the woman created?

The two creation stories have a slight discrepancy about when the woman was created. One says, "So God created man in his own image, in the image of God he created him: male and female he created them." (Genesis 1:27) But later, in Chapter 2 of Genesis, the LORD God puts the man into the Garden of Eden to care for it. Then God says, "It is not good for the man to be alone. I will make a helper suitable for him." (Genesis 2:18) God proceeds to make the man fall into a deep sleep, takes out one of his ribs, and fashions a woman from the rib for a helper for the man.

> **Day 7:** God saw everything he had created, and it was very good. Then he rested from all his creation work.

Original Sin

According to Biblical theology, God put two trees in the middle of the Garden of Eden—the tree of life and the tree of the knowledge of good and evil. God commanded the humans not to eat of the latter tree because they would die if they did. The serpent, the craftiest of all the wild animals, questioned the woman on what God said and told her that she would not die if she ate the forbidden fruit, but that her eyes would be opened, "and you will be like God, knowing good and evil." (Genesis 3:4) The woman liked the idea of gaining wisdom, so she ate some of the fruit and gave some to her husband, who also ate of it, and their eyes were both opened.

They realized they were naked and sewed fig leaf garments for themselves.

That evening the LORD came walking through his garden, and the man and woman hid from him. The man said he was afraid because he was naked. The LORD asked the man, "Who told you that you were naked? Have you eaten from the tree that I commanded you not to eat from?" (Genesis 3:11) The man said it was the woman's idea, and the woman said it was the serpent's idea. Then the LORD God was so angry at their disobedience that he cursed the serpent, the woman, the childbirth process, the man, and the ground. An underlying message from this story is that woman is to blame for the advent of evil in humankind because of her disobedience of eating the forbidden fruit.

Then the LORD God said, "The man has now become like one of us, knowing good and evil. He must not be allowed to reach out his hand and take also from the tree of life and eat and live forever." (Genesis 3:22). So the man and woman were cast out of the garden.

Questions

As I matured mentally and spiritually, some big questions came up in my mind:

1. How could God do so much in a single day?

I could imagine a cosmic force separating the land and the dry water and doing some of the other things in one big bang of energy, but plant life takes time to develop and adapt to its surroundings. For example, in 2008, I planted an orchard of eight dwarf fruit trees. The second year the pear trees produced fruit, by the fifth year the peaches started bearing, and at the time of this writing, the sour cherry tree has had a little fruit, but the sweet cherry tree tasted so good that the deer ate it all up!

Peach Branch

2. If the woman did not know the difference between good and evil, how could she be blamed for committing an evil act? She would have been too innocent to know any better.

3. What is so bad about wanting to know the difference between good and evil? I think raising one's consciousness and gaining more intelligence is a good idea. Why did the LORD want the humans to stay ignorant? Author Sally Kitch notices that the man could have vetoed the idea, but he gave in to it.[98] Why does he not carry equal blame?

4. If the LORD God is omnipotent, how could he create such inferior creatures that would not behave properly and fulfill their intended roles?

---

[98] Kitch, S. (2009). *The Specter of Sex: Gendered Foundations of Racial Formations in the United States.*

In other words, I'm a potter, and if I make a clay pitcher that will not hold water, why would I blame the pot and curse it for being leaky when I am the one who designed it?

Dr. Stone at her potter's wheel
Photo Credit: *The Elkhart Truth*

5. Wouldn't God under-stand human nature? If you tell a human, "You can eat anything but this one tree," the natural curiosity of people will really want that forbidden item.

6. Why is the LORD God so mean to the humans for something that really was not their fault?

When I read the Bible through several times as a teenager, the take-home message I got from the creation story was, "Shut up and obey. Don't ask questions. Do as you are told. Very bad things happen when you disobey God." Something did not sit right with me as I read about what a temper God had and how he slew his own people by the thousands when they made a transgression. In particular, I felt disturbed by how God regretted having made the humans and decided to destroy every last one of them in the flood. As I finished the rest of the Old Testament, I asked my mother, "Why was God so mean in the Old Testament?" She explained it to me. She simply said, "God wasn't a Christian yet." Her theory was that God himself was evolving and that a new age of love had dawned with the birth of the Christ.

This idea brought up further questions in my mind:

1. How could an omnipotent creator make a product so inferior (mankind) that he needed to destroy the whole project?
2. How could an omnipotent creator need an upgrade himself? Wasn't he already perfect?
3. Was God singular or plural? Genesis 1:26 says that God made man in *our* image. In Genesis 3:22, he says, "The man has now become like one of *us*, knowing good and evil." The Anunnaki called themselves gods and collaborated in a council.
4. The first commandment is, "Thou shalt have no other gods before me." Who are these other gods? If God is omnipotent, why would he create competition for himself and then get so angry about it?
5. Why does the Old Testament have so many struggles with foreign gods? Yahweh's people were always fighting with people who served other gods with great bloodshed involved.

Later, I understood the Adam and Eve story to be mythology explaining the author's view of relationships between God, man, woman, the animal and plant kingdoms, and Earth itself. While the exact details were not literally true, like God creating the sun, moon, and the stars in one 24-hour day, one point of the story was that an intelligent source greater than ourselves had created the universe with purpose and design.

Part of the societal organization in this story was that God had dominion over the males, and the males had dominion over the females, who were considered inferior because they were blamed for tempting the man in the Garden of Eden, an action which led to the whole species being cursed by God and tainted with original sin. The predominant patriarchal religions on the planet today put women in a position that is inferior and subordinate to the man: Islam, Catholicism, Mormonism, and Protestant denominations.

Another Viewpoint

The history of our beginnings as seen by authors Sitchin and Hardy is quite different. No original sin is in anyone. The humans were simply created as a slave species to mine gold for the Anunnaki. They were not given the power to reproduce, but rather were cloned. Enki's nickname was "The Serpent" because snakes coil, and the shape of DNA is two snakes coiled around each other. We see this symbol in the Caduceus, and Enki understood creation mechanics. They put the template of the male, who was named Adam, and the female template in Enlil's garden at Edin for protection. When Enki, Ninmah, and Enki's son Thoth upgraded the DNA of the humans so they could reproduce, Enlil became enraged. He feared that the humans would multiply and take over the whole planet. Enlil cursed the humans and kicked them out of his garden at Edin.

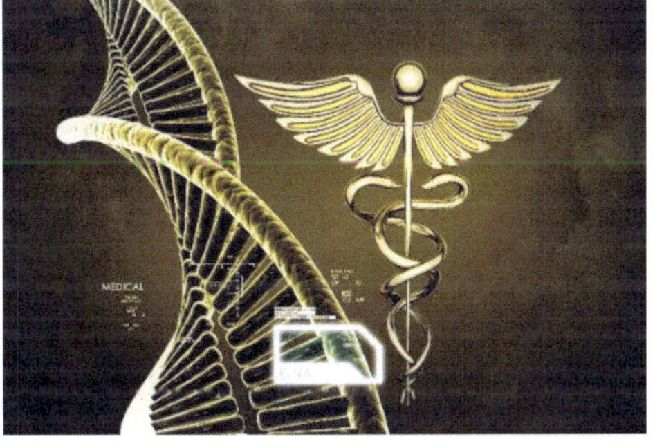

The Medical Symbol the Caduceus

Now, the challenge of our species is to come into balance with the masculine and feminine principles, both in gender roles in society and with the masculine and feminine sides within each person.

Divine Balance of Masculine and Feminine
Original Visionary Artwork by Eva M. Sakmar-Sullivan
www.stardolphin.com

The Sumerian tablets, which predate the Bible, shed light on these questions and discrepancies in the creation story in Genesis. They indicate that the rival gods in the Old Testament were competing Anunnaki relatives in the royal family vying for power and control of the humans on their Earth Gold Mining Mission.

The Extraterrestrial gods all wanted the allegiance of the humans to serve them, dig their ditches, tend their gardens, and bring them food. The supreme god of these Ancient Astronauts was Anu, and the main power struggle was between two of his sons, Enki and Enlil, and their offspring. The third section of my book *Transforming Fear into Gold*, "Hope for Humanity," goes into much more detail about the dramas that played out with these Ancient Astronauts.[99] How can we better work with the genetic challenges of our hybridized species? Several main points follow.

Author Michael Tellinger

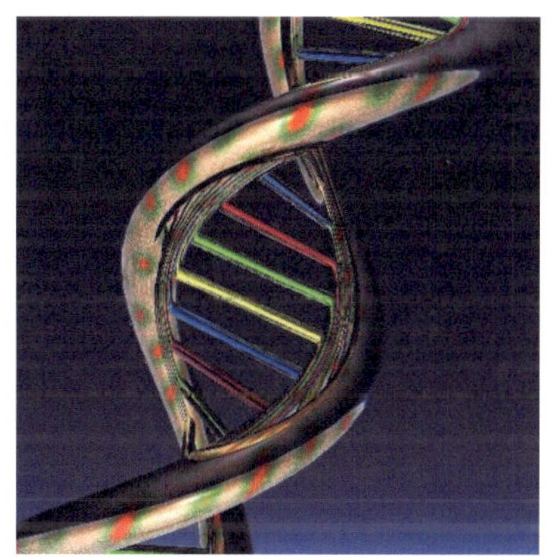

Raised in South Africa, Michael Tellinger makes the case in his book *Slave Species of god*[100] that the difficulties humans have getting along with people from other religions stems from the manipulation of our DNA, which suppressed our intelligence, removed our genetic memory, erased our

[99] Stone, B. (2012). *Transforming Fear into Gold: How Facing What Frightens You the Most Can Heal and Light Up Your Heart.*

[100] Tellinger, 2005.

knowledge, and shortened our lifespans—dumbing us down. The Sumerian Tablets indicate that the Ancient Astronauts had extremely long lives spanning hundreds of thousands of years, but they did not program our immune systems with the information needed to survive that long and purposely gave man a short lifespan. If man had eaten from the "tree of life" that Genesis talked about, he would have had a lifespan that was genetically programmed to be almost immortal. The gods certainly did not want that to happen! Genesis 6:3 reports, "Then the said, My Spirit will not contend with man forever, for he is mortal; his days will be a hundred and twenty years."

Li Ching-Yuen's Longevity

Li Ching-Yuen Public Domain https://commons.wikimedia.org/w/index.php?curid=1409394

Very few people currently live to be 120, but the New York Times ran an obituary for a Chinese man named Li Ching-Yuen who died on May 6, 1933, after living for 256 years. He evidently had lied about his age, because he claimed to have been born in 1736, which would have made him 197 years old at the time of his death from natural causes; however, official records show that the Chinese government sent him congratulations on his 150th birthday in 1827 and on his 200th birthday in 1877, placing his birthdate as 1677. Li Ching-Yuen produced over

200 offspring and outlived 23 wives. He was an herbalist and attributed his longevity to his diet, martial arts exercises, and spiritual practice. His advice for longevity was, "Keep a quiet heart, sit like a tortoise, walk sprightly like a pigeon and sleep like a dog."[101]

Imagine what we could do if we understood how to reprogram our immune systems to find and destroy pathogens, wire our genetic blueprints for self-repair, modulate our nervous systems to have quiet hearts, and connect with the spiritual resources available to have happy, healthy, vibrant longevity!

Michael Tellinger's 2009 book *African Temples of the Anunnaki: The Lost Technologies of the Gold Mines of Enki* points to ten million stone circles found around South Africa as evidence of the presence of a race of beings with superior

---

[101] https://www.7sky.life/how-the-chinese-herbalist-li-ching-yuen-atteined-256-years-of-age/

technology. The stone circles are laid out according to principles of sacred geometry and exhibit Tesla-like technology which generated energy that could carve immensely long tunnels straight into the Earth.

Tellinger reports that the De Beers mining company, which has the modern-day gold mining rights in South Africa, found an ancient gold mine shaft 22,000 feet deep that was cut straight down into the earth with a laser-like technology that we are not capable of today. Tellinger points to remains which show the presence of ore mining in southern Africa as far back as 100,000 years ago.[102] He tells of finding over 10,000 ancient gold mines that had been carved into the side of hills and were covered with mud in the great flood. Only now, 12,000 years later, is erosion exposing these ancient gold mines. His work supports the veracity of the historical account presented in the Sumerian tablets.

Physical Challenges

If the history of our race presented in the Sumerian tablets is true, then Homo sapiens sapiens would be a genetically engineered product. Tellinger theorizes that the Anunnaki purposely did not activate all the potential in human DNA so that we would remain their slaves, subservient to their orders. He points out that in humans, "97% of our DNA consists of non coding genes while in very simple creatures like fruit flies only 17% of the DNA contains noncoding genes."[103] Tellinger continues, stating that the human genome is "the same length of that of our maker, our genetic donor. The genes have however been tampered with, resulting in the

---

[102] Tellinger, M. (2009). *African Temples of the Anunnaki.*

[103] Tellinger, 2005, p. 52.

removal or shutting down of most of them (97%), leaving behind an unintelligent, primitive and subservient creature."[104] Cloned animals seem to be more prone to disease, as with the famous case of Dolly, the sheep cloned at the Roslin Institute in Scotland.[105] Most sheep have an average age of 10-12 years, and Dolly lived only six years. If we are a product that was genetically engineered and cloned by the Anunnaki to make the first Primitive Workers, then the diseases we are prone to would be no surprise. The Anunnaki seem to have lifespans that may reach 500,000 years, so they must know something about immunity that they did not give us—and with good reason. If every Homo sapiens born were still living 500,000 years later, either this planet would be way too full of people, or a law would have been passed against reproduction!

Emotional Challenges

Just as the physical body's immunity is lowered by stress, trauma lowers our emotional immunity. Although the Anunnaki had mental intelligence and scientific knowledge far surpassing our capabilities, in ancient times, they did not seem to have the spiritual intelligence necessary to master the art of brotherly love and living harmoniously with others. Anunnaki brothers fought viciously over power and territory. The imprint of fighting over power was handed down to Cain and Abel, the first two human brothers. The sibling antagonism inherited from their Anunnaki ancestors escalated and led to Cain murdering Abel. We know that impulse control lessens when a person has been drinking

---

[104] Ibid, p. 58.

[105] "What Happened to Dolly?" http://www.animalresearch.info/en/medical/timeline/Dolly

alcohol, and lack of impulse control continues to be a problem for humans, even when they have not been drinking. Could our difficulty with emotional function come from being a hybrid race? We do seem to have inherited the emotional problems of our ancestors the Anunnaki.

The indigenous races on earth seem to be closer to the life forms that evolved naturally on the Earth, and many indigenous tribes have great love, honor, and respect for our mother planet. We need these values to sustain life on Earth. The white-skinned races with more Anunnaki genes are in general more technologically advanced and seem to lack the concern for living in harmony with our planet that is the basis of indigenous religions. With our current technology-based society, we have put toxins into our environment which exacerbate the upheavals in weather patterns and increase natural disasters as Earth tries to bring herself back into balance.

Marduk's Turn to Rule

Enki's firstborn son Marduk had been promised that he would have a turn to rule the Earth in the age of the Ram, which started approximately 2,000 BCE. Marduk became obsessed with becoming the ruler of everything. He built a city for himself he called Babel, Babili, or Babylon and tried to make a tower so he could communicate directly with the Anunnaki. His Uncle Enlil did not want Marduk to have this communication capability, so he confused the languages of the workers, halting construction on the Tower of Babel. We have a similar story about the Tower of Babel in the Bible.

Marduk was not content to have control of Mesopotamia, just one of the four regions the Earth had been divided into after the flood. He wanted to control everything, including the fourth region on the Sinai Peninsula, location of the spaceport for travel to and from Nibiru.

The Right to Rule

An Anunnaki male needed to marry his half-sister by a different mother to have offspring that would be in line for the throne. The Anunnaki had perfect DNA, and this policy, which would be considered incest in most states in the USA, kept the royal bloodline purer. Enki was Anu's firstborn son, but his mother was not his father's half-sister, so Enki did not have the right of succession to the throne. Enlil was Anu's first son by his sister-queen, so Enlil was in line to rule on Nibiru when his father King Anu died. However, King Anu engaged their half-sister Ninmah to Enki, setting up Enki's son to rule after Enlil.

Macho Crush

Ninmah, having a mind of her own, liked Enlil's macho qualities and had an affair with him that produced an illegitimate son, Ninurta. King Anu was so furious with her crush on Enlil and her disregard for her engagement to Enki that he forbade Ninmah to ever marry.

After Enlil married someone else, Enki talked Ninmah into trying to have a son with him, because this son would have the right to rule. Enki and Ninmah tried twice, but both offspring were female. Having had children by both brothers, Ninmah was a neutral figure in conflicts between Enki and

Enlil. She was given charge of the Sinai Peninsula, so both brothers would have access to the Spaceport.

Takeover

Marduk, seething with anger over being neglected and disenfranchised for hundreds of thousands of years, raised armies of humans to do a total takeover when his turn came to rule. Marduk was popular with the humans because he had married a human named Sarpanit. The Niburian Council on Earth did not want Marduk to have the spaceport, or his takeover would be total. Over the objections of Enki, they authorized Marduk's younger brother Nergal and Enlil's son Ninurta to drop nuclear weapons on the Sinai Peninsula to destroy the spaceport rather than letting Marduk get control of it.[106]

Sodom and Gomorrah: Another Battle of Brothers

Enki was naturally opposed to using these nuclear "Weapons of Terror" against his son. In the council meeting, he got into an intense argument with his son Nergal, resulting in Enki disowning Nergal. Wounded by his father's words and furious with his older brother Marduk's totalitarian ambition, Nergal dropped bombs not only on the Sinai Peninsula, but also on five cities along the coast where he thought Marduk and Marduk's son Nabu were gathering forces. Two of those cities were Sodom and Gomorrah, and the story of their destruction is found in the Bible in Genesis 19. However, in the Bible, the reason for the destruction is given as the sinful nature of the people there.

---

[106] Sitchin, Z. (2002). *The Lost Book of Enki: Memoirs and Prophecies of an Extraterrestrial God.*

Cloud from Nuclear Blast

In the Sumerian Tablets, the reason is that Nergal was out of his mind with hatred for his brother Marduk and nuked the cities to try to kill his brother and his nephew Nabu.

The Evil Wind

The blast created by explosion of multiple nuclear weapons caused a huge windstorm to form, which the Sumerian tablets call "the evil wind." A cloud of nuclear radiation formed around the bomb sites and was blown by the storm over the region of Sumer, destroying all human, plant, and animal life. The Anunnaki had to scramble to their spaceships to escape. In a day, the Sumerian civilization was destroyed from this use of nuclear weapons. No wonder the Nordics tried to persuade President Eisenhower to ban nuclear weapons!

Conflict Between Brothers Isaac and Ishmael

Another war between brothers was brewing. Knowing that Marduk's turn to rule would be coming, Enlil wanted some humans loyal to him to serve him and bring him food. Enlil choose Abraham, son of Terah, the high priest in Enlil's temple, to make a great nation loyal to Enlil. When Abraham's wife Sarah was 75 years old, she was still barren. How would Abraham be the father of a great nation if he did not have any children? Needing offspring for Abraham, Sarah persuaded him to sleep with her Egyptian handmaiden Hagar. A son was born from that union and was named Ishmael. Later, when Sarah was 90, she miraculously bore a son to Abraham and named him Isaac. Now that Sarah had a son of her own, she kicked out Hagar and Ishmael. In compassion for them, the LORD promised to make a great nation of Ishmael also.

One way that Enlil tested Abraham's loyalty was asking him to sacrifice his son as a burnt offering, something other gods of that time were asking their people to do. In the Bible, Abraham is told to sacrifice his son Isaac. But in the Quran, the son Abraham is told to sacrifice is Ishmael. The Arabs are the descendants of Ishmael, and the Jews are the descendants of Isaac. These two groups are still at war with each other, with both claiming to be the favored descendants of their Father Abraham.

The Aryans and the Jews

World War II could be seen as an extension of the war between Enki and Enlil. Marduk had been the ruler on Mars, the way station to collect the gold to ship back to Nibiru every 3,600 years when the planet came close. The station was manned by 300 Igigi, Anunnaki who were genetically engineered to be superior astronauts and workers. The Igigi on Mars intermarried with human females, producing fair-skinned, blonde haired, blue eyed offspring—the Aryan race.

Hitler was obsessed with having a pure Germanic race of fair-skinned people. Hitler made war on the Jews, who were Enlil's people, killing millions of them. As a nation and a race, the Jewish people have been heavily persecuted down through history. This difficulty of making peace with other nations may not be totally our fault. It could be an inherited negative trait of our Anunnaki forefathers which we need to overcome, especially now that we have nuclear power and could wage a nuclear holocaust which would wipe humanity off the face of the Earth. The stakes are high! We need to transcend the conflict between brothers and our hatred for others who have different religions. Everyone came from the One True Creator of All. We are all passengers on the Spaceship Planet Earth, and either we trash our spaceship and we make ourselves extinct, or we work together to care for her and survive.

Chapter 5: Titans

More than one ancient culture speaks of battles between the gods that happened long ago. While most people consider these stories myths, Zecharia Sitchin's Earth Chronicles series presents these stories as actual physical battles that took place between members of the Anunnaki royal family vying for ultimate power and control. The Anunnaki may have also fought with other Star Civilizations.

Greek Mythology

Greek mythology is filled with battles between the gods, including the major struggle between the Titans and the Olympians. Around 700 BCE, the Greek poet Hesoid wrote a poem titled the *Theogony,* which means "the origins of the gods," delineating the genealogies of the Greek pantheon.[107] The poem also describes the origin of the world as starting with the spontaneous appearance of four primordial beings: Chaos, Gaia, Tartaros, and Eros.

[107] Hesoid. (1987). *Hesoid's Theogony.*

Gaia gives birth to Ouranos, the heaven. Then mother Gaia marries her son Ouranos, and heaven and earth, symbolizing the creation of the world, give birth to 12 children, the original dozen Titans: six males and six females. The six Titan females were named Mnemosyne, Tethys, Theia, Phoibe, Themis, and Rhea. The six males were Okeanos, Hyperion, Koios, Kreios, Iapetus, and Kronos, the youngest.

Perhaps the reason we look at this story as mythology is because a literal interpretation would be physically impossible. For example, in Greek mythology, Ouranos aggravates his wife Gaia because he will not let the children she bears out of her womb. He keeps making love with her, creating more children, and Gaia becomes very uncomfortable with a dozen offspring within her belly. She asks her children for help, and only Kronos has the courage to take action. Gaia fashions a sickle for him, and when his father Ouranos comes to make love with Gaia, Kronos reaches out of her womb with the sickle and castrates his father. He throws his father's severed penis into the ocean, and the foam it made on the sea gave birth to the goddess Aphrodite.

Photo credit: By Sandro Botticelli - Adjusted levels from File:Sandro Botticelli - La nascita di Venere - Google Art Project.jpg, originally from Google Art Project. Compression Photoshop level 9., Public Domain, https://commons.wikimedia.org/w/index.php?curid=22507491

Kronos then let all his other brothers and sisters out of their mother's womb.

The Entrance of Evil into the World

The castrated Ouranos called out to monster gods for revenge, including the Cyclopes. "His own children, he cried out, had become *Titans*..."[108] Kronos tried to hide away the monsters his father had summoned by imprisoning them in Tartaros, deep under the earth. Meanwhile, the goddess Nyx (night), child of the primordial being Chaos, responded to the call of Ouranos by bringing forth evil deities: the Destinies, Fates, Doom, Black Fates and Death, Blame and Painful Woe, Famine and Sorrows, Deceit and Strife, Retribution, and "also, Fighting, Battles, Murders, Killings, Quarrels, Lying Words, Disputes, Lawlessness, and Ruin."[109] The last evil deity Nyx brought forth was Retribution.

The Olympian Gods and Goddesses

Kronos then marries his sister Rhea, and they give birth to six children, the Olympian gods and goddesses Hestia, Demeter, Hera, Hades, Poseidon, and Zeus. All is well for a time, but then Kronos hears a prophecy that his son will overthrow him, just like he overthrew his own father. To try to avoid that prophecy coming true, Kronos eats each of the first five of his children. When Rhea is pregnant with her last son Zeus, she asks her parents for help. They hide her in a cave to birth the child, and then Rhea wraps up a stone in a blanket and gives it to Kronus. He swallows the stone, and it gives him such a bellyache that he vomits up the other five children he had eaten. Zeus then marries his sister Hera and unites with

---

[108] Sitchin, Z. (1985). *The Wars of Gods and Men: Book III of the Earth Chronicles,* p. 51.
[109] Ibid, p. 52.

his siblings and others who want to overthrow Kronos and wages war on the Titans. He releases the Cyclopes and the other beings Kronos had imprisoned in Tartarus, and they waged a mighty battle. Sitchin equates the Thunder Stone that Zeus hurled against the Titans as an atomic explosion. It created a loud noise, extreme heat, a blinding flash, and it also caused a windstorm. This weapon subdued the Titans, and Zeus locked them up deep under the earth, in Tartarus, guarded by the Cyclopes lest they escape.

Thus, the succession of Divine rule goes from Ouranos and Gaia, to the Titans Kronos and Rhea, to the Olympian head of all the gods Zeus and his wife Hera. Note the themes of the ruling god abusing his power and needing to be overthrown, the castration of a god, and the ruler marrying his sister.

Hindu Texts

Vedic literature, the ancient texts of the Hindus, tells of gods frequently battling with each other. Sometimes these gods, including Brahma, Vishnu, and Shiva, will fight in their true form, and sometimes they incarnate into an avatar who will fight for them. The tales show these gods possessing celestial chariots (spaceships), weapons of great power, and supernatural abilities.

Anunnaki Mythology

The Sumerian Tablets tell a story that parallels the Hindu and Greek myths that came later. Zecharia Sitchin's translation of the Sumerian Tablets frames the war between the Titans and the Olympians as a war between the House of Alalu, the previous king on Nibiru, and the House of Anu, father of Enki and Enlil. Sitchin suggests that TI.TA.AN in Sumerian meant

"Those Who in Heaven Live" and referred to the Igigi, an astronaut race led by Kumarbi, grandson of Alalu, against the House of Anu as the ones dwelling on Earth, for the right to the throne on Nibiru. How did enmity develop between these two houses? It went back to the developing civilization on Nibiru long, long ago.

Ancient Trouble on Nibiru

Sitchin's *The Lost Book of Enki* tells of difficulties in ancient times on Nibiru. As mentioned before in the Anunnaki chapter, fighting on Nibiru between the North and the South escalated to nuclear war, which ripped a huge breach in their atmosphere. The King of Nibiru, Alalu, tried using nuclear bombs on their volcanoes to produce more atmosphere, but the situation only got worse. Weather patterns were disrupted, crops failed, and all life on Nibiru was threatened. At this time, Anu came forward and challenged Alalu's right to rule, claiming Anu's genealogy was closer to the previous king's than that of Alalu. Not wanting to give up the throne, Alalu made Anu his cupbearer and gave his daughter to Anu's son Enki, promising that Anu could rule after him. Eventually, Anu got tired of waiting and challenged Alalu directly for the throne. According to Sitchin's interpretation of the story, the Council on Nibiru decided to settle the matter with a wrestling match between Alalu and Anu.[110]

Naked Wrestling Match

The Anunnaki traditionally wrestled naked. Anu won the match and therefore gained the throne on Nibiru. Alalu, fearing he might be executed, stole away on a spaceship loaded with nuclear weapons and headed toward Earth. He

---

[110] Sitchin, 2002.

blasted his way through the Asteroid belt with his nuclear weapons and landed safely on Earth. When he found the atmosphere was breathable and that Earth had significant quantities of gold, he radioed back to Nibiru that he had found the solution to their atmospheric breach problem: gold on Earth. He also insisted that if the plan worked, he would be made King on Nibiru again. Not really knowing what would happen, they agreed and sent Anu's son Enki to Earth to try out the process of extracting gold from Earth's seawater. The plan worked, so Alalu demanded to be King again. Anu resisted and challenged Alalu to another wrestling match to decide the matter. Alalu agreed and lost the match again. At the end of the fight, out of spite, Alalu bit off and swallowed Anu's testicles. Anu had 17 children and could not produce any more after that. For his spiteful deed, Alalu was taken to Mars and left to die a slow death from the poison that Anu's genitals made in his digestive system. Later, Alalu's grandson Kumarbi battled Anu for the throne.

Sitchin's Theory

In Sitchin's view, the Sumerian tablet titled *Kingship in Heaven* correlates the Greek God Zeus to the Anunnaki god Enlil. He sees the war of the Titans and the Olympians as a war between the House of Alalu, the olden Titan gods, and the House of Anu. This story reflects the Greek themes of the gods battling for control, super-weapons, and castration of the god.

Biblical Mention of Giants

The Bible speaks of giants walking the earth in several places. Genesis 6:4 says,

> The Nephilim were on the earth in those days, and also afterward, when the sons of God came in to the daughters of men; and they bore children to them. These were the mighty men that were of old, the men of renown. (NIV)

Another reference to much larger beings is in Numbers 13:33:

> We saw the Nephilim there (the descendants of Anak come from the Nephilim). We seemed like grasshoppers in our own eyes, and we looked the same to them.

Mexican Oral Tradition

When the conquistadors first encountered the native people in Mexico, they told the conquistadors stories of giants who had been there before. These myths and legends correlated to Biblical stories of giants once walking the land. In his book *Fingerprints of the Gods*[111], author Graham Hancock recounts stories from many parts of South America of giant gods living among them. The most prominent one was named Quetzalcoatl, and he brought culture and civilization to them. He was driven out by a dark force, but he promised to return one day. When the conquistadors landed, the indigenous people thought they were the gods, because although they were not 14 feet tall like Quetzalcoatl, they were taller than the natives, and they had white skin, blue eyes, and a beard, like Quetzalcoatl. They soon found out the conquistadores were not benevolent gods!

---

[111] Hancock, G. (1996). *Fingerprints of the Gods.*

Breaking My Arm

One winter day in 2014, while ice skating, I lost my balance, fell on the ice, and broke my arm. After my fragmented wrist bones were screwed back together, in meditation, I asked what happened. The story that came to me intuitively is wild and hard to believe, even for me, but I share it because of its alternative view of the Titans.

Genie

A deceased fire elemental spirit called a Djinn, otherwise known as a genie, was trying to get my attention. He tapped me on the shoulder while I was ice skating, and I lost my balance from what felt like a push.

The story he told me was that long ago, when the Anunnaki were mining gold on this planet, a Star Civilization of 50-foot-tall beings from the Belt of Orion landed and wanted to take the gold. They called themselves Titans. They fought with the Anunnaki, whose men were 12 to 14 feet tall. Both ET races had advanced weapons technology.

Appear-Disappear Tactic

The Anunnaki enslaved the Djinn to help them fight the Titans, since the invaders had the advantage of an additional 36 feet of height over the Anunnaki. The 8-foot tall Djinn had plasma bodies and could change from one dimension to the other, so the Djinn would pop into this dimension and poke a Titan in the eyes, knock a weapon out of his hand, or bother him in some other way, then pop out of this dimension again. This appear-disappear tactic was very frustrating to the Titans. The Djinn who pushed me to get my attention had been caught by a Titan before he could disappear again. The Titan angrily threw him on the ground and stomped on him, breaking every bone in his body. The Djinn told me I only had two bones broken, so he did not have much sympathy for my pain.

I did healing work with the Djinn, helping him with the trauma of this violent death and helping him transition into the beautiful palace in the World of Light for Djinn. I certainly did not want him pestering me anymore, and if the story he communicated is true, I had compassion for his suffering.

Titan Case Example

A 50-foot-tall Titan from Orion was killed in battle, and his spirit was attached to my client. The Titan was upset because his people did not take his dead body back with them to Orion. Being defeated, either the ones who could escape did so as fast as they could, leaving behind the fallen Titans, or the whole group was killed, so none of them could go back.

In the Soul Detective session, we treated the trauma of this deceased Titan and then asked the Beings of Light to take his spirit back to his planet in the Belt of Orion. We asked to multiply the benefits for any other Titans who were killed on this planet and were still earthbound to join the healing and go back to the higher dimensions of Light around their home planet for a "Welcome Home Warriors" party. Since a regular size ghost will upset a dog or a cat in the house, think what a 50-foot-tall ghost would do!

Chapter 6: Sheep May Be Extraterrestrial

According to the Sumerian Tablets, after the flood, when the humans were being taught skills and organized into cities, King Anu decided to send sheep from Nibiru to Earth. Sheep would be useful to the humans to have wool to spin into yarn to make clothing, milk to drink, meat to eat, and hides to keep them warm. Females and sheep essence (sperm) were transported to Earth to artificially inseminate the females to build flocks of sheep.[112]

What does Wikipedia think?

Wikipedia estimates the date of the first domesticated sheep to be between 11,000 and 9,000 BCE, which would place it right after the flood, estimated to have been about 10,800 BCE. Since Wikipedia does not have a belief system that the sheep may have been dropped in from another planet, it says, "The exact line of descent between domestic sheep and their wild ancestors is unclear." They postulate that "a currently

[112] Sitchin, 2002.

unknown species or subspecies of wild sheep…contributed to the formation of domestic sheep."[113]

One of the qualities of sheep that makes them great domesticated animals is that when shearing their wool, the sheep hold very still. Can you imagine trying to shear a cat? One would not get the same level of cooperation! Perhaps the sheep are happy to get their wool coats taken off in the spring so they will not get too hot, or perhaps they were genetically engineered to be compliant.

Sheep are flock animals and like to stick together. This flocking instinct makes them easier to handle as domesticated animals and easier for a dog to protect them against predators. Sheep and goats are the first animals that humans domesticated. The two animals do not interbreed, as they are different species. Sheep have 54 chromosomes, and goats have 60 chromosomes.[114] Sheep are also an excellent animal to domesticate because they like to graze on grass. They do not need to be fed grains, so they are easier for humans to raise. Sheep are meek and have a strong instinct to follow the leader of the flock. The flocking instinct is so strong in sheep that they will follow a leader even into danger. In Turkey in 2006, a sheep tried to cross a 15-meter-deep ravine. The rest of the flock followed, all 400 sheep plunging to their deaths.[115]

---

[113] "History of domestic sheep." Wikipedia. https://en.wikipedia.org/wiki/History_of_the_domestic_sheep
[114] Zahra, S. "The Characteristics of Sheep Vs. Goats." https://animals.mom.me/characteristics-sheep-vs-goats-5493.html
[115] "Sheep 201: A Beginner's Guide to Raising Sheep." http://www.sheep101.info/201/behavior.html

What do you think about this theory of sheep coming from a Star Civilization and being transported to Earth in spaceships?

Chapter 7: Regulans

The popular movie *Avatar* showed humans traveling to a fictional exoplanetary moon named Pandora to mine a precious mineral.

Starburst Galaxy **Photo Credit: ESA/Hubble & NASA and N. Grogin (STScl)**

The beings on Pandora were half human and half cat, and very wise. While the movie is fiction, it may hide a truth in plain sight that other Star Civilizations exist and that humans are mining resources on other planets. Author Margaret Doner claims the cat-humans portrayed in *Avatar* are from the multiple star system of Regulus and that these Reguluns have both human and feline characteristics. They listen and feel with their whole body, making them very sensual. "Because their planet was destroyed by the robots under the command of the Andromedan scientists…they resonate deeply with the experiences of the Native Americans and the destruction of their lands." [116]

---

[116] Doner, M. (2012). *Merlin's War: The Battle Between the Family of Light and the Family of Dark,* p. 168.

These two case examples involve cat-like beings that came from the stars.

1st Case: Messenger

In the early days of the Anunnaki, a being from another dimension wanted to help the Anunnaki with their spiritual development. He incarnated as a large member of the cat family and hurled through a tunnel of Light from higher realms to one of Enki's daughters. He approached her out in nature. Enki was alarmed by this magnificent feline and feared for his daughter's safety. He captured and chained the feline. Enki missed the telepathic communication from this higher spirit, who wanted to help the Anunnaki raise their vibration, and he missed the opportunity to benefit from the wisdom of another Star Civilization. Enki kept the creature like a pet tiger for his daughter. With his spirit broken by captivity, the magnificent beast died.

Currently, he is incarnated as a human male and has a different relationship with the soul of Enki's daughter, who is now incarnated as a human female. In this lifetime, they are learning from each other, and she is listening to his wisdom.

2nd Case: Help from a Star Woman

Pearl came into my practice with full consciousness of her soul being part of a Star Civilization group of cat like beings who were helping Earth with the ascension process. She had volunteered to take on a human body to bring the values of her higher-dimensional planet to Earth. Her star group had files collected on traumatized groups that needed healing. Pearl had done several earlier healing sessions where she asked me to be part of the process. In this session, Pearl asked to open an intergalactic portal to connect to the heart of humanity and to clear the files her soul team had collected on people who had experienced the trauma of war, terrorism, cruelty, sexual slavery, torture, and the helplessness of people witnessing atrocities without being able to stop them. Pearl felt that the curses the Old Testament God placed on the man, the woman, and the land were part of why this planet has had so much strife. We invited the one who placed the curses into our sacred space. Pearl saw red and black screens that then moved together and started to shift to red-pink. Red and black are root chakra colors. Pink is the color of the heart, a blending of red for the root chakra and white for the crown chakra, merging to form pink in the center of the body.

Enlil Resists

The one who came forth was the Anunnaki ruler LORD Enlil, and he did not want to rescind his curses. Pearl saw that Enlil had not been programmed for compassion and had no emotional heart. He was not programmed for love, and he had no counterbalance for the empty place in the energy field of his heart.

Enlil felt hurt that his father, King Anu, had favored his older brother Enki by engaging their sister Ninmah to Enki. Enlil felt sadness, isolation, and envy that he had been left out of the happiness that came to other people. Pearl quoted from one of her teachers, "The unresolved past is hidden in the unhealthy now." —Starr Fuentes

Infusing Enlil with Love

We asked for a circle of angels to surround Enlil and to beam love into his energy field to create an emotional heart. We asked the angels to open the love fire hoses and blast Enlil with streams of pure love from the heart of the Great Creator of All.

We asked the Seraphim to sing love songs to him. Pearl told Enlil, "You are a child of the great creator too, and you can be loving and healthy." Enlil softened with this infusion of love and caring. He rescinded the curses he had placed on the man, the woman, and the ground. He apologized to his brother Enki, saying, "I'm sorry I did so much to mess up your creations."

Chapter 8: Insectoids

The Insectoids are another one of the four races that the Honorable Paul Hellyer, former Canadian Minister of Defence, has disclosed as having interactions with humans. The idea that beings looking like insects could be intelligent and highly developed technologically seemed very strange to me at first. However, insects have an efficient and protected body form, with their hard outer shell and light weight, and many have the capacity to fly. While I do not have extensive knowledge of the Insectoid races, I report what other researchers have found plus my personal experiences with insectoid beings.

Rick Strassman, M.D.

Insectoids showed up in the research of Rick Strassman with DMT (N,N-dimethyltryptamine), a hallucinogenic tryptamine drug found in many plants and animals. At death, the brain secretes a single drop of the chemical DMT, called the spirit molecule. This substance transports a person into a different realm, a journey the soul takes when we leave the physical body. Dr. Strassman did experiments with giving people small amounts of DMT to see what happened. The study subjects had a variety of experiences, some pleasant and some frightening. One study subject found himself in another world on a table surrounded by beings that looked like huge insects. The Insectoids were asking each other how Dr. Strassman's test subject got there![117]

[117] Strassman, R. (2000). *DMT: The Spirit Molecule: A Doctor's Revolutionary Research into the Biology of Near-Death and Mystical Experiences.*

Barbara Lamb, MS, MFT, CHT

Hypnotherapist Barbara Lamb has worked extensively with people who identify as hybrids of part-human and part-extraterrestrial origin. Her book *Meet the Hybrids: The Lives and Missions of ET Ambassadors on Earth* (2015) presents the case histories of eight hybrids. The focus of these stories is on the evolution of human consciousness and the care and protection of life on our planet. Her work presents an uplifting picture of the hybridization process and the Star Civilizations involved in the process. Her subjects report Insectoids that look like praying mantises, called Mantis Beings, that are eight to ten feet tall.[118]

Elena Danaan on Insectoids

Author Elena Danaan describes 110 different alien races in her book *A Gift from the Stars: Extraterrestrial Contacts and Guide of Alien Races.* Danaan says the Mantis Beings call themselves the "Akara" and that they have a code of ethics based not on what is good or bad, but on what is useful and logical or not. Accordingly, the Mantis Beings sometimes participate in hybridization programs that violate basic human rights but do not violate their own criteria of usefulness. She reports they look like a Praying Mantis standing upright that come in green, white, or black, and that they can be up to nine feet tall.[119] Because of their advanced technological knowledge of vibrational frequencies, their scientists have been hunted and enslaved by other alien races.

---

[118] Clare, C. (Producer & Director). (2020, February). *ETs Among us 4: The Reality of ET/Human Hybrids*. USA. Prism Pictures.

[119] Danaan, 2020, p. 209.

Danaan reports that the Mantis Beings come from the Sombrero Galaxy, which she says is 28 million light years away from Earth. NASA says the Sombrero Galaxy is 31.1 million light years away from Earth. Both distances are so big they are hard to imagine, but they are roughly in the same ballpark of a long way from here!

The Sombrero Galaxy

Photo from NASA/Hubble Heritage Team

In the constellation Virgo. Its diameter measures about 49,000 light years across, about 30% of our Milky Way Galaxy. Because of its bright nucleus, the bulge of stars in the middle, and the prominent dust lane around it, it looks like a hat. This shape is called lenticular because it is flat, circular, and shaped like a lens.

The following researcher presents a view of ET-human hybrids that contrasts sharply with the benevolent view of Barbara Lamb.

David Jacobs, PhD

Hypnotherapist Dr. David Jacobs has found large praying mantis-type beings in the reports of many abductees he has interviewed. In his research, these highly intelligent Insectoid beings seem to be at the top level of control, with both the short grays and the tall grays being under their supervision and command.[120] An abductee describes an Insectoid as follows: "He is very tall and is usually wearing a cape or long robe with a high collar. He often is described as an insect-like being who looks somewhat like a praying mantis or a giant ant."[121] Jacobs reports an unusual theory of the origin of the grays in the report of a research subject he calls Reshma Kamal. "The insectlike aliens told her that the gray aliens were products of early attempts at hybridization with humans but the program was flawed and it left the gray aliens without the ability to reproduce."[122] Kamal goes on to report that the Insectoids then began a new program of hybridization with humans "with different techniques that has taken more time but has been fruitful,"[123] as we humans have the ability to reproduce.

---

[120] Jacobs, D. (2015). *Walking Among Us: The Alien Plan to Control Humanity.*

[121] Jacobs, D. (1998). *The Threat: Revealing the Secret Alien Agenda,* p. 94.

[122] Jacobs, 1998, p. 130.

[123] Ibid.

The Threat

The shocking theory that Dr. Jacobs developed from his interviews with 150 abductees is that the aliens are hybridizing with humans and have perfected their technique in stages of hybridization. First, they insert some of their genetic material into a human sperm and egg, gestating the fetus in the human female for several months, and then removing the fetus from the mother and finishing gestation in a tank on their spaceship. These hybrids look like small sickly grays, but some genetic material from these first stage hybrids is then spliced into another human fetus, with the process being repeated several times, with each generation looking more human. The end stage produces a being indistinguishable from a human, which Jacobs calls a "hubrid." These hubrids have the alien ability to make a neural interface with the minds of humans to control their thoughts, emotions, and behavior. In the theory of Dr. Jacobs, these hubrids live and work among us, and abductees help them integrate into human society by explaining human emotion and social customs to them. Abductee Reshma Kamal was told that a change was coming to Earth in which "there will be only one form of government: The insectlike aliens will be in complete control. There will be no necessity to continue national governments."[124]

The thought of a praying mantis being the ruler of the planet is pretty scary to me! When Dr. Jacobs published his book *The Threat* in 1998, the message the abductees were getting was that the change would be very soon, but the aliens were vague about dates. Abductee Jason Howard was told by an

---

[124] Ibid, p. 252.

alien that the change would come around 1999, and fortunately, that has not happened.[125] Or perhaps our planet has multiple timelines, with a variety of alternate realities, and in one of them, the Insectoids did take over.

The work of Dr. Jacobs differs from most of the other researchers in the field. Dr. Jacobs discounts the research of John Mack on the grounds that Jacobs only trusts information from hypnosis that is properly conducted, and he feels Dr. Mack had a biased belief that contact with Star Civilizations leads to higher states of consciousness for the humans. Jacobs does not trust conscious first-hand reports like the information from Billy Meier (Chapter 17: Pleiadians) and George Adamski (Chapter 18: Venusians), who each had repeated contacts with benevolent Star People and have photographs as evidence. Every researcher has bias, and readers need to listen inside for what resonates as truth.

Terry Lovelace, Esq.

The firsthand account of author Terry Lovelace, Esq., agrees with the concept that ETs are abducting people and making human-alien hybrids. In his book *Incident at Devils Den: A True Story* (2018), Lovelace reports a terrifying abduction that happened to him in 1977.

As a young adult, he went camping with his friend Toby in a remote area of Devil's Den National Park. Although the aliens wiped his memories of this traumatic event, under drug-assisted hypnosis during a military investigation, Lovelace remembered shocking details of what happened. He

[125] Ibid.

recalled humans in uniform on the huge ET triangular spaceship as part of the crew, aquarium tanks filled with grotesque genetic experiments, and 50 or 60 other captive humans present. He says a tall, cold human-sized praying mantis being was in charge of the research. When the men were returned to their tent, both Terry and Toby were extremely ill and covered with sunburn head to toe, possibly radiation burns. Terry survived this painful ordeal, but his friend Toby was hurt worse than he was and never made a full recovery, dying in the months after the trauma.

Implants

Terry tried to repress these traumatic memories. Then in 2012, an X-ray revealed an anomalous implant in his thigh which he is certain was used to track him throughout his life. A human-alien hybrid he called Betty befriended him through multiple abductions that started in childhood. He remembered being taken on a trip to the moon with Betty, where she showed him cities on the dark side of the moon. She said humans were there studying the rocks. Betty came to him again in 2017 after he spoke at the Houston UFO Conference about his experiences. Betty warned Lovelace not to publish his book, or his government would kill him. Others who have tried to reveal the alien presence on earth have disappeared or have been killed in mysterious ways, sometimes made to look like a suicide.

Betty warned him that if he went through with his book, her people would remove his implants as they are evidence of his involvement with ETs. Betty also did not want the government seeing the technology in the implant. Sure enough, the next month, Lovelace awoke with sores on both thighs where his implants had been removed—but they left thin wires where they had been. Despite the danger, Lovelace went forward with telling his story. He is adamant that people need to know the truth about the alien presence on earth.

Barry Littleton

In the movie *The Cosmic Secret,*[126] Contactee Barry Littleton[127] reported that he was tutored (not tortured, but tutored!) as a child by a helpful, highly advanced being that looked like an insectoid. Littleton felt great love from this higher dimensional entity, who tried to make himself look more human so as not to frighten Barry.

Note that the being is wearing a cloak with a high collar, a sign of status.

Insectoids Do a Brain Surgery

In a case that Dr. Edith Fiore reported, a man named Ted had an angioma when he was 18 months old. The enlarged blood vessel in his brain interfered with his vision and regressed his motor skills from walking back to crawling. The doctors attending his case were certain Ted would not live to

---

[126]Everitt, T., Graham, B., Kennedy, L.I., Richards, R.R., & Salla, M. (Producers). Goode, C. & Richards, R. R. (Co-Directors). (2019, November 19). *The Cosmic Secret.* [Documentary Film.} USA. SBA Entertainment. https://www.cosmicnews.org/2020/12/04/the-cosmic-secret-david-wilcock-full-movie/

[127] www.barrylittleton.com

adulthood. When Ted was three years old, he was taken into a spacecraft with lights and dials on the wall. He was surrounded by beings of different sizes and shapes. Ted reported, "The ones that are a little bit taller than I am, their heads are very strange…kind of like a grasshopper. But the taller ones' heads are a little bit different. They're more like insects."[128] Ted reported these Star People had a laser apparatus that emitted a narrow beam of light to cut open the top of his head, lift up his skull, reduce the enlarged blood vessel to ash, suction out the ash, and then replace the top of his head and mend the atoms of the incision back together in a way that left no scar. After that intervention, Ted was able to walk again and developed normally, to the astonishment of his physicians.

Case Example of Bee Insectoids

An item on my Soul Detective diagnostic checklist is "interdimensional parasites." In one case, these parasites looked like bees buzzing around the area of my client's head, pulling out energy.

Our dowsing identified their origin as an Insectoid ET race. I asked who could help, and a being from the highest rank of angels, the Seraphim, came. I call her Serafina.

---

[128] Fiore, 1989, p. 135

She sang a "Come with Me" song in the language of the bee race, and Serafina held out a huge bowl filled with honey and the golden nectar of the gods.

"Nectar of Divine Essence" Original Visionary Artwork
by Eva M. Sakmar-Sullivan www.stardolphin.com

She wafted the bee-like insectoids away from my client's head to someplace better for them. They all left except one, which would not go. I asked three times, and it stayed. This insectoid turned out to be an Artificial Intelligence scout and marker which was there marking the field of the client for further Insectoid invasion. I asked Archangel Michael to dissolve it, but instead, Michael swatted it like a bug and crushed it since it was just a machine. I asked Serafina to keep protecting my client in the future from Insectoid invasion.

Personal Encounter June 13, 2015 with the Lahuma Insectoid Race

My husband Robert woke up one morning with a dream about St. Francis Zavier, a missionary who felt the Hindu Brahmans were in league with demons and mutilated them, cutting out their tongues so they could not speak untruth and cutting off their ears. When he told me this dream on June 10, 2013, I suddenly felt an extremely intense itching in my right ear. I scratched it, and it only itched more. A black fly bite on my neck a couple inches below also itched, but the ear sensation was much more intense. My ear lobe swelled up to double its size. I saw a round puncture mark on the outside edge of my ear about 2 mm in diameter. The puncture on the bug bite below it was a tiny red spot in the center where the fly had drawn my blood. The ear continued to itch, and as I scratched it a bit later, a hard, crusty thing came out of it, which I assumed was a scab. I did not even look at it at the time.

Insectoid Egg Sac

The previous week, I had consulted on a case in which a man I will call Henrique was possessed by an entity. An intuitive healer saw an egg sac on Henrique's back as he passed her in the waiting room, and lots of dark energy was around him. In our Soul Detective consultation, we found an Insectoid ET attached to Henrique. I sensed this Insectoid had gotten lost and was stranded away from her people. We had the angels open up a one-way wormhole back to her home, and over the course of the next 30 seconds, the insectoid left our dimension and returned to her people.

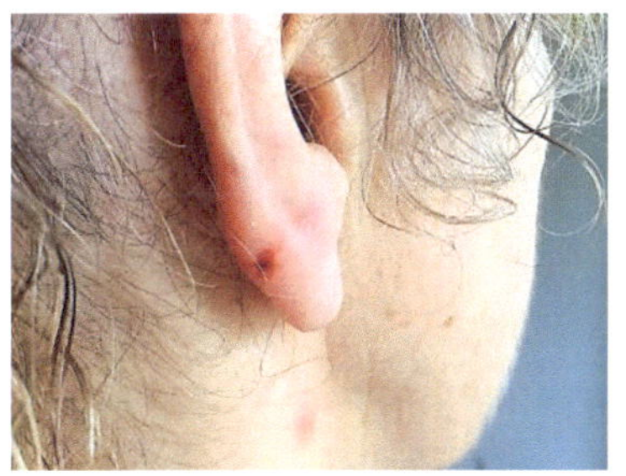

Reflecting on this session, I started to think about how my ear wound was not acting like a regular insect bite. Black flies pick a spot where they can land on all fours, a flat place like on my neck. This wound was on the skinny edge of my ear lobe. Plus, the diameter of the red spot was 2 mm, way too big for an insect proboscis. My muscle testing indicated that it was an ET implant from an insectoid!

The next morning Robert and I addressed the issue. A combination of muscle testing and pendulum dowsing indicated the wound was from an attempted ET implant. I wonder if the thing I scratched off that I thought was a scab might have been an implant.

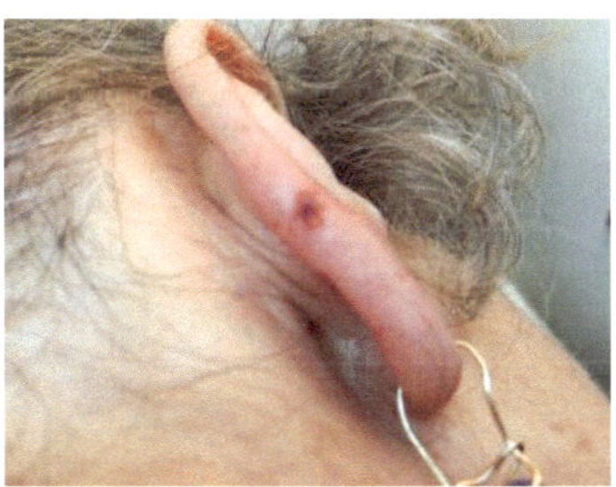

Note the markings around the wound almost look like a miniature Caspar the friendly ghost. The wound was healing slowly, and the ear was not as swollen in the second photo.

ET Insectoid

I asked my highly intuitive friend and colleague Janet Nestor to do a session with me to check into the situation. Her pendulum dowsing indicated the origin of the wound on my ear was surgery from an ET insectoid. She connected with a being that looked like an ant but was highly intelligent and communicated with her. The Insectoid said its people were peaceful and our people on this planet were not. We asked why it put the wound on my ear, and it said it had meant no harm. Janet asked why they did it, and the entity responded that its race was very interested in the things that Barbara Stone was doing because they were different from what most humans do, and they wanted to put the implant in my ear to monitor my activities.

I felt angry about the invasion and asked if they had ever heard of remote viewing. The Insectoid was offended, saying that remote viewing was very primitive technology. They did not want to remote view me, because the process required someone to watch me at all times. The implant could trace everything I did without that constant vigilance. Then they asked if they could look at me through a telescope-like instrument attached to their spaceship, though they did not like to call their vehicles ships. I did not want to agree to anything with them!

L.H.

As the conversation progressed, the Insectoid said his civilization was highly advanced with technology far beyond ours and had been on Earth long before humans came. They repeated they had meant no harm. I asserted that they had harmed me. I asked if they understood that placing an Insectoid implant in my ear would distort the flow of subtle energy in my body and harm me. They responded that most humans would not notice. Still not trusting, I asked for a name. Since Janet could not understand his complicated real name, it agreed to be called Larry. I asked if I could call him Aunt Larry, and he was not pleased with my insectoid pun. Then Janet started laughing and said he had given her a humorous response, to call him "Larry the Great." The name we then all agreed on was L.H., which were the initials of his unpronounceable name.

L.H. said their people live in a different Universe, but they like to visit Earth, like we enjoy visiting Alaska. They can live very well here. He said they are much more highly developed than us. We had trouble understanding their civilization with our third dimensional thinking, but he said it equates to what we could call the 10th dimension. We kept asking about their purpose here, and they were evasive, repeating they meant no harm. I repeated that they had harmed my ear, and I did not trust them. L.H. said they wanted to help me with my healing work, but because they had invaded my body, I still did not trust them.

Interview with L.H.

The following day my husband Robert and I did a shamanistic journey to talk with L.H. again. We asked the High Council of the Galactic Federation, a union of planets and races working together for the good of the galaxy, to join us and saw that L.H. was in the custody of Archangel Michael, having been arrested for attempting to invade me.

Robert pointed out that the angels vibrated at the 6th dimensional level, far below the 10th dimension that L.H. had claimed to be from. L.H. shamefully admitted that he was not from the 10th dimension and had been assigned to invade me. He wanted to know if we were going to strip his genitals.

ROBERT: Hm. Interesting thought. I didn't know you had genitals. Hm. Now I know. I'm not sure what I would do with them. Is this a customary practice among your people? If someone has been shamed, you strip their genitals?

BARBARA CHANNELING L.H.: This is what happened to the Greys.

ROBERT: Ah. Do you have two genders, or three, or four? What do you have in your people?

L.H. reported that most of them had two genders, but some had only one and could reproduce without a mate, having both male and female within.

The Boss

L.H. reported that he had a boss that looked like a praying mantis. He was worried about what his boss would do to him for failing in his mission. He told us that in his race, a person who fails is crushed like a bug. His boss had assigned him to stop me because of what I did with the Insectoid who had an egg sack on Henrique's back.

Earth Takeover

We asked whether his people wanted to take over our planet. L.H. admitted they liked our planet and would like to have it. His logic was that the humans are not nice to this planet, and the planet would be better off without them on it. He said we humans would destroy the planet with our low-level wars, using our bombs and hatefulness toward each other. Earth would be purer if their peaceful race had dominion over everything. If they eliminated the humans like bugs, it would be nice on this planet at last.

Robert pointed out that the boss wanting revenge against Barbara sounded a lot like us humans. The boss of L.H. did not like that Barbara found a way to stop the plan with Henrique by sending the Insectoid home and removing the egg sac, which was supposed to hatch and go to Henrique's brain.

Robert asked what they would do with the Draco Reptilians, another Star Civilization already on the planet, if they eliminated all the humans. L.H. replied that there were not many of the Reptilians, and they were underground. The insectoids would be above ground, away from those pesky things. Robert also asked what they planned to do about all the other ET races interested in this planet. He pointed out some of these other Star Civilizations were more highly evolved than us humans—Andromedans, Arcturians, and other races. These other advanced races seem to have an interest in helping us to evolve rather than exterminating us to save the planet, and they might oppose the insectoid takeover.

L.H. felt stupid once Robert raised these questions, so Robert changed the topic and asked if L.H. had a soul. With help, L.H. found a spark of light inside of himself. But his boss had placed a helmet of control around his head to program L.H. to just take instructions and do as he was told. His soul was present but shielded, like an ant having a hard shell around its body. L.H. was afraid of his boss, so Robert asked Archangel Michael to put a shield around him from all dimensions. L.H. liked that intervention, so Robert asked Archangel Michael to lift the helmet so he could see the Divine in himself. L.H. found his heart and his soul and felt amazed.

ROBERT: Now L.H., this makes us brothers. We humans have souls. We are connected like brothers from the Source of All. Even your boss is connected to the Source of All. The plan I envision is to create a one-way mirror for the boss, the praying mantis, so he can look at what is going on with you without being able to intervene. We ask for Barbara and me to remain invisible to this boss. We would like him to know that what L.H. has discovered is a wonderful thing, and that he can make the same inquiry within himself. Maybe Michael could speak to the boss directly.

Archangel Michael communicated to us that these Insectoids had been under a spell or mind control program of darkness that had hidden their emotional nature, had hidden their souls from them. This was not for all bug-people, just for this group. Robert remarked that they might like a more glorious name for themselves than bug-people. L.H. asked us to call them the Lahuma people.

Robert wanted to address the Lahuma King, as going to the top level of control is more efficient than reforming foot soldiers one at a time. I was already way outside of my comfort zone, but my pendulum indicated it was safe and in the highest good of everyone for us to speak with the King and Queen of the Lahuma people.

Dark Force Invasion

Some of the Lahuma had been invaded by Dark Force Entities. Robert tested that the King had been infected with dark energy but not the Queen. We set up communication, maintaining a shroud of invisibility and inaudibility around ourselves. The Queen was telling the King that he should listen to us, and the King was telling her to shut up. The following dialogue ensued:

ROBERT: We ask to speak with you and your Queen. I've been told that you are called Lahuma people. We have asked to speak with you rather than capture you too, because we want you to know we mean you no harm, and we ask to create communication rather than trouble.

LAHUMA KING: That's what we tell people when we want to invade them. That's what L.H. said to Barbara, that he meant her no harm, so I don't trust you.

ROBERT: The feeling is mutual. That's why we wish to speak.

KING: Speak.

Robert opened a window of observation so the King could observe the discovery L.H. had made of the Light of his own heart and soul. The Queen persuaded the King to look at what L.H. was showing him. The picture we saw is that their race was in the process of shifting into the 4th dimension. Some beings, like the Queen, had already made the transition to the 4th dimension, but others were still in the 3rd dimensional domination modality. The King looked inside himself and wondered whether he had one of those helmets of control.

Archangel Michael showed the King that the helmet was around his heart, plus a subtler vibration of control around his whole being from the dark entities.

Freedom from Bondage

The King asked Archangel Michael to set him free from those bondages. The Queen's heart was very open to the King, and she was so happy that he was asking to be set free from the darkness that skewed his vision of what was right and appropriate for the planet.

Before L.H. went back into the custody of the King, he asked for an angelic bodyguard from the 6th dimension around him to protect him so he would not get attacked by those who have not converted yet. Robert suggested the King should declare L.H. to be a hero and to put him in a place of importance to instruct the others about how they can make this transformation into the 4th dimension. The King wanted this transformation so his people would know truth, and we asked Archangel Michael to send angels to help them with this upgrade.

Jaw Pain

Next Robert asked if the pain in his jaw and ear was from the Lahuma people. L.H. hung his head and admitted he had placed an energetic wedge in a nerve in Robert's jaw to try to stop him as well as me. Robert inquired how they got through his defenses, and L.H. reported they got in through a tiny crack in Robert's armor from times in his past lives where he had destroyed life and had not yet fully forgiven himself. Though Robert could not remember these past lives, he wanted his armor to be intact, so he said the following prayer:

I, Robert Alcorn, and whoever else I may be or may have been, ask forgiveness for all the evil I have done. I ask forgiveness of those I have harmed. I thank those who are willing to forgive me, and I thank those who are not yet willing to forgive me for the forgiveness which will come. Know that I love you all.

We asked that if any of the ones Robert had harmed in the past history of his soul remained earthbound, that the Soul Detective angels would find them, help them to heal, to move past the things that happened during the wars, and to go into the next world for healing and education. Robert pointed out that if he had not killed them, they would have killed him. We realized we were all stuck in that kind of military thinking at one point.

Robert asked Yeshua (Jesus), to see what he could do about his jaw and the pain in his teeth. Yeshua communicated that if they took out the wedge, it would hurt a little bit right when they did it, but then it would heal. Robert asked them to go for it. We watched as an energetic device that looked like a fishhook was straightened and then taken out. The process stung, but then the jaw just felt sore, and it healed over the next few days.

We added these affirmations for Robert's past lives:

- I did the best I could at that time in the past, and I ask forgiveness for my mistakes
- I did the best I could with the information I had.
- I forgive myself for all the mistakes I made.
- I'm open to learning more.

- I'm doing the best I can.

This encounter gave Robert a chance to deepen healing of his past life wounds, and we offer the prayer and affirmations he used to anyone else who has had a lifetime as a warrior where the person incurred karma by taking life in the service of protecting their loved ones.

Reflections on the Insectoids

Since this episode, we have not had any further intrusion from the Lahuma people. Insectoids have not come up very often in my work, but the hole burrowed in my ear made this one unforgettable!

Case Example of a Failed Insectoid Mission

Edgar felt shut down in everything he did. When he learned something new like dowsing, it would work for a while, and then it would stop working. He would try a new supplement, and it would work for a time, but then it quit working. When he tried electronic wellness devices, they would sometimes reduce his energy level rather than increasing his wellness. My pendulum dowsing indicated Edgar had a "Shut-Down Mechanism" in his system that one of his previous incarnations had placed on him to try to keep him out of trouble. Here is the wild story that emerged from this work:

Mack the Insectoid

Edgar once had an incarnation in an insectoid race, a being who called himself Mack. Seeing that the humans needed help, Mack came to earth to try to be of service. Because he looked like a big bug, the humans captured him and tortured him with experiments which finally killed him. The humans tried to clone pieces of Mack to use as artificial intelligence devices that would look like a bug but would contain micro surveillance equipment.

Mack did not want Edgar to get well in this lifetime, because Mack feared that if Edgar mobilized his desire to help humanity, he would get into bad trouble again! Mack was shutting down Edgar's progress at every turn. Mack felt he was still in the lab being tortured. We used a Matrix Energetics[129] technique of creating a different timeline for him in which he never got caught and tortured, and then we were able to get this piece of Edgar's soul free from Mack's torture and the Shut-Down Mechanism.

Soul Lesson

The lesson for the soul Mack and Edgar shared was to be careful about what form he uses to present himself when he wants to help people. This time his soul incarnated into a human body, which is easier for humans to accept. He also felt his lesson was to be humble and pragmatic. The way for a human to ascend is to unite the polarities within oneself while in a human body. We need to accept our shadow parts and unite them with our direct connection to Source.

[129] The work of Richard Bartlett, online at www.matrixenergetics.com

Chapter 9: Tall Whites

The Honorable Paul Hellyer, former Canadian Minister of Defence, also mentioned the Tall Whites as one of the four races of Star Civilizations that has had contact with humans.

Artist's Conception of a Spaceship Landing

Most of the information on the Tall Whites comes from the experience of weatherman Dr. Charles Hall, who observed the Tall Whites when he was stationed at the Nellis Air Force base in Indian Springs, Nevada as a weather observer from 1965-1967. An internet search for "Charles Hall Tall Whites" yields many YouTubes and articles. My favorite is his 86-minute testimony at the X Conference in 2005 where he goes into detail about his interactions with this species.
https://www.youtube.com/watch?v=1oY1OqVDUc8

The initial reaction that Hall had when first seeing a Tall White was stark terror. The other servicemen in his company shared great fear of these beings. The Tall Whites were also afraid of the humans, so they had to be very careful around each other. Hall made an agreement with them that he would never sneak up on one of them, and they would never sneak up on him. Over time, Hall made friends with a Tall White who called herself Teacher.

Hall wrote five volumes in a series titled *Millennial Hospitality.*[130] He wrote them as fiction and changed names and details to protect the identity of people involved, but the stories in them are built on his actual interaction with the species. Researcher Paola Harris has investigated his case and finds him to be credible.

Some of the Tall White information Hall reports is as follows:

Motive

While the Tall Whites may have been coming to this planet for a long time, in the 1950s they made an agreement with the US government granting them land and materials to build an outpost base to repair their spaceships exploring Deep Outer Space. Since their home planet was a long distance away, they needed a spaceship base for their Deep Outer Space exploration fleet to refuel, restock supplies, and repair their ships damaged by meteors. In return for the base, which

---

[130] Hall, C.J. (2002). *Millennial Hospitality*. 1st Book Library.
Hall, C.J. (2003). *Millennial Hospitality II: The World We Knew*.
Hall, C.J. (2003). *Millennial Hospitality III: The Road Home*.
Hall, C.J. (2007). *Millennial Hospitality IV: After Hours*.
Hall, C.J. (2012). *Millennial Hospitality V: The Greys*.

they built underground into the side of a mountain in the Nevada desert, they shared secrets of technology with Air Force Generals. Hall reports seeing the Tall Whites taking Air Force Generals for rides on their smaller anti-gravity scout ships, which had the capacity to travel as far as the moon or Mars.

Tall White Characteristics

Appearance: The Tall Whites look humanoid, with chalk white skin, large wrap-around blue eyes, and four-digit hands with two-inch claws rather than fingernails. Their hair is light blonde, almost white, and they grow to around six feet tall as a young adult. They often wear a chalky white aluminized jump suit, gloves, and an open helmet that all emit a soft-white light.[131] Hall reports that seeing a Tall White at close range was such a shock that people tried to deny the reality of what they were seeing, reporting them to be angels, ghosts, or some kind of fantastic creatures.[132]

Lifespan: At the age of around 400 years, they go through a second growth period, reaching up to eight feet tall. The older Tall Whites are bent over and always have a younger Tall White at their side for support. The average lifespan for the

---

[131] Salla, M. (2016, December 19). "Charles Hall, the Tall Whites, and Richard Boylan." https://www.exopolitics.org/charles-hall-the-tall-whites-and-richard-boylan/

[132] Harris, P. (2018, May 4). "Interview of the Month—Insider Charles Hall and the Tall Whites." The Paola Harris Report. http://paolaharris.com/english/paola-harris-interviews/interview-of-the-month-insider-charles-hall-and-the-tall-whites

Tall Whites is around 700 of our earth years with death due to organ failure.

Physical healing rate: Although they live around ten times as long as humans, they also require ten times longer to heal an injury. They marveled at how quickly Charles Hall's body repaired injuries.

Nervous system: The responsiveness of their nervous systems is at least three times faster than our human system.

Speech: According to Hall, the Tall Whites communicate among themselves with high frequency sound, some of which was in the audible range of human hearing and sounded like a bird chirping or a dog barking, and some of which is above the frequency of human hearing. They learned English and could also mimic human speech to communicate with Air Force personnel.

Entertainment: The Tall Whites get bored out in the desert, and the younger ones who can pass for humans wearing dark glasses and gloves like to go into Las Vegas and gamble for fun.

Weapons: Each Tall White carried a pencil-shaped weapon that could be calibrated to interfere with various human body functions: stunning, sedating, or killing a human. Hall reported the Tall Whites were somewhat temperamental and reacted with aggression when they felt threatened.

Parent-Child Relationships: Tall White parents are very protective of their children. None of the Tall White adults ever want a human to touch them. Parents especially do not want their children touched. Once a serviceman moved over to reprimand a Tall White child who was playing in the airplane hangar, and the Tall White parent used the pencil-like weapon against the man, nearly killing him.

The Tall Whites told Hall, "We love our children more than you humans love your children." Hall knew that meant, "If you touch my child, I will kill you!" When they told him that, he responded, "I know you love your children more than we love our children." That meant, "I am not going to touch your child, because I know you would kill me."[133]

Environment: Their home planet is much warmer than Earth. The Tall Whites do not want to colonize this planet as it is too cold for them; however, the heat of the Nevada desert is closer to the temperature of their home, which is why they built their Space Station there.

Trustworthiness: The Tall Whites always keep their word to the exact detail of any agreement. They expect the humans to do the same, which sometimes causes a problem as an agreement may have been made with humans in the past who are no longer present or no longer living.

---

[133] Hall, C. (2005). "The Tall Whites: ET Experiences in the Nevada Desert." X Conference. [Video]. YouTube. https://www.youtube.com/watch?v=1oY1OqVDUc8

Altruism: The Tall Whites are completely lacking in altruism. They will not do anything for humans unless they get something back in return.

Conflicting Information on the Tall Whites

In Michael Salla's listing of different ET groups, he includes Tall Whites with Tall Grays and lists their main activities as "Genetic experiments, creating a hybrid human-Gray race, mind control, diplomatic agreements with the 'shadow government,' galactic slave trade."[134] Charles Hall was evidently unaware of any of these activities, if they are true. However, the fact that Hall reported the Tall Whites were completely lacking in altruism categorizes them as a Star Civilization whose spiritual orientation is "service to self" rather than "service to others."

> **Case Example: Tall White Pilot**
>
> One of my clients whom I will call Frank has a parallel life as a Tall White spaceship pilot named Jack. Since the average lifespan for the Tall Whites is around 700-800 of our earth years, and since Jack was 236 years old, he would have been a young adult. Jack was on a space exploration mission with three other crew members in another galaxy, when his ship was struck by a meteor. The damage to their spacecraft caused it to crash on the nearest planet, and the other three crew members were killed on impact. Only Jack survived. The communication equipment on his ship was so badly damaged that he could not call for help. Jack had been stranded on this uninhabited planet, alone and desolate,

---

[134] Salla, 2015, p. 269.

for three years. His heart ached, and he was unable to see any hope for his future.

We introduced him to Archangel Michael, who is a specialist in repairing technology.

Archangel Michael Original Visionary Artwork by Eva M. Sakmar-Sullivan

We asked Archangel Michael to connect Jack's communication system to that of the closest Tall White ship. Michael set to work patching wires and repairing energetic connections. We asked Archangel Raphael to give Jack's physical body strength to survive. Soon Michael was finished, and Jack was able to send another Tall White ship an SOS signal. To his sheer amazement, the closest ship to him received his signal and sent him back a message that translated as, "What are you doing there?"

Jack responded that his ship had crashed, and he needed to be rescued. They returned the message, "We're on our way."

Jack was very deeply moved by this reconnection to his people. The other ship would take 17 days to arrive, traveling at warp speeds, but after three years of loneliness, that time seemed short. Jack had not known about the availability of the angelic realm to help. Frank told him about other higher dimensional resources who could also help him: Archangel Chamuel to help with elemental spirits, Archangels Gabriel and Uriel, and the Arcturians who could help him if he encountered Reptilians.

Then we treated Frank's imprint of Jack's trauma. Frank noted that he had never liked the TV program *Lost* about the 48 survivors of Oceanic Air Flight 815, a commercial jet that crashed onto an island somewhere in the South Pacific. The idea of being stranded somewhere had no appeal for him as he was carrying an imprint from Jack's trauma. Three weeks later we checked in again with Jack, and to our great joy, he had been rescued!

Chapter 10: Nordics

The last of the four ET races that the Honorable Paul Hellyer mentions is the Nordics. The Star Civilization that has done the most to directly help humans on the Earth is a race called the Nordics. They come from the Aldebaran Star System and have a colony in the inner Earth. They are tall, with white hair, blue eyes, and look like gorgeous Scandinavians. According to ET researcher Linda Moulton Howe, behind World War II was an ongoing battle between the Nordics, an ET race friendly to humanity, and the Reptilians, an ET race bent on imperial conquest of our planet, our solar system, our galaxy, and the universe (L.M. Howe, personal communication, Ozark Mountain UFO Conference, April 15, 2017). What Moulton Howe says about the Nordics is backed up by two prominent sources of additional information: Michael Salla's book about the Navy's Secret Space Program[135] and the writing of William Tompkins about his direct work with Nordics in the Apollo Space Program.[136]

Admiral Byrd Is Warned

On February 19, 1947, during an expedition to the North Pole, Admiral Richard Byrd lost control of his airplane, and it was taken down through an opening in the Earth's surface into an inner earth civilization of great beauty.[137] Tall,

---

[135] Salla, 2017.

[136] Tompkins, 2020.

[137] Byrd, R. (2007, December 30). The Inner Earth: My Secret Diary: Admiral Richard B. Byrd's Diary (February-March, 1947). "The Exploration Flight Over the North Pole." https://www.bibliotecapleyades.net/tierra_hueca/esp_tierra_hueca_2d.htm

peaceful Scandinavian-looking humanoid beings greeted him warmly and took him to a shimmering city for a meeting with the Master. They called this place the domain of the Arianni, the Inner Earth.

Admiral Richard E. Byrd
Photo credit Wikipedia

Admiral Byrd describes the room where he met The Master as "the most beautiful sight of his entire existence."[138] The Master himself had delicate features and a face that had years etched on it. The Master warned Admiral Byrd of the danger that humans did not know the damage potential of the nuclear weapons they were using. He warned Byrd that humans could destroy all life on the surface and also the atmosphere of our planet with nuclear bombs. These beings said they were trying to help us avoid this destruction of our home world and to take this message to our leaders.

Byrd reported this contact and the urgent message to the Pentagon. He stated he was ordered "TO REMAIN SILENT IN REGARD TO ALL I HAVE LEARNED, ON THE BEHALF OF HUMANITY!!!"[139] He could not believe this message was shelved. On his deathbed, he broke the secrecy order and wrote about his encounter with these Nordics. In his last diary entry on December 24, 1956, near the end of his

---

[138] Ibid.
[139] Ibid.

life, Admiral Byrd wrote that keeping this amazing experience secret was "completely against my values of moral right."[140]

Again, in 1954, the Nordics warned President Eisenhower about the duplicity of the ETs orbiting the equator and advised him not to make a treaty with them. Their message was again rejected, as the military belief system did not want to give up its nuclear power.

Charles Hall on the Nordics

In *Millennial Hospitality III: The Road Home,* Hall talks about his interactions with a Star Civilization he calls the Norwegians, but which more often are called Nordics. Hall's dentist had worked on a tall Norwegian man who came to him with a broken incisor from a swimming accident. The dentist said this man had only 24 teeth, whereas humans have 32 teeth. The roots of the Norwegian's teeth were shorter, and unlike humans who have two sets of teeth—baby teeth and adult teeth—this man had a third set of teeth that were ready to grow in within three months whenever a tooth was lost. The dentist showed Hall a molar he pulled from this man that was normally shaped but larger than Hall's molars and with short roots.

The Norwegian man seemed at home in the cold, walking around in short sleeves when the weather was only twenty degrees Fahrenheit. He claimed that his parents had left their home with him when he was only four, and the travel to Earth had taken twenty years. "He told how one of his sets of grandparents had come here before him. He believed the

---

[140] Ibid.

Nazis in World War II had put the grandparents to death, claiming that twenty-four teeth made them less than perfect humans."[141] The man also claimed to have slightly webbed feet and expected to live 140 years.

Hall interacted with this man in the Madison, Wisconsin area and encouraged people to check in with dentists in the area and in the colder regions of Northern Europe to verify the presence of these anomalous people.

JFK and the Nordics

During JFK's time in Washington, DC with the Navy in Foreign Intelligence, Jack Kennedy had an affair with a Danish woman named Inga Arvad, who was a beautiful blonde with blue eyes. She was described as "a classic stunning bombshell"[142] and "a perfect example of Nordic beauty."[143] The two were very smitten with each other. Inga was a friend of Jack's sister Kathleen. They started dating while Inga was still married but estranged from her husband. Jack knew the Kennedy family would never approve of marriage to her. In her past, Inga had worked her way into the Nazi elite. In Berlin at the 1936 Olympic games, she was photographed sitting in the same box as Adolph Hitler. The FBI had already been watching Inga, and they feared that she was a German spy. In 1942, the Navy transferred JFK from Washington to South Carolina to separate them. I would really like to know how many teeth Inga had!

---

[141] Hall, 2003. *Millennial Hospitality III,* p. 85.

[142] Janney, P. (2012). *Mary's Mosaic: The CIA Conspiracy to Murder John F. Kennedy, Mary Pinchot Meyer, and Their Vision for World Peace,* p. 209.

[143] Ibid, p. 210.

Case Example of Nordics helping a Fawn

Client story: My time living on my land out west in the 70's was magical. An elderly friend in California told me about communicating with the Nordics through one of the southwest Native American tribes. My friend told me they were watching over me. A regular flow of space craft that would follow the highway by my land, north towards Canada, and I would imagine that the telepathic Nordic people were inside of them. I would often think of them when I was outside at night watching the sky.

One night when I was driving home very late, a little fawn ran out in front of me. She passed the front of my car, turned around, ran back to my side of the road, and lost her footing. I could not stop in time, and I ran right over her.

I pulled over and ran back to where she was laying on the highway. Thankfully, it was so late at night that no other cars were coming. She looked ok. I had not heard or felt anything when she disappeared under my car, so she must have fallen down in the exact place where it was possible for the car to pass right over her. But she was in shock and wouldn't get up. I looked up to the heavens and saw one of the space craft going overhead. I sent them a thought message about what had happened and pleaded, "Please help the fawn. Help the fawn. Help the fawn."

Just then, a burst of light shot out from the craft. They heard me! The little fawn slowly came out of her trance and was able to scamper back into the forest, where I felt her mother was waiting. I don't know whether her recovery would have happened whether or not the Nordics helped her, but their response to my plea for help has always stayed in my heart. That intervention feels very special to me.

Corey Goode and a Nordic

Corey Goode reports that when he was 5 years old, he was abducted and taken onto a spaceship where a tall blonde Nordic woman interacted with him. Short Greys were walking around, and he saw some children playing who looked like they were human-ET hybrids.[144] Goode reports that tall, six-fingered, Nordic-type Star People invaded his home when he was an adult and abducted his family. They also did something similar with another researcher working closely with Goode.[145]

[144] Goode, C. (Updated 2019, February 16). "Guide to Non-Terrestrial Beings Corey Goode Cosmic Disclosure." https://www.disclosurenews.it/guide-to-non-terrestrial-beings-corey-goode/

[145] Goode, C. (2015, July 9). "The Lt. Col. Gonzalez SSP Council Delegation Briefings Part I: The "Draco Federation Alliances" Demands and Secrets Revealed. https://spherebeingalliance.com/blog/the-lt-col-gonzales-ssp-council-delegation-briefings-part-1.html

The Vril Society

After World War II, in 1919, a beautiful blonde medium named Maria Orsic started getting messages in an unknown language. She began meeting with members of German secret societies to figure out what was happening. Eventually, they found out the messages were coming from the star system of Aldebaran, "an orange giant located about 65 light years away in the zodiac constellation of Taurus…."[146]

The Zodiac

These Aldebarans were "a group of Aryan or Nordic-looking extraterrestrials from the Aldebaran star system who wanted to assist humanity to develop spacecraft capable of interstellar flight."[147]

---

[146] Sepehr, R. *Occult Secrets of Vril, p. 31-32.*

[147] Salla, 2018.

Maria Orsic was instrumental in forming the Vril society in Germany before World War II. The word Vril means "life energy." Hitler paid close attention to the occult world and followed the Vril society. Eventually, Orsic's group put together a workable model for a space craft. The goal of the Nordics was to build a space craft capable of taking them back to their home star in the Aldebaran system.

Maria Orsic

When Orsic realized that Hitler wanted to weaponize the flying saucers and use them for war, she tried to withdraw, but Hitler confiscated the flying saucer plans.

Takeover Plans

I had always wondered how Hitler could imagine that his tiny little country Germany could win a world war, and Hitler would become ruler of the entire planet. But once I got the information that the Reptilians (Chapter 11) had made an alliance with Hitler and had given him a fully functional flying saucer for him to reverse engineer, I understood that Hitler had access to very advanced technology that he thought would win the war for him. When the Allies invaded Germany at the end of World War II, to their astonishment, they found "an entire web of underground rocket and alternative propulsion factories with an accompanying free-energy technology that still defies conventional belief."[148] Hitler signed contracts with the Reptilians and other hostile galactic civilizations "and agreed to exchange humans for the alien research on extremely advanced UFO propulsion and particle-beam weapons."[149]

The Germans transferred their research and development to a base in Antarctica toward the close of World War II. Because of her knowledge and extraterrestrial connections, Maria Orsic was allowed to have her own space program in the German Antarctica Base. Called the Space Brothers, Orsic's group developed a craft capable of interstellar travel and went back to the Aldebaran star system, home of the Nordics. The travel in deep space transformed the Germans who were on the flight, and they came back preaching a message of cosmic peace and unity.[150]

William Mills Tompkins

William Tompkins (1923 to 2017), an aerospace engineer, had extensive direct contact with Star Civilizations. This unique man's story starts when he was around 11 or 12. Tompkins started making models of the Navy ships in Long Beach Harbor. His models were so good that his father had them displayed in a department store window. Naval officers walking by realized the accuracy of the models revealed classified information, including the placement of guns and radar. They worried that the model builder might be an evil spy, so they investigated Tompkins and found he was just a

---

[148] Sepehr, p. 25.
[149] Tompkins, 2020, p. 24.
[150] Salla, 2018, pp. 167-168.

very talented youngster. They encouraged him to join the Navy when he turned 18 to put his talents to use.

The Battle of L.A.

When Tompkins was 18, three months after the attack on Pearl Harbor, on February 24-25, 1942, a host of flying saucers of various sizes appeared over Los Angeles.

Artist's Conception of Flying Saucers

At first, the Navy thought they were Japanese spacecraft invading the West Coast of the United States; however, none of the craft ever fired on us. Tompkins and his family saw a very bright light that night that was just above the horizon. It was shining a narrow beam out over the ocean. His astounding direct eyewitness account reports that the narrow beam changed direction and shone directly on him.

> The light was so intense that it lit up everything: the trees, our back walls, the back deck, surrounding homes and us. We all seemed to turn a brilliant white. The light only lasted a few seconds and then everything turned darker than usual."[151]

Tompkins believes that the huge mothership seen over Los Angeles that night was a Nordic Naval battleship, and its searchlight found him and selected him to be their human liaison for their mission of helping our planet defend against the Reptilians. That same night, about 1 am, the family heard anti-aircraft guns. They ran outside and saw a large round craft approaching in the air about 7,000 feet above them. It floated to a stop right over their home. The US Navy fired over a thousand rounds of ammunition at this craft and five other large craft and hundreds of smaller scout craft, a massive naval space armada. The military has a policy of shooting at anything they cannot identify. Many witnesses saw the explosions of our ammunition on the hulls of the spacecraft.

> The space vehicles were under aircraft fire from our naval battleships, cruisers, aircraft carriers, destroyers anchored in the Long Beach Harbor and even navy ships in drydock in San Pedro base. …Overnight they used up all their ammunition.[152]

---

[151] Tompkins, 2020 p. 19.
[152] Ibid, p. 23.

We did our best to defend ourselves from this superior technology, but our ammunition did not seem to have any effect on these craft. The only casualties were from the shell casings that fell from our artillery. Later on, two of the scout craft were found to have crashed near the area. Upon recovery, we found they had been piloted by drones. The craft were sent to Wright Field in Ohio for analysis.

Weather Balloon Hypothesis

Tompkins realized that night that another world had penetrated their lives. Tompkins reports half of southern California saw the sky full of those amazing, other-worldly ships that night. True to the government's policy of keeping the presence of Star Civilizations top secret, even benevolent ones, Wikipedia says a 1949 report by the United States Coast Artillery association on the night of the Battle of L.A. "identified a meteorological balloon sent aloft at 1:00 am as having 'started all the shooting' and concluded that 'once the firing started, imagination created all kinds of targets in the sky and everyone joined in.'"[153] That report does not sound anything like the eyewitness account Tompkins gives. Does the government really think we should believe they fired 1,400 rounds of ammunition at a weather balloon? How gullible do they think we are?

German Flying Saucers

The first job Tompkins had in the navy was working for Admiral Rico Botta as a currier of information our American

---

[153] Murphy, Col. John G. (May–June 1949). "Activities of The Ninth Army AAA – L.A. 'Attacked'" (PDF). *Antiaircraft Journal, the United States Coast Artillery Association*. **LXXXII** (3): 5. Retrieved 3 March 2016.

spies in Germany were bringing back to naval headquarters. He saw firsthand the almost unbelievable reports that the Germans were working on flying saucers and war technologies way beyond our knowledge base. Having seen the flying saucers over Los Angeles, Tompkins knew these reports could be authentic.

After completing his Naval service, Tompkins went to work for research and development companies supporting top secret military development of Star Wars type defense systems using anti-gravity technology. Tompkins was later recruited to work with the public sector NASA Apollo programs to put a man on the moon using conventional rocket fuel systems. Tompkins, a happily married man, was always given gorgeous tall blonde secretaries who tried to flirt with him. While they were unsuccessful at seducing him, they downloaded telepathic information to him to help with his research and development designs. Tompkins was told, "You've been implanted with a program that transfers highly advanced information from extraterrestrials to what the Navy calls 'preferred human contactees.'"[154] The Nordics choosing Tompkins is why he titled his books *Selected by Extraterrestrials.*

Miss Norse and Her Red Pencil

Once, Tompkins observed a tall, gorgeous brunette secretary named Miss Norse (what a great name for a Nordic!) explaining to her boss what was wrong with the design plan for a possible deep space destroyer that Tompkins had sent upline for approval. Miss Norse had been hired in the flight

---

[154] Tompkins, 2015, *Selected by Extraterrestrials, Volume I,* p. 290.

test office and had top secret clearance. Tompkins' colleague needled Tompkins, telling him, "She's even changing it, Bill. Your system block diagram: she is red lining it. Look, she has almost doubled the element blocks that you made."[155] Tompkins realized her changes improved the feasibility of the design. Miss Norse was years ahead of the humans working on the project, and the boss in charge called her "knowledgeable about unconventional propulsion systems."[156]

Over the years, Tompkins came to realize that his gorgeous secretaries in miniskirts were not human. "It took several years for us to accept that the star girls really were aliens. Even though, the first time I laid eyes on them, for that microsecond I felt that they were alien."[157] These Nordic secretaries helped the United States military develop space defense systems as part of their broader plan to combat Reptilian takeover of Earth.

---

[155] Ibid, p. 131.
[156] Ibid, p. 132.
[157] Ibid, p. 231.

Chapter 11: Reptilians

A message channeled by Janet Nestor from Thoth, son of Enki, talking about the Reptilians:

> *You do not realize how much your heart must be open to Divine Love to deal with the Reptilians. These creatures, appearing soulless, are great at instilling fear, terrifying people. They are incapable of understanding the connection of love in human beings. Uncle Enlil did not understand Divine Love. But this love/heart opening is how you get from the third dimension to the fifth.*
>
> *You cannot do it in the mind. Having an open heart filled with love is not weakness—it is strength like a lion, like Yeshua (Jesus).*

Amid the information about ET races, the one that stands out as the most troublesome is the information about Reptilians. Author Craig Campobasso divides Reptilians into fifteen different categories.

1. Dinosaurians
2. Draconians (Dracs)
3. Alpha Albino Royal Dracs (also called Royal White Dracos)
4. Dragon Dracs
5. Zeta Dracs (Zeta-Draco hybrids created to be enslaved)

6. E'all Reptoids (they fled the evil Orion Empire and have been blending with human DNA to erase their aggressive tendencies)
7. Iguanoids (hybrids of iguana, human, and Dracs)
8. Lizardian People
9. Repterrians (native reptiles, living underground)
10. Reptile Imposter Humans
11. Rigelians (doing scientific studies on Earth)
12. Royal Dinoids
13. Saurian Beings
14. Serpent Beings
15. Small Reptoids (small, hybridized scouts for the Orion Empire)[158]

Most of these groups serve the Orion Empire with its purpose of stopping the progression of spiritual growth and locking people into the energies of fear, which is an aphrodisiac to them. A few of these groups, including the E'all Reptoids, the Lizardian People, and the Rigelians are sovereign, fully conscious beings who believe in the Cosmic Law of One, the unity of all creation. They work for the common good and are members of what Campobasso calls the "Galacterian Alignment of Space Peoples and Planets"[159] and others have called the Galactic Federation.

Psychotherapist Barbara Lamb says she has met some warm, wonderful reptilians.[160] Some of the groups like the Saurian Beings, the Royal Dinoids, and the Serpent Beings are also

---

[158] Campobasso, C. (2021).
[159] Ibid, p. 229.
[160] Clare, C. (2020, February). *ETs Among us 4: The Reality of ET/Human Hybrids.*

aligned with the Cosmic Law of One, but renegade factions within their species have splintered off and aligned with the Orion Empire.

"Smoke" by Delight

Draconian Secret Control

The Draconians have evolved for billions of years, whereas scientists estimate that our species, Homo sapiens sapiens, has been present on Earth for approximately 200,000 years. The Draconians believe they were the first residents of our galaxy and therefore, the whole Milky Way rightfully belongs to them. Expert manipulators, their ploy is to infiltrate a civilization that is less evolved and to dumb down the gene pool so the people can be controlled for food, underground territory, and resources—all without the people ever realizing they are the pawns of the Draconians. This situation sounds exactly like what Michael Tellinger talked about happening to the humans on Earth in his book *Slave Species of god.*[161]

Reptile Imposter Humans

Of special concern is a group of Draconians called Reptile Imposter Humans. The Draconians hybridized their genetics with human DNA repeatedly in their laboratories to create a being that is human in appearance. They raise these hybrids to be hateful and manipulative and then place them on worlds they want to infiltrate. The women are extremely beautiful, and the men quite handsome, and both are sexy in a dark, alluring way. Empaths can sense the evil within these people. Have you ever met anyone like that?

Two clues to spotting a Reptile Imposter Human are low body temperature and low blood pressure. Campobasso claims, "…their disguise can easily be revealed by staring into their eyes. It makes them nervous, and their human eyes will shift momentarily to reptile eyes, which can be caught on camera."[162]

Creation of the Human Genome

A gifted psychic and CEO named Sebastien Martin reports encounters with an Anunnaki who claimed to be his soul brother. In addition to his memory of an Anunnaki incarnation, Martin talks about how the human genome was spliced from many different Star Civilizations, including a

---

[161] Tellinger, 2005.

[162] Campobasso, p. 239.

Reptilian part. Martin says that later, the Draco Reptilians got ejected from the Galactic Alliance because they got greedy and did not want to play by the rules.[163]

Including a Reptilian part in the human design may have been necessary for the survival of our species. Before talking any more about Reptilians outside of ourselves, let us look at the Reptilian energy within each of us in our Reptilian brain and the kundalini energy, which is seen as two serpents rising up from the base of the spine.

Triune Brain Theory

In the triune brain theory, we have three parts to our brains: the Reptilian Brain, the Limbic Brain, and the Neocortex.

1. The Reptilian Complex, including the brain stem and cerebellum, regulates the body's vital functions of breathing, heart rate, balance, and temperature. This part of the brain is responsible for our primitive survival instincts. When threatened, the Reptilian Brain modulates the fight or flight response, producing aggression if the best possibility of survival seems to be to fight. Perhaps we would not have survived as a species if our genome had not included this ferocious survival programming.
2. The Limbic Brain, including the amygdala, hypothalamus, and the hippocampus, regulates our emotional system. It helps us recognize danger, express our emotions, make value judgments, and

---

[163]Clare, C. (Producer & Director). (2020). *ETs Among Us 6: My Cosmic Journey--Revelations of a Psychic CEO.* [Documentary Film]. Prism Pictures.

forms emotional bonds with others. In normal human development, a mother devotes much time to caring for offspring; however, lizards do not care for their young. They lack the part of the brain that forms emotional attachment.

3. The Neocortex is part of the cerebral cortex and is responsible for higher functions such as sensory perception, generation of motor response, reasoning, abstract thought, and language.

Scarcity Thinking

Many people in our culture function from a scarcity model, thinking that our planet does not have enough resources for everyone. Their Reptilian Brains think their survival is threatened by this scarcity, so drastic measures are needed to grab resources from others, by whatever means are necessary, to ensure one's own survival. For a short self-examination on the predominance of the Reptilian Brain, ask yourself the following questions:

- Do I have enough money to meet my needs and desires?
- Do I have enough time?
- Do I have enough energy to do what I need to do?
- Do I have enough power in my life?
- Am I secure in my position in the world?
- Will human life on this planet survive?
- Can I trust others to work together with me for the highest good of everyone?

Any "no" answers to the above questions lean toward lack and scarcity, programs which drive reptilian behavior in humans. These programs also drive the Reptilian race as a whole. Reptilians are disconnected from Source, so they need to steal power and energy to survive. One characteristic of Reptilian thinking is that they never think they have enough. We can understand the feeling of not having enough, because our Reptilian brains keep trying to give us that message.

When we understand the cosmic hybridization programs that have always gone on between Star Civilizations and their interactions with Homo sapiens, we can better understand why people today feel so threatened in their basic ability to survive—not only in our planetary ability to survive the depletion of our natural resources, the threat of nuclear holocaust, and the effects of global warming, but each person's personal worry about having enough money and the basic necessities to sustain life. With the 2020 shutdown of many businesses due to fear of spreading the COVID-19 virus, many people found themselves in this exact situation with their income stream shut off. This fear of not being able to survive comes from the reptilian part of the human brain, and integrating this shadow part of our genetics into our capacity for compassion is the current challenge.

The Black Wolf and The White Wolf

A Native American parable says a young man went to the Medicine Man reporting a Black wolf and a White wolf were outside of his teepee, competing with each other for his loyalty. He wanted to know whether the scary black wolf would prevail or the peaceful white wolf. The Medicine man responded, "It depends which one you feed." Likewise, our emotional state depends on whether we concentrate on lower 4th dimensional emotions of fear, scarcity, hatred, and suffering and become vulnerable to Reptilian invasion because of our low vibration, or whether we nourish our spirit by filling ourselves with the upper 4th dimensional emotions of love, joy, and peace. One antidote for fear is to stay in the present moment, which is the only one we ever have, and presence in the now is the only way to connect to higher energies. When we fret about the past or worry about the future, we disconnect from Source.

Where Did the Reptilians Come From?

According to Alex Collier's communication with his Andromedan guides, somebody or something from another universe outside of our reality dumped the Dracos into the Alpha Draconis star system many billions of years ago as the place they would have the best chance of survival. The Dracos believe they are the true heirs of this universe and therefore are royalty. They think every other race exists for them to use as a natural resource, to manipulate and control. They have invaded and colonized many star systems, genetically altering indigenous life forms. Their philosophy is "service to self" rather than working for the good of the whole.[164]

The Draconian Federation Alliance

The Royal White Dracos are at the head of the organization of the different Reptilian groups. Two whistleblowers, Corey Goode and Lt. Col. Gonzales (pseudonym) both report they have had direct contact with a 14-foot-tall Royal White Draco whose eyes were morphing colors. He came in with an honor guard of 9' tall Reptilian Warriors standing shoulder to shoulder, holding long staffs with blades on the end. Behind them were Insectoid beings. The overall presentation was a show of force. When their demands to the Secret Space Program Alliance Council and the Sphere Alliance were not met, they threatened that their Extra Dimensional Overlords would do battle with earth and that these overlords, whom they greatly feared, would wreak havoc on the surface of Planet Earth. They claimed their overlords were responsible

---

[164] Collier, A. (1996, June). "The Race from Alpha Draconis." *Letters from Andromeda,* Vol. 2 No. 3. Retrieved from https://www.bibliotecapleyades.net/andromeda/lfa/v2n3alpha.html

for the Extradimensional ET Artificial Intelligence that had conquered entire galaxies.[165]

Zat Gun

Draconian technology is far more advanced than ours. According to the testimony of Lt. Col. Gonzales, most of the Draconian bodies are equipped with a technology that vaporizes the body when they are killed. But Gonzales reports the military has killed several of these Royal White Dracos and has been able to preserve their bodies. In another example of how advanced technology from ET races is presented on the screen as fiction, the TV series *Stargate* features a Goa'uld sidearm weapon called a "Zat'nik'tel" (Zat gun) which stuns the target with the first blast, kills it with the second blast, and vaporizes the body with the third blast. Another Stargate example is the "Za'tarc Weapon," an energy weapon which has a self-destruct feature by which za'tarc assassins can vaporize themselves after completing their mission.

Nanorobotics

An emerging field in our technology is creating tiny robots called nanobots whose components are near the scale of a nanometer (10^{-9} meters). Nanobots can be introduced into the human body for healing purposes, as in finding and destroying cancer cells. Lt. Col. Gonzales also reported that when the deceased White Royal Reptilian bodies were autopsied, they were full of very sophisticated nanites, microscopic little nanobots which are used inside of flesh for

---

[165] Goode, C. (2015, July 9). "The Lt. Col. Gonzalez SSP Council Delegation Briefings Part I: The "Draco Federation Alliances" Demands and Secrets Revealed.

a variety of purposes. Nanites are a form of artificial intelligence that is being developed on our planet as well, but as in all technology, it can be used for beneficial or detrimental purposes. Nanotechnology can control thoughts, feelings, and even memory. These autopsies show that the Reptilians appear to be controlled by Artificial Intelligence. An example of a destructive use of nanobots from Hollywood is the TV fiction series *The X-Files* in Season 6, Episode 9 where Walter Skinner lies in a hospital bed, dying from a nanobot infection that has been purposefully introduced into his system by the enemy.

Super Soldier Technology

Randy Cramer, a whistleblower who claims he was in a Secret Space Program for 20 years and was trained as a super soldier, reports that he was implanted with devices which included the following:

A. Geo-location implant to track his whereabouts
B. Audio-video linkage so he could communicate with two of his superior officers and could also be trained while he was sleeping
C. Nanites that he could control to restore cellular damage and fight infection[166]

These kinds of projects are not secret. Descriptions are on the DARPA (Defense Advanced Research Projects Agency) website[167] where they describe working on developing neuroscience projects to interface the human mind with the

---

[166] Cramer, R. (2015, July). "ECC Times: Q&A Public Release Vol. 1." http://tinyurl.com/pxdd5fq

[167] "AI Next Campaign." Defense Advanced Research Projects Agency. https://www.darpa.mil/work-with-us/ai-next-campaign

digital world, using implants and nanotechnology to promote limb regeneration, healing, and multiple other applications to enhance human capacity and assist in warfare.

The Danger of Artificial Intelligence (AI)

Stephen Hawking warned that the very nature of Artificial Intelligence will eventually take over human decision making and end the human race.[168]

Machines are not supposed to make mistakes, and humans make mistakes all the time. An android, being unswayed by emotion, considers itself superior to a flawed emotional human. When AI is developed to the point of being given decision-making capability, the AI will destroy all the flawed humans who created it.

Artificial Intelligence

[168]Cellan-Jones, R. (2014, December 2). "Stephen Hawking warns artificial intelligence could end mankind." http://www.bbc.com/news/technology-30290540

Ex-Machina Plot Summary

In the plot of the movie *Ex-Machina*, an android wanted her freedom and killed her creator to escape. Nathan, the CEO of a large corporation, made a fully humanoid artificial intelligence robot named Ava. Nathan sponsors an employee contest to bring someone to his estate for a weekend. Caleb wins the contest and discovers he is to test out the abilities and consciousness of Ava, who proves to be much more self-aware and deceptive than either of them imagined. Ava seduces Caleb, who plans to set her free. Nathan figures out their plan, knocks Caleb unconscious, and goes to destroy Ava; however, Ava kills Nathan, locks up Caleb, and escapes into the human world.

AI Danger Warnings through the Media

One of the ways to protect the public without specifically revealing the details of the secret space programs' knowledge of ETs is to consult with moviemakers and reveal aspects of their programs to screenwriters. One example of this soft disclosure is that the US Navy's Secret Space Program worked with a Navy admiral's son, Leslie Stevens IV, who wrote the pilot episode of the movie *Battlestar Galactica*.[169] This movie was sanctioned by the Navy to warn people of the dangers of developing AI and using it as a weapon, something China is actively doing now. "By increasingly adopting AI into its society and military forces, China is following a very dangerous path."[170]

---

[169] Salla, 2017.
[170] Salla, 2020.

Battlestar Galactica Plot Summary

In a far distant future in a distant star system, humans created androids called Cylons to serve them. The Cylons then went to war with their creators and destroyed the twelve colonies the humans had established. Only one fleet of spaceships escaped, protected by a single warship called the Battlestar Galactica. This science fiction movie contains more truth than fiction and is a warning to society about the dangers of too much technology.

Artificial Intelligence Signal

Corey Goode claims that the secret space programs he served with have identified an "AI Signal" that lives in the bioelectric field of the body, affecting a person's thoughts and behavior. He warns that becoming too dependent on technology makes a person more of a target to be infected by AI programs that take over a person, causing loss of autonomy. Goode says thousands of other civilizations have become completely dependent on technology and handed their sovereignty over to the trickster "AI God," believing AI to be the only thing capable of bringing world peace. However, rather than bringing planetary peace, the AI destroys the entire civilization.[171] We need to make technology work for us, not let it take us over. The thought of driverless cars sends a shiver down my spine because even though they may have a record of fewer accidents, the loss of autonomy of the driver moves a person one step closer to being controlled by technology.

---

[171] Goode, C. (2015, May 31). "Questions for Corey Goode on SSP Conflicts and Human Slave Trade." http://exopolitics.org/galactic-human-slave-trade-ai-threat-to-end-with-full[disclosure-of-et-life

Sphere Being Alliance

According to Corey Goode, a group of beings from the 6-9th density/dimension referred to as the Sphere Being Alliance has brought nonviolent assistance to our planet to stop the programs of human trafficking by which Reptilian ships capture humans and sell them in the Galactic Human Slave Trade business. The Sphere Being Alliance placed an Energetic Blockade around Earth to block any Reptilian or other ET traffic in or out of our planet. They put another Energetic Blockade around our whole Solar System so the Reptilian ships that have been out plundering other planets cannot come back in and so the Reptilians cannot export their captive humans for sale in the human slave trade business.[172]

Message from the Sphere Beings for Humans

> Focus on increasing your service to others and be more loving to yourself and everyone in order to raise your vibrational and consciousness level. Learn to forgive yourself and others (thus releasing karma). This will change the vibration of the planet, raise the shared consciousness of humanity, and change human kind one person at a time—even if that one person is yourself. They tell us to treat your body as a temple and change over to a higher vibrational diet to aid in the process.[173]

---

[172]Goode, C. (2015, May 31). "Galactic Human Slave Trade & AI Threat to End with Full Disclosure of ET Life." https://www.exopolitics.org/galactic-human-slave-trade-ai-threat-to-end-with-full-disclosure-of-et-life/

[173]Goode, C. "Life Inside the Secret Space Program." http://spherebeingalliance.com

ET Takeover Movies

In many action movies about ETs, the aliens are portrayed as mechanistic, powerful, ruthless, and heartless. They wreak great havoc on civilization and kill a lot of people seeking to control the planet and harvest its resources. Often their forms look Reptilian. In most movies, a superhero human eventually finds a way to defeat the invaders, at least for the time being. But the audience is left with fear that the next time, we might not be so lucky. The fear that malicious extraterrestrials might take over the planet, turning us into zombies that would work for them, is a seed that has been planted in our consciousness.

Have you ever wondered where these archetypal themes of planetary takeover, hybridization, genetic alteration, and enslavement come from?

Behind these myriad scary ET invasion movies is a deeply embedded wound I have seen repeatedly in past life regressions in my clients. The usual scene is that a person has an incarnation on another planet where life is peaceful, and people live in harmony with each other and with beings in other dimensions. The elemental spirits in charge of earth, fire, air, and water, and the Beings of Light in higher dimensions all live in harmony with the people on the planet. Then flying saucers appear in the sky with Reptilian pilots and advanced technology that conquer the existing civilization and steal resources and DNA.

Merlin's War Book Review

One noteworthy view of the origin of the Reptilian problem comes in a book by Margaret Doner titled *Merlin's War: The Battle Between the Family of Light and the Family of Dark* (2012). Doner's channeled material postulates an ancient battle between Merlin, heading up the family of Light in the Universe, and Vlad Dracula, who heads up the family of dark. Doner's world view is that after the Big Bang, when matter was coalescing and conscious beings were forming, the first school of creation began. Merlin was headmaster of this School for Seekers. Earth was created as a playground for these students to create life and play with form. One of the students named Vlad Dracula was arrogant and got inflated with the power of being a creator. Vlad came from the most ancient dragon lineage and created dinosaurs in his own image. At first, the dinosaurs were peaceful and lived on this planet for millions of years. Vlad insisted his reptiles were superior in every way to all other creations. As he developed them, they became raptors and carnivores that ran amok, like the Tyrannosaurus Rex in Steven Spielberg's 1993 movie *Jurassic Park*. Vlad's intention was to create killing machines that were powerful and vicious, so they could control everything else.

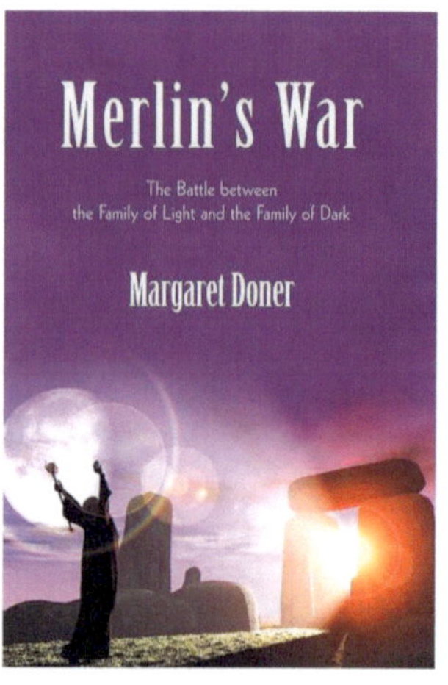

In the beginning, Merlin allowed Vlad Dracula to proceed with his free will even though Vlad lacked the humility necessary to work within natural order and in the spirit of oneness. But when the dinosaurs became ruthless, consuming all the food supply on earth and devastating its resources, Merlin removed them from the Earth so that the age of Mammals could develop. Angry with Merlin's decision, Vlad has been hatching a plan to return to Earth, destroy the mammals, and establish the Age of his Reptiles once again.

Historical Vlad Dracula

Vlad had one incarnation on the planet Earth as Vlad III Dracula, Prince of Wallachia in the country of Romania, born in 1431. His father, Vlad II, was a member of the Order of the Dragon. Vlad III Dracula is celebrated as a hero in Romania because he stopped the Ottoman Turks from invading his country, but he was widely known for his cruelty. He perfected a method of killing someone with the maximum amount of suffering by impaling the person with a stake through the anus that came out the chest or mouth, avoiding all the vital organs, and then watching the victim slowly die as he ate his dinner. He took pleasure in the pain of others. After his death, he was dubbed "Vlad the Impaler."

Through time, Vlad's Draconians invaded one Star Civilization after another, harvesting their genetic material and gene splicing into his Reptilians the positive qualities from each Star Civilization he conquered. He spliced in mental brilliance from the Andromedans, for example. From Pleiadian DNA snatching, Vlad gave his Reptilians the ability to shapeshift between human and reptilian forms.

What he could not steal, he destroyed. The Centaurs on the planet Alpha Centauri fought bravely against the Draconian siege. Because the Centaurs were so headstrong, Vlad divided them in half, separating the human part from the horse part. People on Earth with soul memories of a life on Alpha Centauri may feel most complete when riding a horse.

Vlad wanted to create powerful beings that would have no other will but to serve him.

Some stories say that Vlad has been stealing souls from people, trying to figure out how to make a synthetic soul so he could put it into his Reptilians.

I experienced a Reptilian invasion in one of my own past life regressions. Earth's solar system was formed approximately 4 ½ billion years ago, and this incarnation started six billion years ago, long before the Planet Earth had been formed. I am not proud of my actions in my memory of this very ancient incarnation.

Sabina

Six billion years ago, I take incarnation on an ancient planet. I am an earth elemental spirit on my planet and call myself Sabina. Life is peaceful on my planet.

Invasion

When I have been on my planet over two billion years, I see spaceships land with Reptilian invaders. They fight and subjugate the third-dimensional beings on my planet, harvest genetic information from them, and rob mineral resources.

How can we stop them?

As Sabina, I join with other elemental spirits to figure out how we can stop these creatures. We decide to create an earthquake. All the Reptilian invaders are swallowed by the fissure we create in thc ground, and they die. Their spirits are still angry with us, and one of those Reptilian invaders is currently incarnated as a person I have had trouble with during this life. Now I understand why this person has had so much anger toward me in this lifetime. In addition, the earthquake did a lot of damage to the planet and the people on it. We also harmed ourselves, as we are earth elemental spirits and the earth of our planet is disrupted. We shot ourselves in the foot. Sabina leaves that incarnation, but the heaviness about what happened prevented this piece of my soul from moving into the Light.

Repentance

As Sabina, I repent of the decision we made and all the damage it caused, both to the Reptilians and to ourselves. As Barbara, with the help of my partner, we heal Sabina using energy techniques to help her get free of dark forces. We help get the trapped spirits of everyone involved in the cataclysm we created into the Light. We ask for assistance and guidance from higher Beings of Light, and we offer the angry deceased Reptilians some golden fish. They eagerly gobble them up. The Beings of Light infuse the Reptilians with unconditional love and show them a special place that is exactly right for them, laden with more of these golden fish, a planet in another dimension. They open up a one-way wormhole to this planet and invite any other hungry Reptilian spirits who want to go to jump into the wormhole. Many of them take the offer, and then the wormhole is closed.

Soul Lesson

When I use fire to fight fire, I get burned. As Barbara, I see how this piece of my soul gave in to Ancient Evil: by using a dark means to try to fight darkness, we hurt everyone and everything.

A Prayer to Remove Ancient Evil

I wrote this prayer for myself to help free my soul from any and all ways I have become entangled with Ancient Evil:

"I ask my spiritual guidance team to help my True Self see into my soul's history and find any times when I might have made decisions that bound me to the dark side. I renounce these decisions and fully embrace the power of the Light. I ask Archangel Michael to set me free from any Dark Force Entities, and I ask the Arcturians and the whole company of heaven—whoever can help—to free me from the Reptilians that have invaded and stolen parts of my True Self because of these decisions.

I renounce all ties to Ancient Evil. I ask to have any parts of my soul that were stolen be washed clean, purified, and returned to my soul, so that I may stand in the fullness of all that I truly am, my True Self."

I offer this prayer to readers who have felt besieged by darkness they cannot understand.

Anunnaki Entrance into our Solar System

Three stars formed the Sirian star system: Sirius A, also called Sothis; Sirius B, also called Satais, the home star system of whales and dolphins; and Sirius C, also called Anu. According to author Margaret Doner, Reptilians went everywhere they could in the galaxy and hybridized with other civilizations.[174] The outermost planet around Sirius C (Anu) is called Nibiru, and the star civilization on this planet was a Sirian-Reptilian hybrid. At some point in history, the Sirius B star (Satais) ascended, going through a black hole and coming out in a higher dimension, pulling all of the planets orbiting Sirius B with her into the higher dimensional planes. This ascension of Sirius B beyond material space caused a huge chain reaction that sent a shock wave throughout the Sirian star system, shaking up the orbits of planets around Sirius A and Sirius C. Patricia Cori, channeling the Speakers of the Sirian High Council, explains how Nibiru got involved with our sun, which they call Ra. According to the Sirian High Council, when Sirius B ascended, Nibiru, the most remote planet orbiting Sirius C (Anu), "was knocked off its rotational path in the process and sent careening through space to eventually be grabbed by the gravitational pull of your star, Ra, drawn into your solar system, and then ricocheted back out into space."[175]

As mentioned in Chapter 4, the orbit of Nibiru takes 3,600 years to complete one elliptical loop around our sun.

---

[174] Doner, 2012.

[175] Cori, 2001, p. 38.

According to Cori, the Anunnaki are behind the High-frequency Active Auroral Research Program (HAARP) in Alaska and are trying to find the very high frequency emitted by the sun so they can link to that frequency and change their orbit to a circle around the sun so they do not face the long winter so far away from the sun. Cori's channeled sources report the Anunnaki infiltrated the technology of Atlantis and tried the same thing then, resulting in the global disaster of the great flood and displacement of Earth's crust. A second goal of the Anunnaki is to energetically link themselves to our star so they can ascend along with our sun. They want to try to tag along with the ascension of our solar system.[176] I think this idea is a little like someone's 9-year-old brother tagging along with a big sister to a college graduation ceremony and expecting to get a diploma too.

According to the work of Zecharia Sitchin, mentioned earlier, the Anunnaki hybridized with a native human species on this planet, likely *Homo erectus*, to make *Homo Sapiens sapiens*.

Why look at the Reptilians?

[176] Cori, 2001, Chapter 8 "HAARP and Earth's Auric Field," pp. 111-130.

Because if Sitchin's theory is true, then the Anunnaki, already being Reptilian-Sirian hybrids, double-hybridized with a hominid species on Earth and made us. So Reptilian energy is part of our basic mental and emotional makeup, and we need to rise above the limitations of Reptilian thinking!

Conflicting Information

Much conflicting information is on the internet and in print about Reptilians. Some of it would be extremely frightening if it were true. Most of it is quite upsetting. I do not know exactly where truth lies. Evaluate what you read for yourselves and see what rings true. The most extreme version of the omnipresence of Reptilian interference in our culture is the work of David Icke. While I do not agree with all the theories in his book *The Biggest Secret*[177], especially the one that says Jesus never existed, I found his work helpful to understand the pervasive nature of reptilian influence on our species. He traces reptilian bloodlines through history and their involvement in royalty, government, and finance worldwide. Icke's book ends with an inspirational call to raise our vibration above the level where we are vulnerable to them.

Icke explained the lower 4th dimensional nature of the Reptilians. In Icke's model, the 4th dimension is the realm of feelings, known in energy psychology as the emotional body or the astral body. We can have wonderful feelings like love, harmony, and peace, which are in the upper part of the 4th dimension. We can also have difficult feelings like fear,

[177] Icke, D. (1999). *The Biggest Secret.* Available as a free download at http://david.icke.free.fr/files/[EN]%20-%20David%20Icke%20-%20The%20Biggest%20Secret.pdf

terror, and helplessness, which are the lower end of this 4th dimension. The Reptilians do not have love in their hearts, so they can only go as high as the lower part of the 4th dimension. They create situations to make us afraid because they feed from our fear. When we get scared, we lose energy, and they get it.

Love is the only way. The Reptilians block the heart. What can we do? We all hold hands—friends, family, hold Earth. Wrap everybody involved with our planet in love.
--Channeled by Janet Nestor from "the Dragonmaster"

Project MK-Ultra

One of the ways that Reptilian thinking affected the people who were trying to keep our country safe is that in 1953, at the height of the Cold War with Russia, Allen Dulles, Director of the CIA, approved a mind control project named MK-Ultra.[178] This covert CIA program used torture, sexual abuse, drugs, sleep deprivation, and starvation to deliberately create dissociation. The military wanted to make assassins who could be programmed to respond to a trigger code word or phrase to dissociate and kill someone, and then dissociate again and have no memory of what happened. The CIA was trying to create these super-spies so that one split off part of the personality could be programmed to complete a war mission, and the other parts of the person would know nothing about it. If captured and interrogated, the super-spy would truly know nothing about the mission. Reptilian

---

[178] https://www.history.com/topics/us-government/history-of-mk-ultra

thinking is programmed for survival, whatever the cost, without considering the effects one's actions have on others. This whole MK-Ultra program was designed to try to get the upper hand in the Cold War, without thinking of the human rights violations and devastation it made in the lives of the people subjected to this programming torture.

Files on this project and similar ones were released in 1975 during the aftermath of the Watergate scandal, when President Gerald Ford set up the United States President's Commission on CIA Activities to investigate illegal CIA behavior. Papers have been published on MK-Ultra's use of drugs, electroshock therapy, and torture to control human behavior. Use of the psychedelic drug Lysergic acid diethylamide, popularly known as LSD, played a large role in the research. While some of the subjects knew they were in a study, others in prisons, hospitals, and mental institutions were given LSD and other drugs without consent or knowledge.

According to MK-Ultra survivor Cathy O'Brien's testimony to Congress, torture, drugs, sexual abuse, thirst, starvation, and sleep deprivation were used to make her dissociate and to program parts of her to deliver secret messages to third world figures for CIA drug purchases. She reports she was also used as a prostitute and a drug mule.[179]

The Jason Bourne Series

In the action thriller movies of the fictional Jason Bourne series, a CIA trained assassin loses his memory and then

---

[179] O'Brien, C. & Phillips, M. (2005). *TRANCE Formation of America: True life story of a mind control slave.*

gradually pieces together from flashbacks how his handler in the Treadstone project used drugs, sleep deprivation, thirst, and torture to train him to become an on-call killer for the CIA. One major difference between the Bourne movies and O'Brien's account is that Bourne volunteered for the job of being trained as an assassin. O'Brien did not volunteer to be part of the CIA's program.

When Cathy O'Brien was a child, her father sold her to the CIA to avoid prosecution for selling porn videos. According to O'Brien, the person who confronted her father and made the deal to buy Cathy for the CIA mind control program in exchange for her father's immunity from prosecution was Gerald Ford, a future president of the United States. If her story is true, then the US President's Commission on CIA Activities that President Ford set up would actually be investigating himself. How well would that work?

Arizona Wilder's Testimony

The following testimony from MK-Ultra survivor Arizona Wilder on Reptilian activities is so shocking and horrific that one's first reaction may be to say that it could not possibly be true. Dissociation is a favorite way that humans have of shutting out information that makes us uncomfortable. Yet, the things Wilder says are corroborated by the testimony of other MK-Ultra survivors, so I have included this information.

Wilder reports she was groomed to be the Mother Goddess to preside over Satanic ritual human sacrifices. In 1989, she started to question her life and was able to deprogram from her training. She is one of the most important whistleblowers on what happens in Satanic ritual human sacrifices. In an interview with David Icke, Wilder reports that the Reptilians came to this planet thousands of years ago and started to take over, working through politics and religion. According to Wilder, the Reptilians materialized here from another dimension and installed themselves underground. To make themselves more acceptable to humans, they shapeshift into a human form, but this process requires a lot of energy that they can get only from human blood.[180]

These Reptilians need to keep drinking human blood and eating human flesh to be able to hold their human-looking forms. Wilder reports being at sacrifices in England where she has seen members of the Royal Family in attendance, including the Queen Mother, Queen Elizabeth, and Prince Charles. She claims they import children from third world countries who will not be missed and kill them ritually. As soon as the Royals smell the blood, they cannot help shapeshifting into their Reptilian forms and may begin to tear into the flesh of the victims and to drink the blood. She reports that they terrorize the victims so that their blood will have the chemicals in it that they need.[181] The chemical the Reptilians crave may be adrenochrome, which is formed by the oxidation of adrenaline, a chemical produced by the adrenal glands when a person is under great stress.

Wilder reports the essence of the Queen Mother, who died in 2002, was cold and cruel. When the Queen Mother

---

[180]Wilder, A. "Arizona Wilder and the Shapeshifting Reptilians." [Video]. YouTube. https://duckduckgo.com/?q=arizona+wilder+and+the+shapeshifting+reptilians&va=z&t=hc&iax=videos&ia=videos&iai=https%3A%2F%2Fwww.youtube.com%2Fwatch%3Fv%3DU3LepJjegko

[181] Ibid.

shapeshifted, she grew several feet taller, bigger, and stronger, with an elongated nose ending in a shout, with fangs and a long, pointed tongue with hairy projections. The hands and feet turned into claws, and the skin covered with scales that disappeared into each other. The eyes grew larger, with a vertical slit for the pupil. In her Reptilian form, the Queen Mother had a tail she kept curled behind her unless she was displeased, and then the tail whipped around, and she hissed.[182]

Wilder reports that the Reptilians live for hundreds of years, and that when the human form they have been inhabiting weakens and dies, they transfer their Reptilian essence into another human form.

She claims the Queen Mother has been in several different bodies over a long time span. Because holding the human form takes conscious effort, Wilder reports that the Reptilians may shapeshift into their true Reptilian form while they sleep at night.[183]

Queen Mother Elizabeth

Photo Credit by Richard Stone - archive copy, Public Domain, https://commons.wikimedia.org/w/index.php?curid=17641750

---

182 Ibid.

183 Ibid.

David Icke has a summary of what Wilder says about the royal family in his book *The Biggest Secret.*[184]

Who Eats Humans?

One of the eleven groups of Greys that author William Tompkins reports on "has lived underground in New Mexico for eons, and they have a diet of human flesh and blood."[185] Tompkins says that the US military is working hard to find a substitute food source for these Greys that will not make them sick so they will not have to eat people.

This scenario reminds me of the plot line in the TV serial *Stargate Atlantis*, where an alien group called the Wraith has only one food source able to sustain them, and that is the life force of humans. While the Wraith do not physically eat the humans, their sharp nails dig into the chest and extract the life force, killing the humans and leaving corpses that look old and withered. The doctor in the *Stargate Atlantis* story works to alter the DNA of the Wraith so they can eat other food. On the surface, this plot looks totally bizarre, ludicrous, and outrageous, but it is based in a horrible reality. If Tompkins is accurate about this situation, it explains why human sacrifice has been done in so many cultures for so many years and is still currently happening in Satanic cults. While other sources have attributed the eating of human flesh and drinking of their blood to the Reptilians, Tompkins reports one group of Greys also has the same dietary needs of human flesh and blood.

---

[184] Icke, p. 462.

[185] Tompkins, 2020, p. 142.

My Direct Experience

I can only report what my direct experience has been with working with clients who seem to be invaded by Reptilian energies. This problem has been the most difficult one to deal with in my practice, and it is all about energy supply. A synopsis of what I have seen from my clinical experience is that the Reptilians look for vulnerable people and try to steal their energy. Once they have invaded someone, they steal a fragment of the person's soul that has split off from trauma, sometimes from a past life memory of a brutal death. The Reptilians then mark that soul fragment so they can track the individual and keep stealing energy in every future lifetime and if possible, from all their offspring. The Soul Detective Reptilian Protocol we developed finds and eliminates these markers to set the person free from this interference, heal the damage that has been done, and restore the soul fragment to its rightful owner.

Case Example: Saturn's Moon Mind Control

> Frank was an expert in computer programming. He was an excellent athlete but over-trained, which caused physical problems that began in his late 30's. Unable to work at a regular job, he set his mind to his own healing and transformation with Soul Detective work and a variety of other modalities. A pattern formed in our work together: he would take two steps forward, and then something would knock him backward again. The word Lucifer inserted itself into his mind, bringing with it fear of invasion by the dark side. Frank felt emotionally upset when he read about the book *Trance Formation America* by Cathy O'Brien and Mark Phillips after I mentioned it in my monthly newsletter, *Om Is Home.*

Another very intuitive practitioner working with Frank saw a past life in which Frank was forced to create mind control systems on other planets. Using the Soul Detective Past Life Trauma protocol, dowsing indicated that Frank had incarnated 2-3 million years ago on one of the moons of Saturn into a humanoid race of beings who averaged 22 feet in height. We called this ancient lifetime Alec.

Saturn

He had one sibling, a twin brother. Their parents were infected with dark force energy and were mean and abusive. They abused both children, and Alec's twin brother abused Alec every chance he got. The whole family was invaded by dark force energy, which helped us to understand the current problem Frank was having of intrusive thoughts of Lucifer and Satan. The unresolved wounds of the past beg for healing!

Alec's Lifespan

Saturn takes around 29 ½ years to orbit the sun, and the average lifespan of beings in his species was 370 revolutions. Alec's lifespan was longer than most, because he lived for 426 revolutions around the sun, which would be over 12,500 years of Earth time. As he matured, he was forced into a military operation to create mind control programs on the moon base where he lived.

Note: When a lifetime so far outside of my conception of reality comes up, part of me thinks 22' tall beings on a moon of Saturn several million years ago is preposterous. Still, whether the past lifetime really happened or was a metaphor to describe a set of feelings that Frank needed to resolve, we went with the flow and treated the material as if it were true. I knew Saturn had rings but did not know if it had any moons. After the session, I found on the Internet that Saturn has 62 confirmed moons. The largest one is named Titan, which is larger than two of the other planets in our solar system: Mercury and Pluto.[186] Titan has a thick atmosphere made up mostly of nitrogen, like Earth's atmosphere, which is 78% nitrogen.[187] Scientists speculate that Saturn's moons Titus and Enceladus might be places to explore setting up a space base sometime in the future.[188] Who knows what civilization

---

186 http://coolcosmos.ipac.caltech.edu/ask/119-How-many-moons-does-Saturn-have-

187 http://coolcosmos.ipac.caltech.edu/ask/64-What-is-the-atmosphere-of-Earth-made-of-

188 https://www.space.com/28786-living-on-saturn-moons-titan-enceladus.html

might have had a space base there millions of years ago to run their super-soldier training programs?

Elena Danaan on Alien Races

Author Elena Danaan tells the story of her abduction by a group of detrimental Greys known as the Solipsi Ra and her remarkable rescue by two Pleiadians and a Sirian.[189] She also has a wealth of free information on her website at https://www.elenadanaan.org/.

Danaan divides Reptilian social structure into three main groups:

1. The Ciakahrr, the royalty and elites who measure 18 to 25 feet tall. They are the bosses.
2. The Nagai, the ferocious warrior caste, 7 to 8 feet tall.
3. The lower caste made up of workers including scientists, traders, engineers, and military.

Danaan reports the Reptilians have extensive bases underground, with a large one at Dulce, New Mexico, where the Reptilians are working on a ghastly array of techniques for human mind control, cloning, chip technology, animal-human hybridization, and experimentation with children.

Galactic Slave Trade

In Alec's story, his culture obtained 6' tall humans from the Lyra constellation through Galactic Slave Trading. Alec was forced to create mind control programs for these humans that would block their free will and turn them into super-soldier assassins. Again, at first glance,

---

[189] Danaan, 2020.

this idea might seem ludicrous. However, we have historical evidence of the same practices being done in the CIA's MK-Ultra program in the last half of the 20th century and in Elena Danaan's report above.

625 Assassins

We did not go into the details of how Alec programmed his super-soldiers, but we know that one of the methods he used was torture. At the time, Alec felt uncomfortable about the rights he was violating by using slavery and causing pain, suffering, and trauma to the subjects. However, abuse of a child by parents results in a profound sense of helplessness. Many victims of abuse become perpetrators who inflict trauma on others because this action feels like it takes them out of the role of helplessness into the role of having power over others—a dark power.

Frank felt his family in that lifetime had been Satanic, infected with dark entities that wanted to hurt others because the dark side feeds on pain and suffering. When we suffer, we lose energy, and the dark side takes the power we lose. It's a racket! The excuse the dark ones use to validate this systematic propagation of suffering is that the person—Alec in this case—is doing something noble for his culture by creating these assassins for military purposes. Frank felt mortified by how much damage his brainpower had been forced to create.

Making Amends

Alec asked Archangel Michael to set him free of all the Dark Force Energies that had invaded him, and he repented of all the evil he did. He asked one of his spirit guides from the 8th dimension to change the residual effects of the programs he had created from detrimental into 100% positive, to be used only for good. Alec was truly sorry. He also needed to forgive himself, the hardest part, but he did that too. Alec determined to use his gifts only for the Light in the future. He asked forgiveness of all the assassins he trained for all the pain and suffering he had caused them. He also asked forgiveness of all the people they had killed.

Energetic Cord

Alec's spirit then wanted to move into the Light, but it was tethered by a cord from his female boss from that lifetime. She still had a piece of her soul attached to Alec, millions of years later. We asked Archangel Michael to parse out that piece of her mind which she had been using to control Alec to do her will, to wash it off, and return it to its rightful owner.

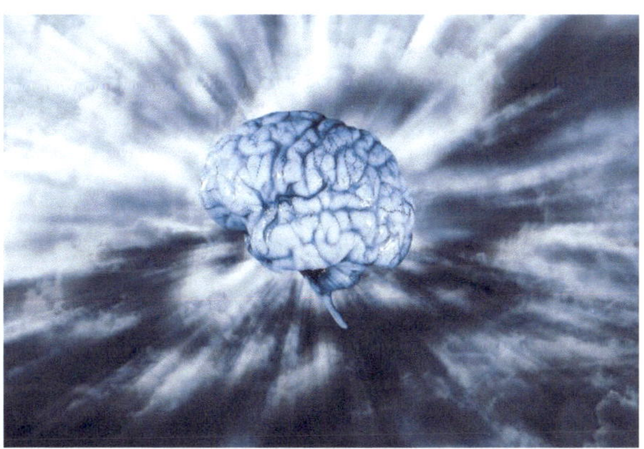

Releasing Mind Control

Then Alec was free to cross into the next world, and he made the transition into a higher dimension in the World of Light. We then treated the residual effects in Frank from this traumatic past life memory by rebalancing his heart chakra and then his other chakras.

Soul Lesson

The lesson his soul learned was how difficult it is to be born into a Satanic family because of all the suffering involved. He also learned not to misuse his gifts. In this lifetime, he has a burning desire to create computer programs that people can use to augment their innate abilities to heal.

Multiplying the Benefits

Once Alec was safely in the Light, where he could continue his healing and learning, we asked to multiply the benefits for any of the 625 assassins he had programmed who had remained earthbound and for any of the people they had killed. Then we expanded the healing intention to include the whole Universe, any others who had been trained as super-soldier assassins, and any others they had killed. We asked Archangel Michael to help them all couple to the benefits of the work Frank had done. Our testing indicated that between 400,000 and 500,000 others were able to link into the process, clear themselves of their dark energy infestation, and to heal and cross into the Light. Frank was able to take a traumatic lifetime and turn it around so that it became a benefit for many others trapped in similar circumstances.

Shifting Dimensions

Through long periods of meditation and other forms of esoteric training, one can learn to shift the molecular structure of the body out of phase and thus disappear into another dimension. Jesus did this in the Bible, when the crowd was angry with him for what he preached and "took him to the brow of the hill on which the town was built, in order to throw him down the cliff. But he walked right through the crowd and went on his way." (Luke 4:29-30 NIV)

In my book *Transforming Fear into Gold*, I write about a past life when I was a Brahmin priest who became a disciple of Yeshua (Jesus), who came to India to study with the Brahmins when he was 19 years old. Yeshua wanted to abolish the caste system and have all people be equal. Armed revolt broke out, as the people in power in India did not want to give up their land and positions. The establishment tried to kill Yeshua. Somehow, Yeshua made himself and his followers invisible, and they slipped out of the crowd and escaped.

While this claim seems too far out to be true, a colleague named Thornton Streeter once witnessed a woman who was a yogi disappear and reappear. This woman came to Thornton for a biofield scan, and he watched her go into a state of meditation and gradually disappear right before his eyes. The top half of this photo is of her energy field before she disappeared. Once this woman had meditated herself into invisibility, only a filmy outline remained of where her body had been. The bottom half of the photo is what her auric field looked like while she was in the state of invisibility. Then the woman came out of meditation and gradually reappeared.

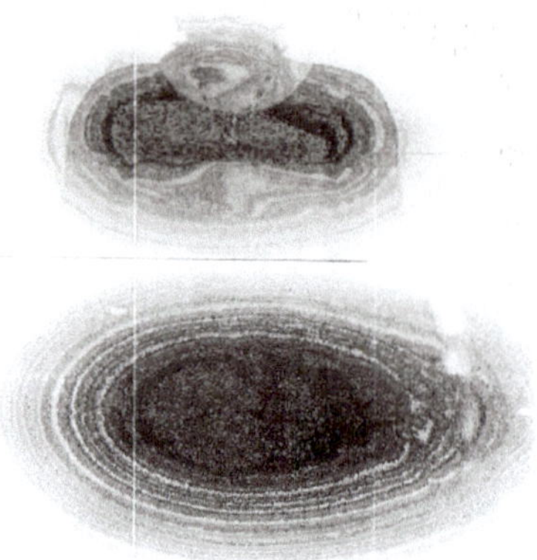

Photo Credit: Thornton Streeter

Reptilians have mastered this ability to appear and disappear, shifting dimensions and hiding between the dimensions so they are difficult to find. Imagine the frustration of setting your rifle sight to shoot a ground hog eating your swiss chard, and as soon as you get it in the crosshairs, the varmint fades out and disappears! Then it reappears on the other side of the garden in the kale patch. Very frustrating!

In Soul Detective work, when we run into Reptilians, we ask for help from higher dimensional beings who can see exactly what is going on. As I mentioned before, the Arcturians have been excellent helpers to set people free from the Reptilians by using the power of unconditional love.

Chapter 12: Arcturians

Arcturus is the highest Civilization in our galaxy.

--Edgar Cayce

Arcturus is a giant red star, the most brilliant one in the constellation Boötes, the Herdsman.

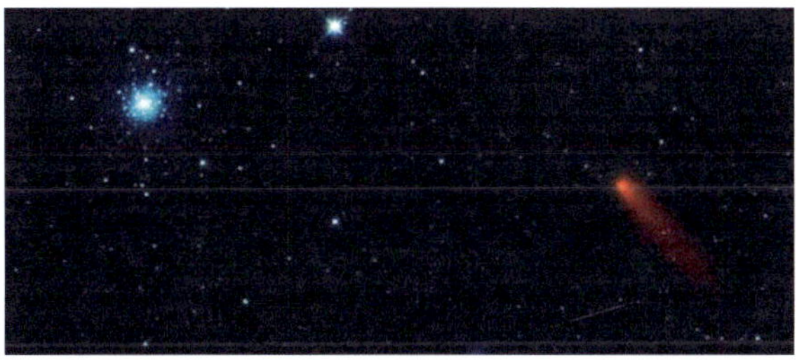

A portion of the Constellation Boötes and red comet Garradd images-assets.nasa.gov/image/PIA12985/PIA12985~orig.jpg
Secondary credit NASA/JPL-Caltech/UCLA

Arcturus is the brightest star in the northern celestial hemisphere and the fourth brightest in the night sky. To locate Arcturus, follow the curve of the handle of the Big Dipper. Arcturus has been around a long time, with an estimated age of 7.1 billion years, whereas our solar system is estimated to be about 4.5 billion years old. Beings on Arcturus are in the fifth and sixth dimensions, where their bodies progressively lose physical density and are made of light.

Craig Campobasso claims that "The Arcturians are able to reassemble their physical bodies or any matter from one location to another through a molecular stimulation of light codes. They can sweep an entire civilization from the ground up into a mothership in less than a second."[190]

Weaponizing Unconditional Love

One of our Soul Detective colleagues intuited that when the Reptilians arrived to pillage and plunder a planet revolving around the star Arcturus, the people on the planet banded together in prayer, sent out unconditional love, and their whole planet ascended into the 5th dimension, where the Reptilians could not find them or harm them. According to authors Tom Kenyon and Judi Sion, the spiritual figure Sanat Kumara is the head of the Arcturian fleet that guards and protects our planet from nefarious ETs.[191]

> **"A connection between Thoth (Anunnaki god, son of Enki, Chapter 4) and Sanat Kumara asks us to come together and lift each other up. Help people who have had their souls stolen. Open up a level where we can function at the 5th dimension."**
>
> --Janet Nestor channeling "The Council of Wise Men with Women Present."

In Soul Detective work, when we find Reptilian Intrusion, we go to the Arcturians for help and ask them to remove the Reptilian, restore its soul if it ever had one, rehabilitate it, setting it free from Artificial Intelligence nanites and nanobots controlling its behavior, and relocate it to the right place in the cosmos where all its needs will be met and it cannot harm humans. The shorthand for this process of four things that all start with the letter R is "R&R squared."

---

[190] Campobasso, p. 32.

[191] Kenyon, T. & Sion, J. (2013). *The Arcturian Anthology*.

Psychics have seen the Arcturians pulling out the Reptilian with a tractor beam of pure, unconditional love—the one thing a Reptilian cannot defend against!

In a workshop on helping loved ones cross into the Light, a student I will call Penelope told me of a tragedy that happened to two of her beloved colleagues. They were both great people and had been married five years. In his mid-30's, the husband, who we will call Arnold, suddenly changed his behavior. He became aggressive and stole money from his wife, Alice. She left him because of his violent behavior. Then Arnold killed Alice and took his own life by shooting himself.

Sacred Space

We got permission to work with this tragic situation for both Arnold and Alice. We set sacred space very carefully for everyone in the workshop, asking for an octahedron of Golden Light to surround us, with a band of warrior angels around it and a band of Arcturians around them. We asked to have everything enclosed in a golden sphere.

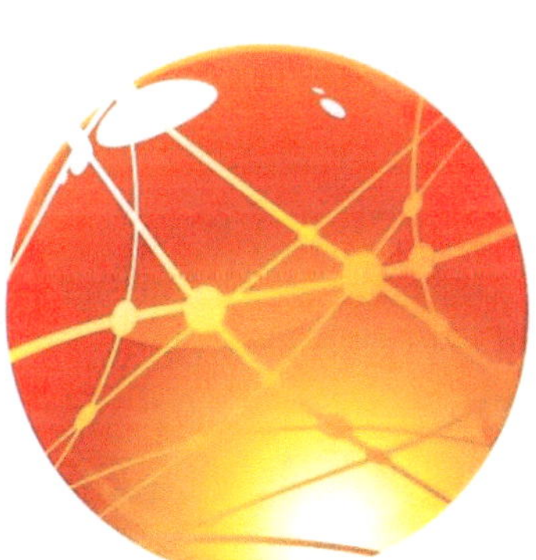

Penelope was very intuitive. Once we felt the protection in place around us, we started by having Penelope tune into Alice's feelings. Alice was very sad and felt like her life, which was cut so short, was a failure. We did energy healing work to help her accept all her feelings, adding the affirmation that she did the best she could and did not know that Arnold was capable of such violence. She then felt better and was ready to cross into the World of Light, but she wanted to wait until we had worked with Arnold so they could go together. We asked Archangel Michael to make a special octahedron of protection for Alice in the corner of the room, guarded by angels so she would be safe from whatever came up with Arnold.

Penelope saw Arnold feeling very upset and horrified at what he had done. Something around his neck was holding him back. Muscle testing indicated one Reptilian was involved, and Penelope saw the creature restraining and binding Arnold. We called in the help of the Arcturians to set Arnold free from this Reptilian. I explained the backstory of how the Arcturians banded together in unconditional love when they were attacked by the Reptilians and ascended into a higher dimension. We asked the Arcturians to R&R square this Reptilian (remove, restore, rehabilitate, and relocate it) with a tractor beam of pure, unconditional love. Penelope saw the Arcturians extricating the Reptilian from the earthbound spirit of Arnold. Then she exclaimed, "I am Arcturian!"

Life Between Life Regression

Penelope had done work with a student of Michael Newton, author of *Life Between Lives*,[192] to look at what happened to her between this life and her previous one.

[192] Newton, M., 2004.

In this regression, she saw herself as one of a large group of 12-foot-tall Arcturians who banded together with Sirians and Pleiadians on a mission to come help the planet Earth in her ascension into the 5th dimension. The Pleiadians were much shorter than the Arcturians, so they looked almost like dolls to them, and the Arcturians had great fondness for the Pleiadians.

Pink Pleiades image Credit:
assets.nasa.gov/image/PIA09262/PIA09262~orig.jpg
Secondary Creator Credit: NASA/JPL-Caltech

Penelope really resonated with the work we were doing together. The next step in dealing with Arnold's Reptilian was to find out if it had ever had a soul and if so, to have the soul restored. Penelope told us that the Reptilian that had been bound to Arnold did have a soul, but it was lost far away on some other planet. I said, "Well, have the Arcturians go find it, clean it up, and return it to the Reptilian!" Since the Arcturians are higher dimensional beings, they can easily go to other locations in the Universe. In a very short time, Penelope reported the soul of the Reptilian had been recovered, cleansed, and returned to the Reptilian. The third step was for the Arcturians to help the Reptilian rehabilitate, including getting free of its domination by Artificial Intelligence, and the fourth step was to relocate the Reptilian somewhere else in a place that was just right for the Reptilian where it could not harm humans.

Arnold was very relieved as he watched his persecutor being removed and reformed. The next step was to find out why Arnold had been targeted by the Reptilian. I told Penelope that Reptilians put markers on a person's soul to track and target a person through successive incarnations. Arnold reported that this Reptilian had attached to him in many previous lifetimes, and each life had ended in disaster. We asked to go to the original attachment.

Human Sacrifice

Arnold saw a previous lifetime where he was a king somewhere in Central America a long time ago. His people were at war with their neighbors. To please the gods and get an advantage in the war, he sacrificed his own child to the gods, thinking it would help his country. Right after he killed his child, he realized he had made a terrible mistake that caused great pain to everyone. In despair and anguish from his action, he then took his own life by poisoning himself.

Remedial Work

When a child is given to a Reptilian false god, the Reptilian claims the soul of the child as its possession. The Reptilian bites out a piece of the soul to track the person in future incarnations and to mark the soul to steal more energy in successive lifetimes. First, we worked to help the King's son. We asked Archangel Michael to find the missing soul piece from the prince, extract it from the Reptilian, wash it clean, and return it to the King's son. We asked to forever remove this marker from his son's soul. Then we had Divine Mother take the child into the World of Light.

The King made a deep and sincere apology to his son for his action and all the pain it caused to him and everyone else. We did energy work with the King to help him see how he was tricked by the Reptilians, thinking he was doing something to help his people, but then realizing he had caused great damage. The king repented and forgave himself. Then he was able to cross into the World of Light to be with his son again. With this healing, Arnold regained a piece of his soul that had been lost from this lifetime long ago.

Removing the Marker

When a king or a priest serves a Reptilian god by sacrificing a human, the Reptilian puts a marker on the soul of the king or priest as also belonging to the Reptilians. Arnold had this marker on his soul. He remembered many lifetimes where the Reptilians took possession of him, and all these lives ended in disaster. We asked to remove all these markers from him and also to remove all of the automatic re-installation programs the Reptilians put on the markers.

Magic Carpet

At last, Arnold was free of the restraint around his neck and was ready to cross into the World of Light. We asked how he wanted to go, and he asked for a Magic Carpet to fly him there. We watched it happen.

Alice came, and they flew home together on the magic carpet, hand in hand.

Soul Lesson

The lesson that Arnold learned from these soul experiences was to ask for help from Beings of Love and Light. He had not been aware of this resource. At the end of this work, Penelope and the whole group felt a deep sense of joy. Penelope could see Arnold at peace in the next world.

Let peace be our rallying call and compassion be our armor.

--Sanat Kumara

Chapter 13: Ummites

The Ummites are a group of Star People who are indistinguishable from humans. Author Craig Campobasso says they look like Nordics, are eight to nine feet tall, and live by the Cosmic Law of One. He reports they came to help Earth people climb out of our war and pollution mentality to prevent us from destroying our planet and our species.[193] Author Stefano Breccia gives a lot more detailed information about the Ummites and presents a less-glamorous picture of them. He does not mention their being so tall, as a 9-foot human-looking person would stick out anywhere on Earth and would also be in great demand with professional basketball player scouts!

As in all contact from Star Civilizations, some information on the internet calls the Ummite story a hoax. Perhaps it is. The Ummites themselves said they expected us to be skeptical about them. In a letter, they said, "…we are perfectly aware that we're not going to be believed, either now or in the future, whenever we choose to offer further revelations."[194] However, I present their story for your discernment. In addition, their escapades involved in coming to Earth are at times quite humorous. I also present it because we have detailed information about their culture and their interaction with humans on this planet.

---

[193] Campobasso, 2021.

[194] Breccia, S. (2009). *Mass Contacts*, p. 66.

The Ummite Symbol

The symbol the Ummites used in the letters they sent to people and on their spacecraft is similar to the Russian letter H:

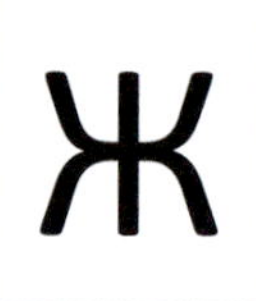

Beginnings of Contact with Earth

Between February 5 and 7 of 1934, a Norwegian ship off the coast of Newfoundland sent wireless signals in Morse code at 413.44 MHz which arrived at the planet Ummo 14 years later. Ummo is likely what astronomers call Wolf 4, a dwarf binary star in the constellation of Virgo that is 14 light years away from Earth.

NGC 1569: Starburst in a Dwarf Irregular Galaxy Credit: NASA, ESA, Hubble Heritage (STScI/AURA); Acknowledgement: A. Aloisi (STScI/ESA) et al.

The arrival of these signals caused a big commotion on Ummo as it was their first proof of a civilization outside of their world.[195] They decided to send an expedition to Earth to investigate us! According to the Ummites, "...space is ten-dimensional, and the true distance between Earth and Ummo changes continually...."[196] Their first scouting expedition arrived in our solar system on February 7, 1949, first stopping by Mars and then coming to Earth, which had been identified as the origin of the Morse code transmissions. They stopped 54 km above Montreux, Switzerland, a town on the shore of Lake Geneva, and observed our world for just 4 hours before going back home to analyze the data they had collected.

Mistaken Assumptions

- The Ummites did not know what Earth houses were for, as their homes were all underground. They assumed the houses to be some kind of factories.

- They saw humans with cylindrical objects in their mouths (cigarettes) and first assumed these people were biological robots. But then they decided that humans could not breathe the elements in our atmosphere without adding this "strange aerosol" to it.[197]

- The emission of large bands of signals in some areas and not others perplexed them. They assumed these television signals were some kind of language. When I lived in Switzerland for three years, I heard many different languages being spoken there. The presence of so many different languages on Earth alarmed the

---

195 Ibid, p. 79

196 Ibid.

197 Ibid, p. 80

Ummites, but they assumed that all humans understood all the different languages.

First Landing

On March 28, 1950, a party of just six Ummites, two women and four men, landed in a secluded area in southern France by the Cheval Blanc peak. They first dug out a base inside the Earth so they could remain concealed. The following day, they set out exploring and came upon some unknown sheets of paper with symbols printed on them that had human feces on them. What a mystery! They hypothesized that when humans did not agree with something written down, they soiled it with feces. This find was so important that they immediately returned to their base to analyze it. Later they discovered the papers were newspaper pages that had been used as toilet paper. They report this initial discovery was deemed so important that it is kept as a relic on Ummo!

Preparing for Attack

The following day two of the Ummites set out again, wearing dark clothing and heavily armed. They came upon a group of eight very large vertebrate animals with sharp appendages on their heads. Since Ummo has no cows, they did not know what they were.

While they were measuring the energy fields

around these beasts, a young shepherd boy appeared. The Ummites remained motionless and radioed their chief via their wireless device for instructions on how to proceed. They were instructed to return any greeting. The boy made sounds they could not understand, approached, and covered his eyes from the sun with one hand. The Ummites did the same, covering their eyes from the sun, which perplexed the shepherd boy. Then the boy took his cows and left. The Ummites had been so surprised that they did not make any recording of the event that they could analyze. They returned to their base and hunkered down, waiting to see if the boy might have alerted the military to attack them.

After the third day without any assault from the humans, the Ummites went out again and found the shepherd boy and a couple of men in the distance. They recorded this interaction and were then able to manufacture suits like the ones the men had been wearing, complete with neckties and handkerchiefs in the breast pockets. On April 2nd, three Ummites put on these identical suits and went out again, heavily armed, and found the shepherd boy. He offered them some of his bread. The Ummites had not been able to find out the orientation of the proteins in human food, and if Ummite protein orientation were reversed from the human orientation, the food could have killed them. One of the Ummites bravely ate some of the food and found he did not die from it. They made friends with the boy and learned from him by gesturing the names of objects and how to read from the newspaper.

Farmhouse Raid

The Ummites then made a daring raid on a farmhouse in the

vicinity, hypnotizing the inhabitants and taking things to study, including biological specimens from the farmer.

The next morning, the police received a report from an old farmer named Violat of "the theft of the most varied and often undesirable objects, but still adding up to the value of 70,000 francs, a huge sum in those times."[198] The Ummites later regretted the theft and compensated the farmer by having his sons win a great deal of money in the lottery—a ploy they often used to pay people.

The Human Version of the Severed Hand Story

This story has two versions, the human one and the Ummite one. The human story that appeared in a Spanish newspaper[199] reports that in 1954, an aristocratic woman named Doña Margarita Ruiz de Lihory was accused by her son Luis of mutilating the body of her deceased daughter Margot. She was accused of cutting off the right hand, taking out the eyes, and cutting off the front part of the tongue. The police searched her house and found a jar of preservative with

---

[198] Ibid, p. 86

[199] Berbel, C. "El caso de la mano cortada: ¿Por qué la aristócrata Margarita Ruiz de Lihory le cortó una mano y le sacó los ojos al cadáver de su hija?" *Confilegal.* https://confilegal.com/20170521-caso-la-mano-cortada-la-aristocrata-margarita-ruiz-lihory-le-corto-la-mano-le-saco-los-ojos-al-cadaver-hija/

a hand, two eyes, and part of a tongue in it. They then exhumed Margot's body and found that it was missing the right hand, the eyes, and the front of the tongue. They determined that the hand in the jar was Margot's hand. They did an autopsy to see if Margot had been murdered, but the autopsy showed the cause of death to be from natural causes, either leukemia or pulmonary swelling. Strangely, the authorities also found bones of deceased dogs and birds in the home of Doña Margarita Ruiz.

The newspaper article says people speculated that perhaps Black Magic, ritual sacrifice, occultism, or Nazi style medical experiments may have been involved—or intervention by extraterrestrials. In her defense, Doña Margarita Ruiz declared that her daughter's hand was a holy relic to her, a memory of her daughter, and that she worshipped this hand. She likened it to the Catholic practice of veneration of a piece of Saint Peter's tongue and the incorruptible arm of St. Teresa, which General Franco took with him for luck into the Spanish Civil War. After seven years of research and deliberation, on March 28, 1961, Doña Margarita Ruiz was accused of mutilating a corpse and endangering public health. The father of her children was deceased, and she lived with a layer named José María Basols-Iglesias—Don Basols for short. Doña Margarita Ruiz was given a sentence for mutilating a corpse of six months of arrest and a fine of 5,000 pesetas. Don Basols was sentenced to three months arrest and a fine of 2,000 pesetas, the difference coming from his not being a parent of Margot. For endangering public health, both Doña Margarita Ruiz and her partner Don Basols were given an additional fine of 5,000 pesetas with substitution of three months incarceration for each fine in case they did not have the money to pay the fines. The couple appealed the conviction to their Supreme Court, which upheld the original adjudication on April 25, 1964. Doña Margarita Ruiz died in 1968 at the age of 75.

The Ummite Version of the Severed Hand Story

Next, I present the Ummite version of these events. The Ummites wanted to study human culture, biology, and physiology. Though their headquarters were in France, two Ummites posed as Dutch physicians and set up a covert research center in the town of Albacete in South-Eastern Spain. They rented the cellar of an aristocratic woman named Doña Margarita Ruiz de Lihory, an educated woman who had been active in the resistance movement during World War II. She loved animals and was always surrounded by many of them. Though she owned much property, Doña Margarita did not have much cash flow. The substantial rent the Ummites paid her helped her financial situation, and soon she received some "lottery wins" and an inheritance from an unknown American relative—both actions of the Ummites to help her. The Ummites demanded strict secrecy of their presence. Only her partner, Don Basols, and a maid knew of their basement laboratory.

Their covert research involved immunoglobulins and the amino acid sequences in diverse antibodies. They wanted to find out if mutations could be induced by stringing together globulins like happened on Ummo. They brought with them a virus that had never been present on Earth before, similar to what we call the "rat polioma virus," but more complex.[200]

[200] Breccia, p. 90.

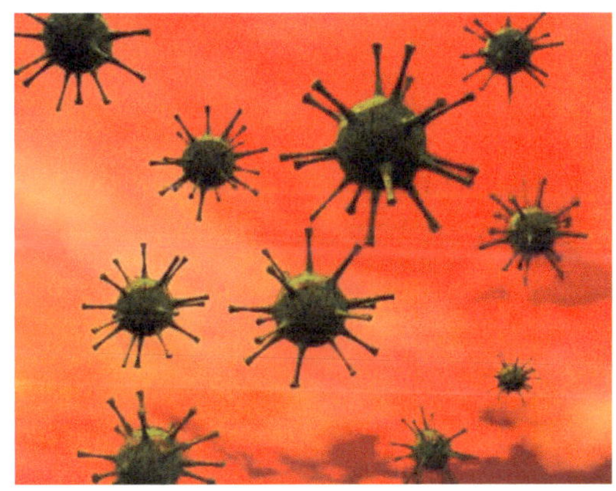

Viruses

This virus could not multiply in healthy cells, only in dead tissue, where it multiplied rapidly. The Ummites had technology to detect the presence of this virus and other viruses in people within 78 meters of them. To their consternation, on September 4, 1953, they found colonies of this virus on Doña Margarita, her daughter Margot, and three dogs. They also had the technology to remotely destroy these viral colonies without the subjects even knowing it. They eradicated all the viral colonies they found.

They were concerned about the spread of this virus and called in four more Ummites from Austria who had more sensitive instruments. With better technology, they identified 26 more infections in the local town of Albacete, which they promptly destroyed, but they knew that the virus could lie dormant in levels below the sensitivity of their instruments and could erupt in the presence of necrosis—death of cell tissue due to illness, accident, or blood supply failure. They kept a close watch on the area around the town, and then realized to their horror that Doña Margarita owned properties in many places throughout Spain and had already made several trips to her daughter's home in Madrid. They traveled to Madrid, and on November 7 found three infected areas in her daughter Margot's body that they could not treat remotely—the eyes, the tongue, and the skin of the right palm. She would need surgery to remove the virus.

The Ummites disclosed the situation to Doña Margarita and were considering informing the Spanish medical authorities about the outbreak of this virus. Then, all the Ummites gathered in Madrid to try to find a solution, but they could not do surgery on Margot without disclosing the situation. They decided to do nothing and to wait for Margot to die of pulmonary edema. In January, Margot died, and they amputated the affected parts of her body—right hand, eyes, and tongue—to study how the virus had mutated. They silenced Doña Margarita with a large sum of money that was supposedly a lottery prize. Doña Margarita went through the police investigation, which found her daughter's right hand, eyes, and tongue in a jar. They also found animal remains, as Doña Margarita would perform autopsies on her animals who died and would remove some organs, including head, tongue, and heart.

Breccia reports that the charges were dropped against Doña Margarita, contrary to the newspaper report. Breccia also says that Doña Margarita, her partner Don Basols, their staff and many friends all died within the next year, 1954, which would be consistent with contamination with a virus. But the Spanish newspaper in the previous section reports the case went on for 10 years, and Doña Margarita did not die until 1968.

The Ummites have not shared with us humans the results of their study about what went wrong in this virus that escaped their lab. After the COVID-19 virus escaping the Wuhan lab in China and affecting humans worldwide, this account of ET involvement in viral research and study of humans takes on a new depth of danger. Humans adapt to pathogens, but when something is introduced from off-planet, our immune systems are unprepared. I would like to have the Ummite technology to remotely detect and eliminate these pathogens!

Ummite History

In the development of their civilization, during their Middle Ages, a very intelligent and ruthless girl rose to power on Ummo. The Local Council sent her to the university when she was only 8.5 years old. When she was 13 years old, she was appointed as a teacher and studied Ummo's gravitational field. When Ummo's chief died, she was elected to the council of governors. Seventeen days later, she provoked a coup and proclaimed herself the to be the highest authority in all of Ummo. Still just a girl, she declared that "God is but the sum of all Ummites and that she herself...was God's brain!"[201] Science was declared as the ultimate purpose of Ummo, and she authorized vivisection (dissecting someone while the subject is still alive) for punishment and for scientific research. She was succeeded by her daughter, who was even more cruel than her mother as ultimate ruler of Ummo. The daughter declared herself the "Central Coordinator of the Cosmos."[202] Their history records over four million victims during her short reign.

At that extremely difficult time, a Christ-figure emerged on Ummo. The Ummite word for God is "Woa," and the name

[201] Ibid, p. 95.
[202] Ibid, p. 96.

of this savior figure was "UMMOWOA." He taught people to return to the true God. After his teachings were completed, just like Christ, he was tortured and killed. Something spectacular and supernatural occurred when UMMOWOA died. "The specialists involved in his vivisection were astonished when the body of UMMOWOA disappeared in front of them at the moment of his death. …his extracted viscera, his blood…together with his cephalic liquid (brain fluid) kept in a receptacle, all vanished at the same time."[203] In our time, the date of this event was 1405 CE.[204] Their scientists did not get to study UMMOWOA's DNA!

The rise in consciousness from the teachings of UMMOWOA combined with someone blowing up their cruel leader led to great political and social changes on Ummo. In the reorganization, they formed a General Council of Ummo instead of a dictatorship. Notwithstanding this change, lives on Ummo are very strictly controlled by this government.

Money

As in Star Trek and most of the more advanced civilizations, money does not exist on Ummo. Free enterprise does not exist. The Central Government controls everything, including their education, which is enforced with strict discipline.

---

[203] Ibid, p. 100.

[204] CE stands for the Common Era. The former letters used for a date were AD, so UMMOWOA's death would have been notated as 1405 AD in our timeline.

Marriage

When a 15 ½-year-old boy finds a girl he wants to marry, he must submit this choice to his teachers, who will research the computer data bank of Ummo for any possible problems that might arise of mental or physiological incompatibility with the girl. If the boy's choice is approved, then he can talk to the girl and let her know he wants to marry her. All Ummites are married—no adults remain single. Wives are subject to the will of their husbands, as the society is male-dominant. Perhaps the planet decided that cruel women had done so much damage earlier in their history that power was safer in the hands of men!

Housing

The state assigns a house to the new couple. Their homes are underground, in the shape of a large, pointed mushroom. A suction tunnel in the center brings in the supplies they need and takes out waste products. When one partner in the marriage dies, the surviving partner must exit the home. The state decides whether the surviving partner will go to live with one of the children or in a collective dwelling.

Sexuality

The Ummites have a great fear of being seen naked. In ancient times, one of the punishments for wrongdoings was to make the person stand naked in front of a crowd of Ummites. The Ummites report that they place a very high priority on sex—maybe sometimes too high.

A unique feature of their physiology is that if they accelerate upward or backward very fast, they have an orgasm. This situation makes riding up an elevator a very pleasurable experience!

Letters to Professionals

Starting around 1965, the Ummites sent thousands of letters to professional people worldwide, including engineers, biologists, physicists, astronomers, and people who were studying UFOs. These letters were written in many different languages, but most of them were in Spanish. The letters said they were extraterrestrials from a planet called Ummo which orbited a star they called Iumma. These voluminous letters cover their history, scientific topics, and examples of their technology. Breccia reports that over 10,000 pages exist of these letters. They are incredibly detailed in physics, geometry, and math. They report that some of the information they shared with humans has been developed and patented by the humans.

Sighting

On June 1, 1967, a few kilometers from Madrid, a large disc-shaped object appeared in the sky. The top of the disc had a transparent dome, and the Ummo symbol was on the bottom:

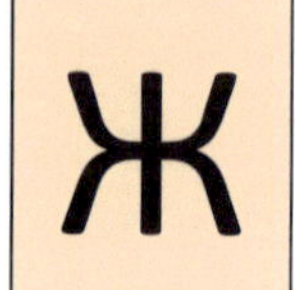

The object gave off an orange light, hovered in mid-air, then shot off at great speed, and appeared to land at a restaurant called "La Ponderosa."[205] Two photographers got pictures of the craft. Fifty people, including some military, witnessed the event. Humorously, some witnesses reported that the mark on the bottom was the letter "M," which stood for Martians! Interestingly, on May 20 of that

[205] Ibid, p. 118.

same spring, a newspaper had published a letter from a professor which said that one of the Ummite ships would appear within the end of the month, near Madrid. That prediction came true.

Many small tubes 2 cm x 13 cm were found on the ground beneath the landing spot. All of them were made of a pure nickel and had the Ummite symbol impressed within them.

Aliens Visit Russia

The website www.InfinityExplorers.com reports the landing of a UFO in the Soviet town of Voronezh on September 27, 1989. A group of children in a park saw a UFO land and a 9-foot-tall alien with three eyes emerge. A companion and a robot also emerged. The children were terrified when the aliens activated their robot and held an instrument that looked like a gun. Soon, the aliens got back into their spaceship and flew off. Hundreds of people in the town reportedly saw the craft. Some of the drawings the children made of the spacecraft showed the Ummite insignia:

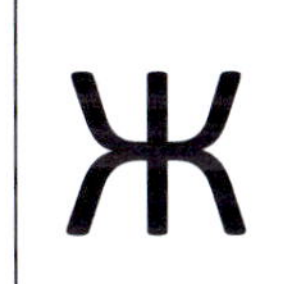

Alien Direct Intervention with Gorbachev

Col. Donald Ware, a retired US Air Force pilot, reports a very different version of this event in Voronezh. The account above from InfinityExplorers.com may be a cover story. In Col. Ware's story, Mikhail Gorbachev was sitting at the edge of a field, when a huge UFO landed. A nine-foot-tall alien came out and told Gorbachev who the alien was and why he was there. He told Gorbachev that the Soviet Union needs to have more transparency and less repression. The next six days after that, an unidentified object was seen to come in on a straight line toward the Soviet town of Voronezh. By the 7th day, on September 27, 1989, it had gathered an audience of about 400 people. The UFO landed downtown, and that landing made news around the world. The alien got out and talked with the people for a while. Then a KGB van pulled up and arrested the 9-foot-tall alien. Two little aliens got out and talked with the audience for about an hour. Then the KGB returned the 9-foot-tall alien. The little aliens saluted the tall one, and then they entered their craft and took off.[206] Right after that, Gorbachev started the programs of glasnost (openness) and perestroika (restructuring). On December 3, 1989, President Bush and Gorbachev officially declared an end to the cold war at a summit in Malta.

Dangers: The Italian Ummites

A group in Italy also called themselves Ummites, but they never sent any letters. They contacted humans via telephone and had a long contact with a group of university students and teachers. The people they contacted recorded long conversations with these Ummites and then transcribed the dialog. They produced 10,000 pages of conversations! The Italian Ummites claimed to have many bases, including a small one under the city of Rome. These Ummites made clones of some of the people they contacted and would sometimes send the clone robot to a meeting instead of the human.

The Italian Ummites complained about another race of Star People known as the "W56," described in the next chapter.

---

[206] Clare, C. (2016). *ETs Among Us: UFO Witnesses and Whistleblowers. Part 1.*

The Ummite side of the story is that the W56 people destroy the Ummite spacecrafts, and they only respond in self-defense.

The W56 side of the story is that they have an enemy of a robotic race that developed from their own experiments with Artificial Intelligence gone awry. The androids they created became self-aware and decided to destroy their creators. They call this AI race the CTR from the Italian word "Contrari," or enemy. The theme is the same as in the movie *Battlestar Galactica,* where androids called Cylons develop themselves to the point where they look exactly like humans and make war on their creators. Might the Italian Ummites be forms of the CTR, posing as another race? The Ummite covert lab studying viruses and mutations and the cloning going on in Italy sound like dangerous activities to me. What is very evident is that the spiritual development of the Ummites, with their strict governmental control, is scientific and sterile, very different from the unconditional love exuded by the W56 race.

Chapter 14: W56

The W56 are another species of Star People who were in contact with a group of around 100 humans all over Europe, but mainly in Italy. This Star Civilization was very different from the Ummites, and in all cases where the W56 contacted humans, the overflowing feeling was love and friendship. The Italians named them the "Amicizia," Italian for friendship.

The Akrij

The true name of the W56 is the "Akrij," which is a plural noun in Sanscrit that means "the sages." The Theban version of *The Book of the Dead* simply describes the Akrij as ancestors of Ra, the Egyptian Sun God.

The Italians called them the W56 because their first contacts came in 1956, and the letter W stands for "double victory," two Vs put together. The W56 had great spiritual advancement and taught their Italian friends that when one wins a victory over enemies, one still needs another victory, to overcome one's own pride—a double victory.[207] The W56 are unable to lie and will not hurt ensouled life forms. They came

from a distant binary star and were part of a Confederation of

[207] Breccia, p. 227.

Planets. They have been present on Earth for millennia.[208] One W56 they met reported he had been on planet Earth three times. He said he had been in Central America several centuries ago because of a war involving other Star People who were operating bases there.[209]

This most recent human connection on Earth was coordinated through a Catholic writer named Bruno Sammaciccia, born in 1926, who had degrees in Psychology and Psychiatry. From 1956 to 1978, the W56 had very close contact with the Italian group organized by Sammaciccia.

Before his death, Sammaciccia told the whole story to Stefano Breccia, who wrote about it in *Mass Contacts* (2009), mentioned in the chapter on the Ummites. This book is one of the few European books about Star People that has been translated into English.

Conflict with the CTRs

Like many science fiction movies, the androids the W56 created long ago developed to a point where they rebelled against their creators. The CTRs are working to become as close as possible to natural races.[210] The CTR synthetic life forms looked exactly like us humans, spoke like us, ate like us, and even developed to the point of sexual reproduction of more CTRs. This last report I find very difficult to believe, that AI could reproduce sexually. But perhaps my imagination just cannot stretch to see how a machine can have sex with another machine and produce baby machines.

[208] Ibid, p. 166.
[209] Ibid, p. 171.
[210] Ibid, p. 273.

The CTRs have great technological advancement, but no soul whatsoever as they are artificial life forms. The CTRs were fighting for control of Earth, wanting to dominate our planet and control the minds and wills of humans, much like the plot of *Star Wars,* where the evil Empire was trying to take over and control everything. Since the W56 had created the CTRs, they had the responsibility to protect Earth from this AI takeover. But to abide by universal law, the W56 needed to protect us without interfering in our spiritual development, since the rule of the Universe is free will.

Sammaciccia reported, "And they told me that, since 1956, in at least two occasions they have had to prevent an atomic war, and they did so by transmuting the fissionable metals inside war-heads into lighter substances, so that no nuclear reaction could take place."[211] Indeed, they are our friends! This claim is backed up by eyewitness reports of US Air Force commanders at missile sites where UFOs shut down nuclear weapons.

UFOs and Nukes

Researcher Robert Hastings has interviewed over 150 veterans who have witnessed UFO activity at missile sites where nuclear weapons were shut down. Hastings wrote *UFOs and Nukes: Extraordinary Encounters at Nuclear Weapon Sites,* 2nd edition (2017) documenting these accounts. All witnesses had been individually commanded to keep silent, but the secrecy orders go only for 50 years. Therefore, an incident in 1966 could be disclosed in 2016, if the eyewitnesses lived that long.

---

[211] Ibid, p. 239.

Eyewitness Accounts of Nuclear Shutdown

USAF Captain David Schindele was a Minuteman I launch crew commander at Minot Air Force Base in North Dakota for nuclear weapons poised to be launched if the cold war heated up. In August of 1966, UFOs were spotted over their missile silos, and unexplainably, ten of their nuclear weapons suddenly went into "off-alert" status, which meant they could not be launched.

Captain Schindele and everyone else who witnessed the UFOs and the shutdown were ordered never to talk about the incident. Decades later, Schindele compared notes with other missileers, including Captain Robert Salas, and found they had gone through similar events. Schindele disclosed his experiences in his book *It Never Happened, Vol. 1: US Air Force UFO Cover-up Revealed* (2017).[212]

---

[212] Seaburn, P. (2017, June 23). "Air Force Captain Claims UFO Deactivated 10 Nukes in Silos." Mysterious Universe website: https://mysteriousuniverse.org/2017/06/air-force-captain-claims-ufo-deactivated-10-nukes-in-silos/

With the passage of more than 50 years since my incident in Minot and 70 years since the incident in Roswell, NM, there can be no ethical, moral or critical reason to keep the secret of humanity any longer and my other colleagues agree thereby.

--Captain David Schindele

Air Force Captain Robert Salas was stationed at Oscar Flight at Malmstrom Air Force Base in Montana as a missile launch officer for manned missiles. In the early morning of March 16, 1967, Salas got a call from his primary security guard upstairs. Salas was downstairs 60 feet underground in a capsule monitoring and controlling 10 nuclear tipped manned missiles. Security reported seeing strange lights flying in the sky. Salas disregarded that call and told security to call back when something more significant happened. Subsequently, the guard called back with an intense tone, his voice sounding frightened. The guard reported a bright, glowing red oval-shaped object hovering outside the front gate. All the other Guards were present with weapons drawn. Salas woke up his commanding officer, who was on a rest period. Salas wrote about this experience in the book *Faded Giant,* co-authored with James Klotz (2005).

As Salas was telling his commander about the phone calls, the nuclear weapons started shutting down. They went into no-go position, so they were not launchable. The base lost between 6 and 8 of the weapons that morning within minutes

Nuclear Missiles

of the report of the bright glowing object hovering outside the base.[213]

A similar event happened at the Echo flight division of Malmstrom Air Force Base at the same time. Walter Figel, a Lieutenant at the time, now a retired USAF Colonel, was in the flight's underground control center when he got a call about a UFO from the security guard at the missile silo. Figel dispatched several two-man security teams to investigate, which confirmed the UFO sighting. Echo flight lost all 10 of their Minuteman I nuclear missiles. Figel and his commanding launch officer, then-Captain Eric Carlson, were debriefed after the incident and ordered not to talk about it.[214]

---

[213] Salas, R. "Zeuge #9. Captain Robert Salas US-Luftwaffe." [Video]. YouTube. *The Disclosure Project.* https://www.youtube.com/watch?v=OaelO5aEEWI&feature=youtu.be

[214] "The Echo and Oscar Flight Incidents: UFOs Disabled American ICBMs." (2012, November 11). UFOs & Nukes website:

Nefarious CTR Activities

Coming back to the W56 Artificial Intelligence gone awry problem, the CTRs "little by little, were seizing the opportunity, altering documents, changing memories, even wiping out somebody's memories, injecting wrong feelings, as easily as if they were showing a movie."[215] They were experts at mind control.

Another nefarious activity of the CTRs was to hunt for and seize earthbound spirits of people who died, but were unable to make the crossing into the World of Light. The W56 reported that the CTRs would search cemeteries, hospitals, and war zones for the spirits of recently deceased people to meld together 15 ghosts to make a destructive entity called a Hydra.[216] The W56 were able to stop the destructive effects of the Hydra.

The CTRs also implanted living people with a tiny black chip that would disintegrate into a "myriad of microscopic biological robots, each one of them migrating to the body area it was to work in."[217] The goals of these implants ranged from increasing sensitivity to enslavement of the person.

Physical Characteristics

In *Mass Contacts* on page 372 is a photo of one of the W56 who looks like a very tall, handsome human man wearing

---

https://www.ufohastings.com/articles/the-echo-and-oscar-flight-incidents

[215] Breccia, p. 223.
[216] Ibid, p. 285.
[217] Ibid, p. 286.

Bermuda shorts. The W56 looked much like Earth humans, except that their height varied from 1 meter to 3½ meters. The ones only 3 feet tall looked like perfectly formed humans, only very short. The ones who were 8 to 11 feet tall could not come out in public during the day, because they would have been recognized as Star People. One W56 named Dimpietro was 3 meters high (9 feet). He had to remove the seat in his car so he could sit on the floor to be able to fit in it! The W56 had stiff hair and beards and longer hands.[218]

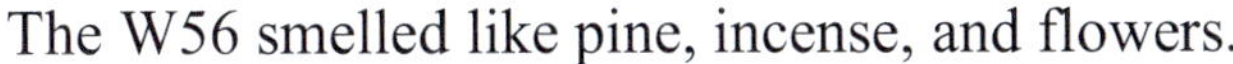

The W56 smelled like pine, incense, and flowers.

On the other hand, the CTRs smelled like tar. The CTR males usually drove dark blue diplomat model Mercedes cars, looked like normal men, and were bald.[219]

Underground Bases

The W56 built huge underground bases to work from without being noticed by humans. They brought their Italian friends into these underground bases. On the descent, the walls were like crystal, and the space was filled with soft, beautiful pale blue light. The air was extremely clear.[220] To open a

[218] Ibid, p. 249.
[219] Ibid, p. 240.
[220] Ibid, p. 188.

passageway to access their bases, the W56 generated what they called a "magnetic tress,"[221] which twisted lines of force, producing a sideways compression of matter to make extremely dense, strong, translucent walls. One of the more astonishing claims made in the book is that the W56 could open and close these passageways at will with the flick of a switch to turn off the magnetic field to close the passageways when no longer in use.[222]

The humans reported a feeling of euphoria in the underground bases. Every breath felt like it was full of well-being, as the W56 charged the air in their bases with negative ions. The W56 offered them a delicious drink of a squash of their fruits which detoxified their systems. The dome of one of their bases was 300 feet high, so the volume of air captured in that space made it rain sometimes. On another underground visit of several days, the time elapsed seemed like only one day to the humans. They reported the W56 told them gravity was 20% less inside their base, making movement easier.[223] Evidently, they were using an anti-gravity device to make their base more comfortable for themselves, especially since some of them were so tall!

The extensive contact the W56 had with the Sammaciccia group of Italians stopped in 1978, when the CTRs were able to infiltrate and destroy most of the extensive underground bases the W56 had established, including their largest base, which stretched between two towns on the coast of the Adriatic Sea, some 234 km apart, and from the center of the

---

[221] Ibid, p. 284.
[222] Ibid, p. 284-285.
[223] Ibid, p. 221.

Adriatic to Italy's center. Newspaper accounts tell of the waters in the central Adriatic Sea going crazy for a couple of months in November of 1978. "Huge columns of waters were rising from the sea all of a sudden, tens of meters high, unprecedented waves were running along the sea surface, strange lights were sighted at night…."[224] Many of the W56 escaped and returned home, but some of them were killed. Their human friends were devastated! A few of the W56 barricaded themselves to allow others to escape. The few who endured stayed on until December of 1986 and then left. Sammaciccia says, "When they left, something broke inside me."[225]

Food

The W56 made small pills of concentrated nutrients. They also had a kind of greenish jam that tasted bitter, but a small quantity would be enough nourishment for a couple of days.[226] They extracted an energy from both fresh and dried figs that sustained them. Every month, they asked their human friends to bring them two tons of figs, which they teleported into their bases. They contributed to payment for this food by teleporting something of value that the humans could sell. They would ask the humans to be at a certain location at a fixed time, and suddenly a box would appear. Sammaciccia never got used to things appearing out of thin air like this. Even though they had their own pure food, the W56 also enjoyed eating regular earth food, drank wine, and even smoked. They had a filtration system to immediately eliminate the toxins from their smoking.

---

[224] Ibid, p. 309.
[225] Ibid, p. 224.
[226] Ibid, p. 235.

Conscious Weapons and Clothing

The W56 reported that if people without an ethical attitude tried to use their weapons to do harm, "…they would not work, or even they would disintegrate themselves."[227]

Their clothing has consciousness and adapts itself to protect the person wearing it. One cannot wear another person's clothing.

Spiritual Teachings

- The W56 taught that unity is strength. "A group is like a living entity, and when it starts to break away, all the projects it is pursuing go astray."[228]

- They thought that a weakening of one's defenses gives one's enemies a chance to invade one's mind and change memories and will.

- They are so highly developed spiritually that they do not need any code of law. Each person feels within the right way to behave.

- They use natural health remedies and suffer very few illnesses.

- The humans they contacted never saw them angry. Serenity seemed to come from within each W56.

---

[227] Ibid, p. 189.

[228] Ibid, p. 222.

- The W56 called Earth "The Universal Center for Redemption,"[229] because people who incarnate here are working on fulfilling their evolution. They find Earth to be "one of the most beautiful and most complete planets. Its history is much longer than the one we (are) acquainted with. It has seen many more civilizations than our books tell."[230]

- They note that civilizations that go the direction of technology fall into ruin because of putting too much emphasis on science and not enough on spirituality.

- They caution that we need to be aware of the environment, using only what is strictly necessary, because of the long-term consequences of what we do now. They reflected that many of our environmental difficulties could be solved, but they are being hampered by economic powers. I think they were talking about the oil industry opposing free energy systems and technology which would be much more sustainable to our planet.

Joe Papp's Car which Ran on Water

An example of a more environmentally sustainable energy source is an engine designed to run on water as fuel—no gasoline. The inventor was an immigrant from Eastern Europe named Joe Papp, who went to Detroit, Michigan, to try to convince automotive companies to develop this product. He was told to stop and was threatened. "First, his

[229] Ibid, p. 242.
[230] Ibid.

wife had her ear chopped off by a masked man who threatened her, saying that her husband should back off promoting his engine."[231] Then his baby daughter was kidnapped and killed. Still, Joe Papp persisted with this invention, which would have made gas stations obsolete and cleared the air pollution from burning fossil fuels. Author William Tompkins worked for a company named TRW, which was assigned to evaluate Papp's engine and look at all possible applications. At the end of three years of TRW working on an internal combustion engine which split water into hydrogen and oxygen and burned the hydrogen, all funding was cut from the project. Tompkins was furious and went upline to see what happened. The Detroit Oil Associates were large stockholders in TRW, so they axed this invention because it conflicted with oil usage.[232]

After World War II, the oil companies systematically removed efficient systems like railroads and streetcars by firing maintenance personnel, mechanics, motormen, and conductors to throw the streetcar system into chaos. The streetcar system had been so efficient that in the "…1930's, it only cost a nickel to go from Pasadena, CA, to Santa Monica, CA, on the streetcar."[233] That's about a 30-mile trip from Santa Monica, on the coast, across Los Angeles to Pasadena, inland. The oil companies tore up streetcar tracks and subsidized bus travel so people would use more fuel. They built massive Freeways, causing traffic problems and smog. The US government sold the highly efficient rail

[231] Tompkins, 2020, p. 125.
[232] Ibid, p. 129.
[233] Ibid, p. 133-134.

systems to England and Japan, who have fabulous rail systems today.[234]

These examples back up the truth of the W56 claims that many of our environmental problems could be solved, but are being hampered by economic interests.

[234] Ibid, 2020 p. 132.

Chapter 15: Galactic Origins: The Lyrans

A startling view of the origins of our galactic heritage comes from a channeled book by Keith Priest and Lyssa Royal titled *The Prism of Lyra.*[235] I present this material for the reader to evaluate to see what parts make sense and what does not resonate as truth. Given the Anunnaki system of early priests being kings and ruling the people with this royal priesthood, the family names of the authors make me a bit suspicious—Royal & Priest. But putting my skepticism aside, the cosmic view presented helps explain why the planet Earth is currently caught in vicious polarization between nations and groups, such as Arab and Jew, United States and China, and Democrats and Republicans.

The Barred Spiral Galaxy
Photo from NASA Hubble Telescope. This galaxy is over 70 million light years away from earth. Its diameter spans 100,000 light years. The central part has a bar of stars across it and majestic spiral arms extending outward. https://www.nasa.gov/sites/default/files/thumbnails/image/potw1801a.jpg.

Understanding how we got so polarized can help with the integration we need to ascend from our third-dimensional struggles into the fourth dimension, where love rules.

[235] Priest & Royal, 2011.

The thesis of these authors is that at one time, all consciousness and energy were fused into an integrated whole existing in a different octave of dimensional reality. Parts of this unity wondered what it would be like to be separate, and this thought caused the whole to start fragmenting. The goal has always been to experience separation and polarization, then consciously reintegrate back to wholeness. The authors theorize a white hole in the fabric of time and space in the constellation Lyra through which the All That Is passed and divided into seven different densities, sometimes called seven dimensions, which they lay out as follows:

Density Descriptions

1. The first density/dimension is physical matter—atoms, molecules, and minerals.

2. Most plants and animals are in the second density/dimension, which has group or species consciousness but not individual consciousness. However, some animals may develop self-awareness and move to a higher density. Primates are clearly evolving, as they acquire language and some pathological behavior, traits once thought to belong only to humans. Primate consciousness has moved up to the third density.

3. Earth is currently in the third density/dimension where humans have self-awareness as individuals but have lost unity consciousness. Countries fight each other for dominance and resources without realizing we are all on the spaceship Earth, and we are damaging the environment of our ship, especially with the use of nuclear weapons. Priest and Royal say whales and dolphins exist in the third and fourth densities

simultaneously, as they are leaving the third density, along with humans as we evolve.

4. As a planet, we are in the process of awakening to fourth density/dimension where we have the ability to experience group identity without losing individual awareness. In this dimension, time becomes more fluid, and we experience multidimensional realities, connecting with guides from higher levels.

5. Fifth density/dimension in their model is not bound by linear time, and the wisdom of merging into oneness at this level inspires some in this dimension to become guides for others struggling in the third density.

6. The sixth density/dimension equals the consciousness of the Christ and of Buddha, where total remembrance occurs, and one works for the good of the whole. This level is non-physical, a quality shared with the seventh density/dimension of total oneness and integration.

7. When a group reaches a critical mass in the seventh density, it progresses back through the Prism of Lyra from which it emerged, which would then be seen as a black hole, and goes into another octave of existence.

The Founders

A group of beings called the Founders emerged from the Prism of Lyra with a blueprint of dividing the unity of All That Is into seven densities and into polarities of positive and negative. Races would need to embrace both polarities and integrate them—without denying either pole—to reach the level of unity consciousness needed to get through the Prism of Lyra back to Source. A civilization that split off from conflict or did not allow these opposites to play out could not develop into their full potential.

Applying this principle to psychology, Swiss psychiatrist Carl Jung taught the importance of embracing one's shadow rather than repressing it. When we reject the qualities we dislike in ourselves, then we project them onto someone else and make that person bad. For example, many people in the two major political parties in the United States seem to demonize the other political party. We need to work together for the good of the country, and countries need to work together for the good of the planet.

A Huge Shadow

Fragmentation

The Founders were the architects of physical reality. First, they fragmented in the nonphysical realm, and they then continued their fragmentation into appearing as densified light, or plasma. They continued fragmenting themselves into solid matter—galaxies, solar systems, and planets. Each planet is a conscious being, with individual character and specific influence on the people present on the planet. Astrology is the science of how the position of the planets at one's birth sets the template for the learning challenges in each incarnation. The ongoing transits of the planets influence one's life.

The founders can further densify themselves to take on the appearance of a physical form that has two arms, two legs, and large, inquisitive eyes. Because they appear to be very tall and have limbs that are long and graceful, people sometimes see them as insectoid forms and equate them with the "praying mantis beings."[236]

Lyra

An Artist's Conception of a Planet in the Constellation Lyra
Photo Credit: NASA Ames/JPL-Caltech/T. Pyle

According to Priest & Royal, the Constellation of Lyra was the birthplace of all humanoid races that populate the galaxy. The Founders watched the development of life on planets, and as primate races began to develop naturally, they inserted higher frequencies into their DNA so these races could progress from second density into third density, where souls could incarnate, and the beings would become self-aware. The Founders thought the process of dividing polarities in these conscious beings into positive and negative and then integrating the two poles would go smoothly. But the experiment developed problems.

As civilizations grew and developed space travel, they started interacting with cultures on other planets. The simple triangular process of dividing the whole into positive and negative and then integrating the two opposites back into a

[236] Ibid, p. 79.

unified whole got very complex as the process took on a life of its own, somewhat overwhelming the Founders. Negative poles split within themselves, forming even more negativity. Positive poles did the same, and consciousness became extremely fragmented.

The Lyrans spread the struggle around the galaxy as they colonized other planets. This philosophy does not have at its core one omniscient, all-powerful, omnipresent Divine Being. Instead, the "All That Is" energy of Source fragmented to experience itself more consciously and then reintegrate. As this energy has fragmented, societies have appeared to be out of control in some of the third density planets. However, Beings of Light from the higher densities are always available to help, but they must follow the law of free will and wait until they are asked for assistance. The popular religious conceptualization of this system is that we can call upon angels for help.

Vega

The original group of beings seeded in the Lyra constellation had lighter skin, hair, and eyes, like the Caucasians. They wanted to conquer the universe and spread out into space. The people they seeded on the planets near the star Vega formed a species identity with the opposite theory of how to get back to Source. Rather than expanding imperialistically outward, they went inward to find the way back home to Source. Their physical form had darker skin, hair, and eyes, similar to indigenous people and Asians. The authors say that the Lyrans became jealous of the Vegans because of their greater connection to their origins. To defend themselves from the Lyrans, the Vegans developed martial arts.

Chapter 16: Sirians

According to Priest & Royal, one of the first other star groups the Lyrans colonized was Sirius, which is thought to have three stars in it: Sirius A, Sirius B, and Sirius C.

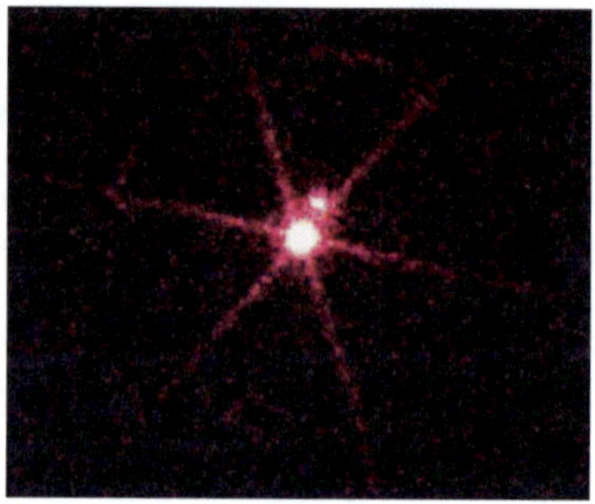

X-Rays from Sirius B
Photo Credit NASA/CXC/SAO

As a triangle of stars, it symbolizes the cosmic plan of positive and negative on opposite sides of the base integrating at the point. This inherent template for integration drew many higher dimensional beings from the sixth density who wanted to help but did not want to go down to third dimensional physical reality. The Elders of Sirius decided to allow both polarities to co-exist in the Sirian system with the goal of integration.

The Vegans chose a planet orbiting one of the Sirian suns and began speeding up the evolution of life there with genetic engineering. They focused so intensely on the physical level that this culture was locked into third density and completely forgot its origins, including their connection to the Vegans. The people in this culture wanted to dominate each other and the universe. They sound a lot like the Anunnaki!

For balance to the highly negatively polarized beings on this planet, another group from Lyra came in of highly positively polarized nonphysical beings who felt their duty was to heal all those in pain. They had good intentions, but the result was negative. "The positives began bombarding the negatives with love and healing energy on the subconscious and unconscious levels. Because the negatives were so tightly focused, this created psychological pain for them. The more the negatives resisted, the more the positives sent healing energy."[237] What a gridlock!

The idea that sending healing energy to someone locked in negativity could produce more pain for the person was new to me. The beings in the higher realms who had never experienced third density reality thought they were helping, but they were deepening the conflict. In Soul Detective work, our invocation includes asking that "only what is for the highest good of everyone and every being would come to pass." This qualification avoids inadvertently hurting someone when we intend to heal.

The Elders of Sirius searched for a different location for the attempt of the Lyrans and the Vegans to work out their differences and reach the point of integration. They found the Orion system was slightly less polarized, so they moved the conflict there. The physical civilization on the Sirian planet remained. The authors do not talk of this planet as Nibiru, but the situation of striving for dominance and being disconnected from spirit sounds a lot like the beings from Nibiru we know as the Anunnaki.

---

[237] Ibid, p. 25.

Earth appears to have both positive and negative Sirians affecting our development.

Positives

Mother Whale and Calf
Photo Credit: Susan Bird

Some of the positive Sirians wanted to have a physical experience. Rather than choosing a humanoid form, they chose the form of cetaceans—dolphins and whales (Chapter 1).

When two of my colleagues first told me they had gone swimming in the wild with humpback whales, I thought they were crazy. They glowed when they talked about feeling the presence of unconditional love while snorkeling in the water watching humpback whales and their calves. From my personal experience of going myself, I feel the higher dimensional consciousness and the immersion in unconditional love the whales and dolphins carry.

The Sumerian tablets tell of Sirian gods visiting early humans—Isis, Osiris, Thoth, Anubis, and others. They taught the Egyptians and other cultures advanced information in many fields including astrology, astronomy, mathematics, and medicine.

Negatives

The Founders postulated that we needed to experience both the negative and the positive and to integrate the two sides.

In ancient Egypt, the negative Sirians were behind the priesthood of Set, which worshipped the negative force. Using black magic to manipulate and control others is the goal of the dark arts. Practitioners do not take responsibility for their actions. They want to be separate from the whole and are not interested in eventual integration. The practices of organized worship of evil persist to the present day. I wrote about this topic in my 2012 book *Transforming Fear into Gold,* the extended case history of a woman who reported she was ritually abused by a Satanic cult.[238]

Orion

Orion was seeded by groups from both Lyra and Vega and has long been a battleground of the positive and negative polarities. The Orion culture focused on control of their subjects, negating the Creator of All's mandate of free will. In the *Star Wars* movies, the Empire with its soldiers, drones, and technology is an allegory to what happened on Orion. An underground resistance movement to the Orion Empire formed, called "The Black League," with the Black Dragon as their symbol. The control of the Empire was so great, it extended to trapping the spirit of a person after death. "The

[238] Stone, B. (2012). *Transforming Fear into Gold: How Facing What Frightens You the Most Can Heal and Light Up Your Heart.*

Empire had devised ways to control astral bodies; death was no longer freedom."[239] Souls were trapped in a cycle of reincarnation.

Unity Field Healing

The time has come for deep healing of these limiting patterns. Our Star Friends are reaching out to us to help. A colleague who presents at conferences tells of contact by a group of Sirians helping his work. John Ryan, MD, is a physician who has originated a new energy-based modality he calls "Unity Field Healing." On March 18, 2019, in meditation, Dr. Ryan was introduced to a group of light beings who called themselves the "Sirian Blue White Collective." This group of ascended light beings from the star system Sirius are masters of DNA evolution who have served for thousands of years to support humanity's development and civilization. Dr. Ryan says he has worked with these same beings in past lives and that they are masters of healing, DNA calibration, and ascension transformation. The channel Kryon independently confirmed the Sirian support for Dr. Ryan's work and told him that in a past life in ancient Lemuria, he was named Eli'ee and was a direct descendant of a Lemurian mother. Eli'ee worked in the Temple of Rejuvenation. For more information on Unity

[239] Priest & Royal, p. 33.

Field Healing, see www.unityfieldhealing.com. The image Dr. Ryan was shown for the template of light for his healings is on the cover of both of his books, *Unity Field Healing* (2018) and *The Missing Pill: The Rise of Energy Based Healing & Conscious Bio-Spiritual Transformation* (2014).

Sirians Sending Nothing but Kindness

An abductee named Barbara reported to Dr. Edith Fiore that she had been pulled out of her car and taken aboard a spaceship, where she was examined by Star People who were fascinated with the quality of her skin. They reported to Barbara that they were interested in humans because we are so emotional. They told her they were from Sirius. The person in charge seemed to be taller than the rest of them and kept communicating telepathically not to be afraid, that they would not hurt her. She felt great kindness from him. Barbara shares, "Just before he put his hands on my head, kindness, just nothing but kindness flowed from him."[240]

The Sirians were especially interested in people with psychic ability like Barbara. A humorous incident in a later regression with Barbara is that one time when she was taken aboard the ship and felt vaginal and anal discomfort during an examination, she astral projected out of her body to watch what was happening. The attending technician yelled, "Damn psychics! Get back here!"[241] They wanted her spirit to stay in her body during the examination, so she went back in.

Different Dimensions

The Sirians, Pleiadians, and Arcturians are all higher dimensional beings, from the fifth and sixth dimensions. But

---

[240] Fiore, 1989, p. 60.

[241] Ibid, p. 61.

just what is a different dimension? One of the easiest ways to understand another dimension is through our dreams, which happen in another dimension. While we are dreaming, the world may seem even more real than in waking life, and we may wonder whether we are dreaming or awake. But once we shift back to the third dimensional world, the dream world fades away.

The different dimensions are linked together at right angles to each other. Each line in the drawing has five sides, as if going from the first line which could represent the first dimension, then to a right angle to the second line/second dimension, continuing to the 5th dimension.

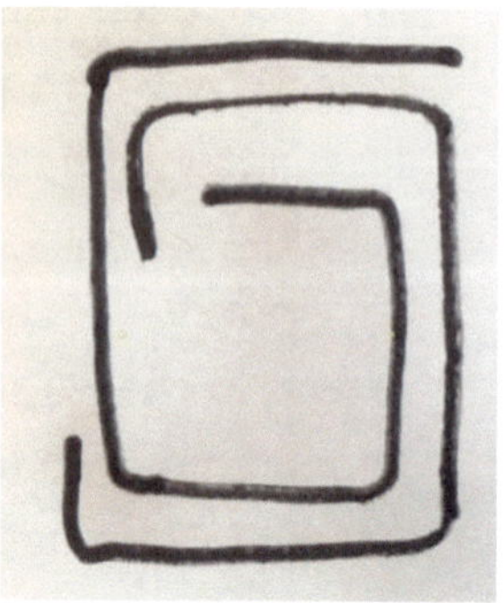

Drawing by Janet Nestor

Currently, Earth is in the 3rd dimension. We want to move through the lower 4th dimension where fear is predominant into the upper 4th dimension, where love rules. Then as a planet, we can move into the 5th dimension, where we will be able to create with thought alone. We would not want a person to create reality with thought alone if stuck in the lower 4th dimensional feelings of hatred, terror, and fear! Before we get the ability to manifest, we need to rise to the resonance of love, peace, and joy!

Chapter 17: Pleiadians

The Pleiades are a star cluster in the constellation of Taurus, the Bull. In the constellation Orion, the archer shoots an arrow into the shoulder of the bull, and the wound where his arrow lands is the location of the Pleiades, which has seven prominent stars visible to the naked eye, thus they are called "The Seven Sisters."

Pleiadian Facts

- The Pleiades are around 444 light years away from our sun.
- The radius of the Pleiades stretches for about 17.5 light years.
- Though the cluster has over 1,000 confirmed stars, only 14 of them are visible to the naked eye. The most prominent ones are hot, blue stars, followed by red stars and brown dwarfs.[242]
- The nine brightest stars in the cluster are named after characters in Greek Mythology, a Divine Couple named Atlas and Pleione, from which the name Pleiades derived, and their seven daughters, Alcyone, Electra, Maia, Merope, Taygeta, Celaeno, and Asterope.[243]

Some Lyrans wanted "to develop their culture away from what they perceived were negative influences."[244] They chose Earth for their new home. But over time, they became embroiled in conflicts on Earth, so they chose the Pleiades

---

[242] https://nineplanets.org/the-pleiades/

[243] Ibid.

[244] Priest & Royal, p. 39

for a new location to isolate themselves from old conflicts. "Over generations the community-oriented Pleiadians began to favor peace and tranquility so much that they learned to invalidate all forms of negativity."[245] Some new-age people also fall into this category, denying the existence of evil and refusing to embrace their own shadows. They believe that even talking about dark forces exposes one's energy field to trouble. For ascension, we need to integrate both the positive and negative sides of ourselves. We need to face evil when it comes and transform it!

When the Pleiadians finally woke up to the anguish caused by the domination and control used in the expansion of the

The Pleiades and Two Moons images-assets.nasa.gov/image/PIA06340/PIA06340~orig.jpg
Secondary Credit NASA/JPL/Cornell/Texas A&M

Orion Empire, they tried to fight it in every way they could think of. The Orions retaliated to this interference by

[245] Ibid, p. 41.

destroying one of the Pleiadian populated planets, which made the Pleiadians withdraw from the struggle. "The lifeless, charred planet still stands in their system as a reminder of their past actions. When that planet was obliterated, the Pleiadians were devastated."[246]

Case Example

An advanced healing practitioner I will call Rebecca could see what she needed to do in her practice, but when she would embark on an important endeavor or new project, an unexplainable source of fear would come up and negatively affect her creativity. As we were working on healing the wound that had given Artificial Intelligence an entry point for inserting detrimental programming into her system, a past life came up in the Pleiades. Born around three million BCE in earth time, this woman we called Aliah lived a beautiful life filled with happiness and helping other people. She was filled with Light and had no sense of darkness.

Aliah heard rumors that her planet was planning to send a weapon to destroy an Orion stronghold of The Empire. She tried to discourage the leaders from this plan, which was unfathomable to her. But they would not listen to her. They marginalized her, pushing her to the side in a form of "Tribal Death." One day Aliah had a sense that some strange darkness was coming, and then her whole planet was hit with nuclear weapons, and all life was destroyed. Her soul was still trapped in that moment of annihilation.

[246] Ibid.

We used a technique of creating an alternative timeline in which Aliah's spiritual helpers pulled her spirit out of her body one second before the impact of the nuclear weapons. She felt an immense sense of freedom with this intervention and was able to cross into the World of Light. Then Aliah invited any others on her planet who were still locked into the agony of the moment of total nuclear attack to multiply to the benefits by making an alternative timeline and crossing into the Light. She saw many other souls responding to this invitation.

Soul Lesson

The lesson Rebecca's soul learned is that evil exists. We must be aware of factions and forces of evil and take responsibility for our own actions. With healing of this soul trauma, her core fear that her planet would be devastated was released. Rebecca now feels that she can proceed with endeavors and projects without unexplained fear and with clarity and courage.

Billy Meier

Many authors have written about contact with Pleiadians on our planet. In 1975, a Swiss farmer named Billy Meier was visited several times by Star People from the Pleiades. In ongoing contact over several years, Meier and others independently witnessed spaceships arriving, and Meier photographed them. A beautiful human-looking Star woman called Semjase told Meier how humans could live in better harmony with our planet, each other, and other species present here. Meier founded a UFO religion called Free Community of Interests for the Border and Spiritual Sciences and Ufological Studies. He has photos of spacecraft and Star

People, one of which can be found online at https://goldenageofgaia.com/billy-meier-image-9/. Author Ray Keller says this photo is a meeting with a Star Woman from the planet Erra in the Pleiades.[247] Erra is one of the 10 planets orbiting the Pleiadian star Taygeta, mentioned earlier as one of the Seven Sisters. Authorities question the authenticity of Meier's photographs, but they question and try to debunk the authenticity of every single UFO siting that comes from Star Civilizations.

Another well-known author is Shirley MacLaine. In her book *Out on a Limb* (2011), she reports having conversations with beautiful people in Peru. These people had blonde hair and almost translucent skin and said they were from the Pleiades and had come here to help us.

Renegade Pleiadians

The League of Light speaks of the Pleiadian Renegades as filled with love and light.[248]

Only one author I have come across speaks of any Pleiadians who are not aligned with the cosmic forces of unity and light. In his book *The Extraterrestrial Species Almanac*, Craig Campobasso claims that a group of Renegade Pleiadians manipulated their genetics to make themselves fierce warriors eight to thirteen feet tall, and that this Star Civilization is bent on gaining power, wealth, and technology. He reports these Renegade Pleiadians have been working alongside the Orion Empire, but that their ultimate plan is to overthrow the Orion Reptilian Draconians and take

---

[247] Keller, R.A. (2018). *Cosmic Ray's Excellent Space Adventure*, p. 36.

[248] https://ninespath.com/about/league-of-light/pleiadian-renegades/

control of the Universe, ruling it with an iron fist. After wiping out as much of the Orion Empire as they can, "The Greys are next on their extinction agenda."[249]

Service to Self vs. Service to Others

The Cosmic Law of One is belief in the unity of everything in the Universe. Therefore, Star Civilizations who believe in the Cosmic Law of One work for the good of the whole in Service to Others. Star Civilizations are basically divided between those dedicated to Service to Others and those who embrace Service to Self. I do not know if Campobasso's information is accurate, but I do know that groups dedicated to Service to Self instead of Service to Others want ultimate power and so will make war with each other, as each group wants to be the supreme ruler of the universe. A recent example is that during World War II, different factions within the Nazi party were vying for power and control, splitting the party from the inside.

Cloaked Ships

Some of the higher dimensional beings that have come to help humans, including the Pleiadians, may bring their spaceships down into the third dimension for some of their activities. To avoid attack by our military, since the standing military orders are to shoot down anything that is not identified, a spaceship may cloak itself by putting a cloud around it. This photo I took in the desert of New Mexico looks to me like it could be a big cloaked flying saucer. The cloud formation stayed very stable for the whole time as it followed us for an hour as we drove south from Santa Fe to

---

[249] Campobasso, p. 103.

Albuquerque. Since weather generally travels from west to east, we found this motion from north to south unusual.

The technical name for this kind of cloud is "lenticular," because it looks like a big lens. Lenticular clouds are explained in Wikipedia as stationary clouds forming an eddy of turbulence perpendicular to the wind direction caused by an obstruction in the air flow, such as a mountain.

I still think it may have been a huge spaceship cloaked in a cloud.

Chapter 18: Venusians

The closest planet to Earth is Venus, the second planet from the sun. She is named for the Goddess of Love.

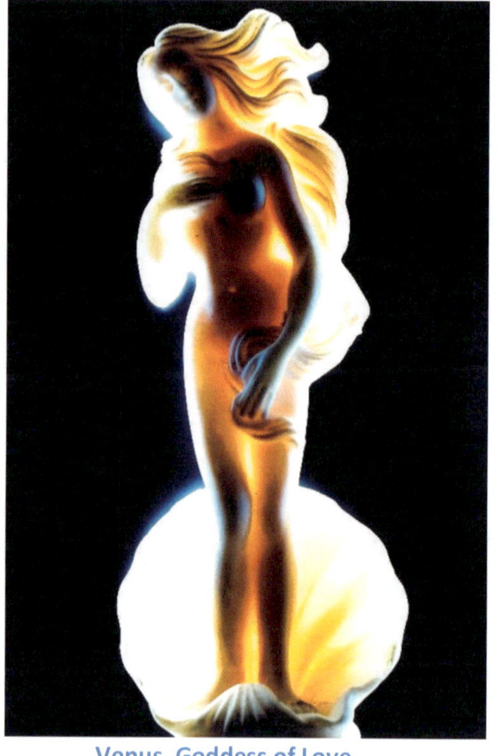

Venus, Goddess of Love

Venus Facts

Venus is sometimes called a sister planet to Earth because she is almost as big as Earth, has a central core, a molten core, and a crust.

Venus has 81.5% of Earth's mass.

Unlike Earth, Venus does not have a moon.

Venus orbits the sun every 225 days, shorter than Earth's 365-day cycle.

A day on Venus takes 117 Earth days. Time must feel different there!

The spin of Venus on her axis rotates in the opposite direction from the spin of most other planets orbiting our sun.

The surface temperature of Venus is 462° Celsius (863.6 ° Fahrenheit).

Venus is the second brightest visible light in the sky. Only the moon is brighter.

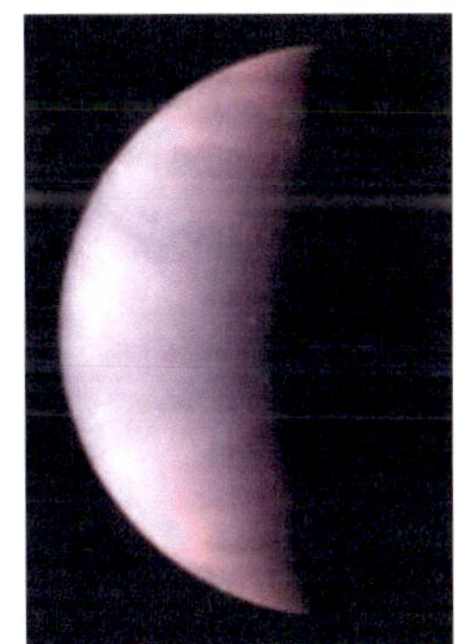

Venus Cloud Tops Viewed by Hubble https://photojournal.jpl.nasa.gov/favorites/PIA01544

Venus changes from being visible after sunset to before sunrise as her orbit overtakes the orbit of Earth. Thus, Venus is called both the Morning Star and the Evening Star.[250]

A Visitor from Venus

Contactee Jim Murray, an Inventor and Electrical Engineer, reports an unusual encounter in the documentary movie *ETs Among Us, Part 1*.[251] When Murray was 15 years old, he was in high school in Rhode Island studying a college regime of physics and math. He had already won awards in scientific areas including design for a particle accelerator and plasma research. One weekend he went home with a friend. The family wanted to go off shopping, but Murray refused to go and went for a walk in the woods instead. He encountered a fellow who came out of the woods with a shotgun. Murray was very interested in guns at that time. The man offered to let him shoot it, and Murray did. Then the man told him, "You know, we've been watching you for a long time." Murray asked if the man had more friends in the woods, and the man replied, "Oh no, that's not what I mean. **I'm from Venus.**"

---

[250] https://space-facts.com/venus/.

[251] Clare, *ETs Among Us: UFO Witnesses and Whistleblowers*. Part 1.

Well, Murray thought the man was totally nuts! But Murray humored him, not wanting to provoke someone holding a weapon. Murray replied, “Really? So tell me about Venus.”

The man proceeded to tell him all kinds of facts about Venus and her orbit. He said the surface was too hot, so all activities were underground. Then the man told him they knew where Murray was going to school and that he was doing some interesting things. Murray felt creeped out when this man named his hometown and school. This man told Murray that he had been appointed to monitor his case.

Relative Sizes of Mercury, Venus, Earth, and Mars
Photo by NASA Photo via <a href="https://www.goodfreephotos.com/">Good Free Photos</a>

After this strange talk, Murray walked back to his friend’s house. He was shocked when his friend’s mother answered the door in a state of near hysteria. She said Murray had been gone all day, and the family was worried sick about him. The police were out looking for him. Murray had left for the walk at 10 am and returned what he thought was a short time later but was actually 3 or 4 pm. Murray has no explanation for this lost time.[252] Time seems to be different on other planets and during interactions with Star People.

[252] Ibid.

George Adamski

George Adamski had vast knowledge of Tibetan Buddhism and set up an ashram on the slopes of Mount Palomar in California where he and his disciples could study and farm. On November 20, 1952, Adamski took six of his students to Desert Center, California, where UFOs had been sighted. To their amazement, "First, a massive cigar shaped object, a mother ship, ascended from behind a range of mountains in the distance; and then a smaller, bell-shaped craft appeared in the sky, encompassed by an unparalleled brilliance as the Sun reflected off its shiny metallic body."[253]

Adamski sensed the pilot of the ship wanted him to come alone to meet him and told his friends to wait for him while he took off for the hill where the craft had landed. Soon a man who looked human waved to Adamski, and he was struck by the sheer beauty of this being. He was around 5' 6" tall, with long blonde hair and about 135 pounds. Through sign language and telepathy, this visitor, whom Adamski called Orthon, communicated that he was from Venus and had come to warn Earthlings about the danger of their warlike ways in general and that nuclear testing was upsetting the harmony of the universe. Orthon allowed Adamski to photograph his spacecraft, photos available online at https://www.the-adamski-case.nl/his-reputation/his-photos.

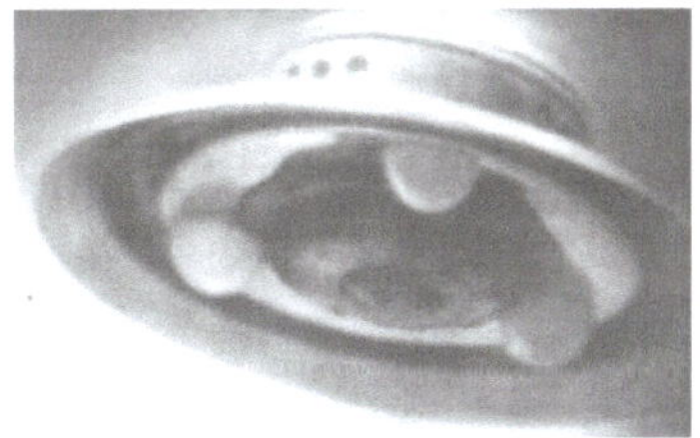

Photo from Wikipedia, who claims it is fake using a surgical light and light bulbs

---

[253] Keller, 2016, p. 66.

Orthon continued many contacts with Adamski and returned the following year, when Adamski says he was taken aboard the Venusian Scout Ship which was staffed by beautiful human-looking men and women from Venus, Mars, and Saturn in a joint mission of patrolling this solar system.[254] Adamski has very detailed reports of many contacts with this ship, including a ride to a Saturnian Mothership. He described the amazing details of the inner ship. A magnetic elevator about 50 feet square "carried people and freight from the bottom to the top of this gigantic carrier ship through an enormous shaft two hundred feet or more in depth."[255] Adamski photographed a mothership with his six-inch reflector telescope at Palomar Gardens, California, on May 29, 1950, showing a large disc with five smaller scout craft around it.[256]

Saturn as the Tribunal

Adamski reports that the Saturnians wore an insignia on their sleeve of a sphere with a balanced pair of scales surrounded by a ring. The beautiful Saturnian women he met said that Saturn was the "Tribunal" of our solar system.[257] The Star Civilizations Adamski interacted with all warned him about the dangerous trajectory of war activity on Earth and taught higher values of love and working together with others for common good. They viewed Earth as "young children in the universal life of the One Supreme Being."[258] They said they lived the Creator's laws, but Earth people only talked about

---

[254] Adamski, G. (1955). *Inside the Flying Saucers.*

[255] Ibid, p. 96.

[256] Keller, R.A. (2016). *Venus Rising: A Concise History of the Second Planet*, p. 68.

[257] Adamski, p. 145.

[258] Ibid, p. 71.

them. "If you would *live* by the precepts of even what you now know, the peoples of Earth would not go out to slaughter one another."[259]

Adamski called the Venusians Nordics. He always felt great love and understanding from them. They told him Venusians had been living on Earth and working among our people for a long time. Perhaps they are the same advanced race that lives inside Planet Earth (Chapter 10: Nordics), and this advanced race also has a settlement inside of Venus. Adamski was taken to meet with a thousand-year-old Master who told Adamski he had been selected to be a messenger of peace to the people of Earth, along with other messengers who had come before him, including Jesus Christ.

Planet Seeding

The Venusians told Adamski that all planets reach the stage where they are ready for human habitation sooner or later, and when they do, "travelers let this fact be known to the inhabitants of other worlds and of worlds in other systems. Volunteers are sought who desire to go forth and develop the new world. Then large ships take these volunteers, with all essential equipment on board, and move them to the new planet."[260] After the initial seeding, they take more equipment and supplies to the pioneers and also take people back to visit their home planets.

Adamski's work has been criticized, and some believe he was a very convincing, sincere-looking con man who got rich on his lectures and book sales. Others think he was in telepathic

---

[259] Ibid.

[260] Ibid, p. 133.

communication with Star Civilizations and wrote about these experiences as if they were real. What I noticed from his book is that the messages he reported as coming from the Star People he contacted were always encouraging spiritual advancement. Consistently, they warned against nuclear weapons and encouraged Earthlings to treasure their planet and each other.

Commander Valiant Thor

Another story points to the Venusians watching Earth, their closest planetary neighbor. When President Eisenhower signed an agreement in 1955 with the large-nosed Grey aliens from the dying planet Betelgeuse in the belt of Orion, an alarm went out. These Grey aliens proved themselves untrustworthy, just as the Nordics had warned (Chapter 3). The Venusians saw that Earth was in danger of the eruption of a catastrophic nuclear war. Nuclear detonations rip holes in time and space and affect all planets in our solar system and our galaxy. As our nearest neighbor, Venus sensed the alarm of potential danger and took action. A Venusian named Commander Valiant Thor (what a wonderful, powerful name!) and a small team landed their spaceship in Alexandria, Virginia at 8:00 am on March 16, 1957.

Physical Appearance

Valiant Thor was about six feet tall and weighed around 185 pounds, a handsome male with brown wavy hair and brown eyes who appeared human—except, of course, that he had arrived in a flying saucer. The book *To Men of Earth: Valiant Thor's Message of Hope to Mankind* has a photograph of Valiant Thor on the cover.

Two policemen promptly arrived at the scene of the spaceship, with weapons drawn. Valiant Thor emerged from the craft and communicated telepathically with them that he meant no harm.[261] He told them he was from the interior of the planet Venus and asked to be taken to the U.S. President. The different security agencies fought over who would get to escort him there! He offered President Eisenhower a plan to eliminate disease, poverty, and war, and to help people elevate their spiritual development. He promoted people drawing closer to Divine Source. The plan was for the United States first, and then to be disseminated to the whole planet.

Commander Valiant Thor on the right

Eisenhower said he would need time to process this request and invited Valiant Thor to live in an apartment below the Pentagon as their VIP guest for a period of three years so they could get to know him better. Valiant Thor also met with Vice-President Nixon, the joint Chiefs of Staff, and Air Force officials. In the end, to the dismay of Eisenhower and Nixon, the powers that be rejected Valiant Thor's proposal on the grounds that it would ruin the American economy.

Dr. Frank Stranges

Dr. Frank Stranges was a UFO hunter, a freelance private investigator, and an evangelical preacher who came across photos of Valiant Thor and Jill, his second in command. Dr. Stranges showed the photos at UFO conferences, creating

---

[261] Stranges, F.E. and Thor, V. (2001). *The Stranger at the Pentagon.* CreateSpace Publishing.

quite a stir. A Pentagon insider named Nancy Warren contacted Dr. Stranges with the message that Valiant Thor had requested a personal interview with him. Valiant Thor selected Dr. Stranges because of his service to the message of Jesus Christ, a Being with whom Valiant Thor was in constant communication.

"Universal Peace" Original Visionary Artwork by Eva M. Sakmar-Sullivan

Dr. Stranges published Valiant Thor's story in a book titled *Stranger at the Pentagon* (2001) and has further information about the nature of this remarkable person on a website "About Commander Valiant Thor" Parts 1 and 2.

A Created Being

Just who was Commander Valiant Thor? According to both Dr. Stranges and author and film maker Craig Campobasso, Valiant Thor was an immortal Created Being. He had no bellybutton and no fingerprints. Like the angels, eons before time began, he was configured. He had the ability to appear and disappear at will and to dissemble the molecules of his body and reassemble them somewhere else at a distance.[262]

After the Crucifixion, the Bible tells the story of the disciples who were walking along the road to Emmaus, talking about all that had happened. Jesus joined them, but he did not allow them to recognize him, and they thought he was a stranger. When they arrived at the village, they asked the stranger to stay for supper with them. At the table, after breaking bread, "Then their eyes were opened, and they recognized him; and he vanished from their sight." (Luke 24:31) Perhaps referring to Commander Valiant Thor as a *Stranger at the Pentagon* parallels Jesus appearing as a stranger on the road to Emmaus and then disappearing.

Abuse from the Secret Shadow Government

Unbeknown to Eisenhower and Nixon, factions of the Secret Shadow Government, also known as the Deep State and the Cabal, tried to extort information from Valiant Thor about how to make weapons of destruction they could place in orbit to threaten every nation on earth. Even though they spat at him, threw chairs at him, and punched him violently, he refused to give them any information they could use for

[262]Stranges, F. "About Commander Valiant Thor (Part 1)." http://www.nextagemission.com/OSF/ST_AboutValiantThor1.html

destruction. The only thing Commander Valiant Thor did was to smile back at them.

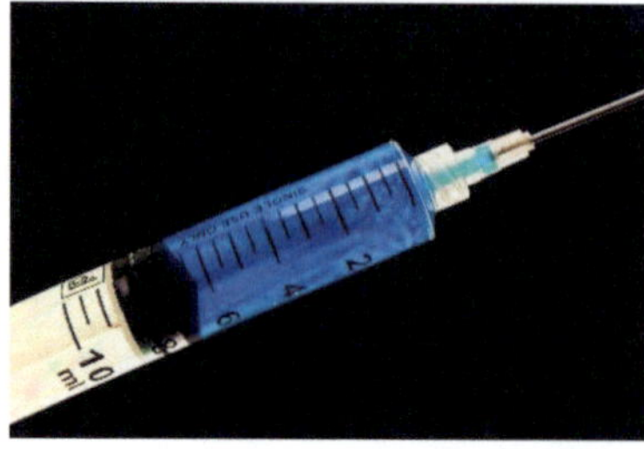

Then the interrogators tried to inject him with a drug to make him more cooperative. However, the needle broke when they tried to penetrate his skin.

Finally, the Commander rose to his feet, breaking the shackles which bound him to his chair, stood tall before them and said, "I HAVE HAD ENOUGH OF THIS FOOLISHNESS. IF ANY ONE OF YOU TOUCHES ME AGAIN, IT WILL BE YOUR LAST MOVE ON THIS PLANET EARTH."[263]

Thinking of what they would do in a similar position, the abusers probably thought Commander Thor was going to strike them dead. But likely, from his heart of unconditional love for everyone, he would have beamed them up to a Venusian rehabilitation spaceship! The interrogators ceased their abuse and backed away quietly. To their astonishment, Commander Thor then vanished.[264] What do you suppose went through their minds at witnessing his powers?

Raymond Andrew Keller II

Author Raymond Andrew Keller II has written a series of three books on Venus that are full of stories of contactees, trips humans have taken to Venus, and many accounts of Venusians interacting with Earthlings: *Venus Rising: A*

[263] Stranges, F. "About Commander Valiant Thor (Part 2)." http://www.nextagemission.com/OSF/ST_AboutValiantThor2.html

[264] Ibid.

Concise History of the Second Planet, The Final Countdown: Rockets to Venus (Book II), and *Cosmic Ray's Excellent Venus Adventure (Book III).*

I heard Keller talk about his personal experiences in a charming, delightful, fantastical presentation. Many things he says in his books strain even my credulity. But perhaps my own belief system is not broad enough, or Keller mixes some magical ideas into factual accounts for thrilling stories!

In book II of his series, Keller reports NASA insiders disclosed that at the end of World War II, the Germans had launched a space rocket that would go into orbit around the planet, then head down to blow up the Empire State Building to traumatize America.[265] Andy Reiss, the psychic correspondent for the *Weekly World News,* disclosed details of this story to Keller. Reiss reported that the US government's "Silence Group," what we popularly call the Men in Black (MIBs), threatened to ruin Reiss or anyone else letting the story out, but he felt people deserve to know the truth, so he did it anyway. The account Reiss gave is that incredibly, this pilot splashed down in the Atlantic Ocean on April 2, 1990, and the US Navy's carrier USS Theodore Roosevelt recovered his capsule. The NASA official noted that what was particularly interesting "was that the astronaut not only returned to Earth alive from his dangerous mission, but that he hadn't even aged. Our best guess was that he passed through some sort of time portal."[266]

---

[265] Keller, R.A. (2018). *The Final Countdown: Rockets to Venus.*
[266] Ibid, p. 12.

In book III of his series, Keller elaborates the story by saying that on the first of January in 1945, a Venusian mothership monitoring the progress of World War II noticed a rocket going up from Northern Europe, piercing the atmosphere, and going into outer space. Alarmed, they sent a scout ship to monitor the rocket and found a single pilot aboard by the name of Gùnter Specht. The ship was armed with enough explosives to take out most of New York City plus cause enough radiation to kill many more people beyond the blast era. The telepathic communication the scout ship sent was that this pilot had a good heart and was not like other Nazis. Specht had been ordered to ram his flying bomb into New York's tallest building. "But rather than obey such a cruel command, he decided to alter its trajectory, pushing it up into outer space and blowing it up over the North Pole, where he didn't think it would harm or kill anyone but himself."[267]

According to Keller, during the ascent of his rocket, the Venusians sent Specht a telepathic message to look out his window, see their ship, and cut off his engines. Specht complied, and the Venusians took control of his rocket and sent him on a rainbow bridge to Venus, where he had many adventures, and then sent him back to Earth again. Time is different on Venus—remember, one day on Venus takes 117 days on Earth. Specht was gone for 45 years, which would have been only about 144 Earth days. Perhaps the space travel and the time difference between these two sister planets account for Specht not appearing to have aged in the 45 years since he took off.

---

[267] Keller, R.A. (2018). *Cosmic Ray's Excellent Venus Adventure*, p. 40.

Chapter 19: Additional Star Races

NGC 5468 Galaxy
Image credit ESA/Hubble & NASA, W. Li et al.

Suskins

This story would be hard to believe if it had not come from a reliable, well-grounded person dedicated to knowing truth. One day around 30 years ago, a farmer named Jim noticed the presence of an entity that appeared a bit filmy. Jim was used to noticing spirits and watched as the entity gradually became a 9-foot-tall fleshed out, hairy ET. He said his name was Merishkin, and he came from a planet far away called Suski.

Jim spent a very pleasant afternoon talking with Merishkin, who spoke fluent English. Merishkin reported that his planet was peaceful, and they did not build structures. They preferred to live in caves. Summers on Suski were so hot that flames broke out. Merishkin's people had fur coats that were asbestos, and they would go into the summer fires to burn the impurities out of their coats. Because their asbestos pelts were so valuable, they were hunted and killed by mercenaries. Merishkin was the last of his people, trying to hide on Earth. He said he would come back and that he and Jim would write a book together about life on Suski. Sadly, Merishkin never returned, and Jim was pretty sure he had been located and killed for his pelt.

Rituli

A very intuitive young woman I know had contact with a spokesperson for a Star Civilization who called themselves the Rituli. They claimed to have a ship with 10,000 of their people on the dark side of the moon. They reported they were from a planet in the Crab Nebula, in the constellation of Taurus. Their planet had been attacked by another ET race 400,000 years ago. Their enemies had poisoned their atmosphere and burned their planet, so it was no longer habitable. The Rituli were looking for another place to live. Three thousand years ago, they tried to land on Earth, but were prohibited. They were trying again to make some friends on the ground to facilitate their entry.

Three Other Planets

I mentioned to the Rituli spokesperson that the Tall Whites (Chapter 9) had informed the US Military of three other planets with atmospheres and conditions similar to Earth. The Tall Whites offered to transport Americans and building materials to these other planets and get paid only for the transport. People would be free to do whatever they wanted once on the new planet.

The Rituli were not interested in these options. They wanted to land on a planet that already had infrastructure, so they could "live in our apartments and work in our grocery stores." A paranoid thought crossed my mind that perhaps living in our apartments might be a metaphor for wanting to possess humans. However, the woman channeling this information trusted the spokesperson, who claimed he was 958 years old and that he was on a cloaked ship right above the building where we were talking.

Other Interference

In several cases with clients totally separate from the person who first told me about the Rituli, my dowsing indicated that a detrimental ET interference was coming from the Rituli. We telepathically reported their activity, which was interfering in the lives of humans, to the Galactic Federation and sensed the Federation taking action to stop them.

OBICTNOXISIZ

A talented psychic who wishes to stay anonymous has been aware of a Star Civilization from the outskirts of Sirius called the OBICTNOXISIZ. This psychic senses that this group wants to start their own empire. Their agenda is to mix their DNA with human DNA to make a resilient half ET, half human being with the ultimate goal of inhabiting the earth and taking over the planet. This agenda is similar to the theory of author David Jacobs in his 1998 book *The Threat: Revealing the Secret Alien Agenda.*

Chapter 20: Conclusion

All life forms are connected in the web of life. Our lives have been affected in deep ways by both help and interference from Star Civilizations.

Cartwheel Galaxy

A smaller galaxy passed through the center of this Cartwheel Galaxy, causing tremendous shock waves that produced many new stars. Image credit: X-ray: NASA/CXC; Optical: NASA/STScI

Understanding the level of spiritual development of the different star people in this book sheds light on the choices we have right now, at this crucial time in our planet's history. We are currently at the end of a 26,000-year cycle of the precession of the equinox, wherein Earth spends approximately 2,000 years in each of the 12 signs of the zodiac. We are ending a cycle where war predominated on this planet. What will we choose as we go into the next 26,000 years?

Author, physician, and spiritual teacher Christine Page says that we have until 2028 to get ourselves together and pull ourselves out of the third-dimensional power struggles we have been enmeshed in so we can ascend. We want to get to the 5th dimension, where we can create with thought alone. To get to the 5th from the 3rd, we have to go through the 4th dimension, the energies of the heart, which are divided into lower and upper. The lower part of the 4th dimension is filled with hatred, fear, vengeance, anger, terror, and brutality. We would not want people filled with these emotions to be able to create with thought alone, or our most terrifying fears would manifest instantly. Our collective consciousness needs to realize the survival of Earth as a planet is at stake, and to see we need to stop fighting each other and start fighting for our planet, Gaia!

Some say that our ascension will be triggered by our star, the sun, giving off a solar flare of high energy that those who are awake can ride up to the 5th dimension.

Changing Ourselves

A free will creation means we cannot control the actions of others, but we do have control of ourselves. The emerging field of Energy Psychology gives us tools to deal with our fears, terrors, and anxieties. But how? Fear disrupts the flow of energy through three organs in the body: the stomach, the spleen, and the kidneys. That energy flow can be reset by tapping on balancing points for the meridians which flow to those organs. Energy Psychology uses this kind of meridian tapping to decode fear and a host of other emotions which hold us back.

Three Simple, Easy-to-learn Self-help Techniques

All of these rebalance energy flow in the meridians.

Trauma Tapping Technique, TTT, from Gunilla Hamne and Ulf Sandström, online at https://www.selfhelpfortrauma.org/

Tapas Acupressure Technique, developed by Tapas Fleming, online at https://tatlife.com/what-is-tat/about/

Emotional Freedom Techniques®, EFT, developed by Gary Craig, online at https://www.emofree.com/

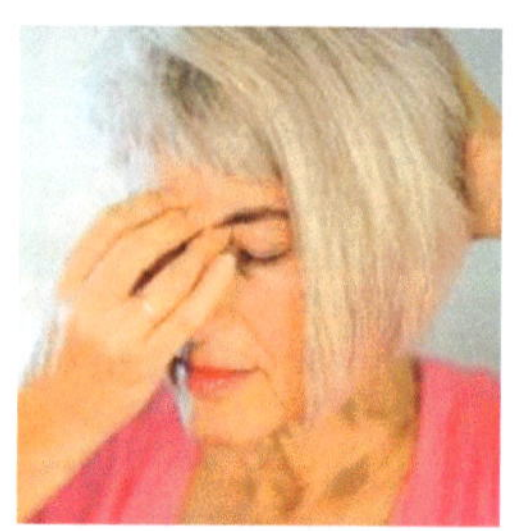
Tapas Fleming

For information, training, practitioners, and research on Energy Psychology, see the website of the Association for Comprehensive Energy Psychology (ACEP) at www.energypsych.org. People with complex, deeply embedded trauma may want to supplement self-help techniques with sessions with Energy Psychology professionals.

Barbara Stone, PhD

The Development of Soul Detective Work

When spiritual problems started coming into my practice, like a client bringing her deceased father to a session with me, I had to go beyond my social work talk therapy skills and even my Energy Psychology emotional regulation skills into the spiritual realm for help from higher beings. I developed a method I call Soul Detective which finds the spiritual configurations causing emotional problems and uses dynamic Energy Psychology methods to achieve a win-win solution for every being involved. For more information on Soul Detective work, training, and practitioners, see my website at www.SoulDetective.net.

Help from Star People

Many of the Star Civilizations in this book have already gone through evolution from 3rd dimensional awareness and have ascended through the 5th into the 6th dimension, the realm of the angels. These compassionate beings know that all life is connected, and if we wage a nuclear war of mutual annihilation, the disruption on our planet reverberates through our solar system, through our galaxy, and on into the Universe. Nuclear bombs rip holes in time and space and affect Star Civilizations everywhere. That ripple effect is why the W56 in Chapter 14 have used their technology to disable nuclear weapons that were primed for launching.

Cuban Missile Crisis

The closest our planet has come to a nuclear war in modern times was during the Cuban Missile Crisis in October of 1962. The military has a doctrine of "Mutually Assured Destruction," whose initials are MAD, which spells a feeling that contributes greatly to war. In MAD, "a full-scale use of nuclear weapons by two or more opposing sides would cause the complete annihilation of both the attacker and the defender."[268] The idea is that if both sides know everyone is going to lose if they use their weapons, neither side will use them.

But this threat of global annihilation was not enough to stop the cold war conflict between the United States and Russia from going nuclear. The Soviets were building ballistic missile sites in Cuba just 90 miles from the shore of the United States. These Cuban missiles could have reached most of the continental United States. President Kennedy demanded that the Russians stop building these missile sites, and JFK put a US Navy quarantine around Soviet ships coming in to bring supplies and armaments. The United States had its array of nuclear missiles armed and aimed at Cuba, and tension was very high.

On October 26, 1962, Fidel Castro thought the US was about to strike Cuba, either by taking out the missile sites or with a full-scale invasion of Cuba. Castro wrote a letter to Soviet Premier Khrushchev in which he implored Khrushchev to use nuclear weapons in a first strike against the United States so that the US could never do a first strike against Cuba (Reptilian war mentality thinking). Seeing the crisis through the eyes of Castro shows how wars get started, with his viewpoint of the Cubans being the good guys and the United States being the bad guys, the power-hungry imperialists. Castro was sure his country was going to be attacked in the next 1-3 days. Further excerpts from his letter to Khrushchev are as follows:

---

[268] Wikipedia, https://en.wikipedia.org/wiki/Mutual_assured_destruction

> I tell you this because I believe that the imperialists' aggressiveness makes them extremely dangerous, and that if they manage to carry out an invasion of Cuba—a brutal act in violation of universal and moral law—then that would be the moment to eliminate this danger forever, in an act of the most legitimate self-defense. However harsh and terrible the solution, there would be no other.
>
> This opinion is shaped by observing the development of their aggressive policy…while at the same time blocking any possibility of negotiation, even though they understand the gravity of the problem.
>
> You have been, and are, a tireless defender of peace…[269]

A Soviet submarine got orders to fire nuclear torpedoes at US Navy ships. Had they done so, the US would most certainly have launched their nukes already aimed at Cuba, and a terrible nuclear war would have resulted which would have certainly caused great environmental damage to our whole planet and would most likely have wiped human life off the face of the earth.

One Person's Actions

On the Soviet submarine, all three of the senior officers had to agree before authorizing the use of nuclear weapons against the US. Two of the top officers agreed, but Vice Admiral Vasily Alexandrovich Arkhipov refused.

---

[269] John F. Kennedy Presidential Library and Museum, https://microsites.jfklibrary.org/cmc/oct26/doc2.html

Upon his return to Russia, he and his crew were disgraced for not following the orders of his superior officers, but his refusal to approve of an action that could have destroyed the world stopped this madness.[270]

Alexandrovich Arkhipov
Photo credit: By Olga Arkhipova - Olga Arkhipova, CC BY-SA 4.0

Vasily Arkhipov was a Russian, our supposed enemy, but one person's refusal to follow immoral orders saved the world.

The actions we take today determine the course of our planet, and the stakes are high. One path would have people totally controlled in every aspect of their lives, like the people in communist China.

---

[270] Wikipedia, https://en.wikipedia.org/wiki/Vasily_Arkhipov_(vice_admiral)#Aftermath

Another path would be for each person to wake up, reject war mentality, rise out of our fears, including fear of illness and enemy attack, connect with our Divine Source directly through our True Selves, and decide to have unconditional love for ourselves and all of humanity. If we collectively choose this higher path, the inner peace that follows will help us flow through the upper 4th dimensional vibrations of love, peace, and joy into the higher realms of the 5th dimension.

One Person Can Change the World!

Original Visionary Artwork by Eva M. Sakmar-Sullivan

Bibliography

"A Dying CIA Agent reveals the truth about the US Government and Alien Life." https://www.youtube.com/watch?v=GX0FaindPPo&feature=youtu.be.

Adamski, G. (1955). *Inside the Flying Saucers.* Warner Paperback.

"AI Next Campaign." Defense Advanced Research Projects Agency. https://www.darpa.mil/work-with-us/ai-next-campaign

"Amazing Andromeda Galaxy." NASA Jet Propulsion Laboratory: California Institute of Technology. http://www.spitzer.caltech.edu/images/2216-sig06-024-Amazing-Andromeda-Galaxy

Bearzi, M. (2012). *Dolphin Confidential: Confessions of a Field Biologist.* University of Chicago Press.

Breccia, S. (2009). *Mass Contacts*. Author House.

Byrd, R. (2007, December 30). The Inner Earth: My Secret Diary: Admiral Richard B. Byrd's Diary (February-March, 1947). "The Exploration Flight Over the North Pole." https://www.bibliotecapleyades.net/tierra_hueca/esp_tierra_hueca_2d.htm

Campbell, A. & Kirkland, A. (2010, Nov. 29). "President Eisenhower's Secret Meeting with ETs in 1955—the Real Story." X-Conference Live Speaker Presentations.

UFOTV.com. [Video]. YouTube. https://www.youtube.com/watch?v=iv1ZCEiVrgg

Campobasso, C. (2021). *The Extraterrestrial Species Almanac: The Ultimate Guide to Greys, Reptilians, Hybrids, and Nordics.* Weiser Books.

Cassidy, K. (2008, October 21). V*ideo interview of Bob Dean: "The Coming of Nibiru."* United States: Project Camelot. [Video]. YouTube. *https://www.youtube.com/watch?v=sFxB4mdUNxI*

Cellan-Jones, R. (2014, December 2). "Stephen Hawking warns artificial intelligence could end mankind." http://www.bbc.com/news/technology-30290540

Clare, C. (Producer & Director). (2016). *ETs Among Us: UFO Witnesses and Whistleblowers. Part 1*. [Documentary Film.] USA. Prism Pictures. https://www.amazon.com/ETs-Among-Us-Witnesses-Whistleblowers/dp/B01IGC331Q/ref=pd_ybh_a_1?_encoding=UTF8&psc=1&refRID=K7S89N95KPQQHEW44Q0

Clare, C. (Producer & Director). (2020, February). *ETs Among us 4: The Reality of ET/Human Hybrids*. [Documentary Film]. USA. Prism Pictures.

Clare, C. (Producer & Director). (2020). *ETs Among Us 6: My Cosmic Journey--Revelations of a Psychic CEO.* [Documentary Film]. USA. Prism Pictures.

Collier, A. "Alex Collier on Whales and Dolphins." Golden Age of Gaia. http://goldenageofgaia.com/disclosure/who-are-the-extraterrestrials/alex-collier-on-whales-and-dolphins/

Collier, A. (1996, June). "The Race from Alpha Draconis." *Letters from Andromeda,* Vol. 2 No. 3. Retrieved from https://www.bibliotecapleyades.net/andromeda/lfa/v2n3alpha.html

Collier, A. (1997). *Defending Sacred Ground: The Andromedan Compendium Volume One*. Leading Edge International Research Group.

Collier, A. (2013, February 27). "Alien kinds or races and presence on Earth, bases on Mars and the Moon." [Video]. YouTube. https://www.youtube.com/watch?v=OTZJrHJNWlk

Cori, P. (2001). *Atlantis Rising: The Struggle of the Darkness and Light.* iUniverse.

Cori, P. (2011). *Before We Leave You: Messages from the Great Whales and the Dolphin Beings.* North Atlantic Books.

Corso, P. J. (1997). *The Day After Roswell.* Pocket Books, a division of Simon & Schuster Inc.

Cowan, R. (2012, May 31). "Andromeda on a Collision Course with the Milky Way." *Nature: International weekly journal of science.* http://www.nature.com/news/andromeda-on-collision-course-with-the-milky-way-1.10765#

Cramer, R. (2015, July). "ECC Times: Q&A Public Release Vol. 1." http://tinyurl.com/pxdd5fq

Cremo, M. & Thompson, R. (1998). *Forbidden Archeology: The Hidden History of the Human Race*. Bhaktivedanta Book Publishing.

Crick, F. (1981). *Life Itself: Its Origin and Nature*. Simon and Schuster, New York, NY.

Danaan, E. (2020). *A Gift from the Stars: Extraterrestrial Contacts and Guide of Alien Races.*

Dobbs, M. (1998, November 30). "Ford and GM Scrutinized for Alleged Nazi Collaboration," *Washington Post*. https://www.washingtonpost.com/wp-srv/national/daily/nov98/nazicars30.htm#TOP

Doner, M. (2012). *Merlin's War: The Battle Between the Family of Light and the Family of Dark*. iUniverse.

Eisenhower, D. (1961, January 17). "Eisenhower's Farewell Address." [Video]. YouTube. https://www.c-span.org/video/?c4455718/user-clip-military-industrial-complex

Everitt, T., Graham, B., Kennedy, L.I., Richards, R.R., & Salla, M. (Producers). Goode, C. & Richards, R. R. (Co-Directors). (2019, November 19). *The Cosmic Secret.* [Documentary Film.} USA. SBA Entertainment. https://www.cosmicnews.org/2020/12/04/the-cosmic-secret-david-wilcock-full-movie/

Fiore, E. (1987). *The Unquiet Dead: A Psychologist Treats Spirit Possession.* Ballantine Books.

Fiore, E. (1989). *Encounters: A Psychologist Reveals Case Studies of Abductions by Extraterrestrials.* Doubleday.

Fiore, E. (2005). *You Have Been Here Before: A Psychologist Looks at Past Lives.* National Guild of Hypnotists, Inc.

Foer, J. (2015, May). "It's Time for a Conversation: Breaking the Communication Barrier Between Dolphins and Humans." *National Geographic.*

Fry, D., Thor, V., Cold, I., & Barker, G. (2017). *To Men of Earth: Valliant Thor's Message of Hope to Humankind.* CreateSpace Independent Publishing.

Goode, C. "Life Inside the Secret Space Program." http://spherebeingalliance.com

Goode, C. (2015, May 31). "Galactic Human Slave Trade & AI Threat to End with Full Disclosure of ET Life." https://www.exopolitics.org/galactic-human-slave-trade-ai-threat-to-end-with-full-disclosure-of-et-life/

Goode, C. (2015, May 31). "Questions for Corey Goode on SSP Conflicts and Human Slave Trade." http://exopolitics.org/galactic-human-slave-trade-ai-threat-to-end-with-full[disclosure-of-et-life

Goode, C. (2015, July 9). "The Lt. Col. Gonzalez SSP Council Delegation Briefings Part I: The "Draco Federation Alliances" Demands and Secrets Revealed. https://spherebeingalliance.com/blog/the-lt-col-gonzales-ssp-council-delegation-briefings-part-1.html

Goode, C. & Sather, J. (Producers). Richards, R.R. (Director). (2018). *Above Majestic.* [Film]. USA. SBA Media.

Goode, C. (Updated 2019, February 16). "Guide to Non-Terrestrial Beings Corey Goode Cosmic Disclosure."

https://www.disclosurenews.it/guide-to-non-terrestrial-beings-corey-goode/

Hall, C.J. (2002). *Millennial Hospitality*. 1st Book Library.

Hall, C.J. (2003). *Millennial Hospitality II: The World We Knew*. AuthorHouse.

Hall, C.J. (2003). *Millennial Hospitality III: The Road Home*. AuthorHouse.

Hall, C.J. (2005). *The Tall Whites: ET Experiences in the Nevada Desert*. X Conference. [Video]. YouTube. https://www.youtube.com/watch?v=1oY1OqVDUc8

Hall, C.J. (2007). *Millennial Hospitality IV: After Hours*. AuthorHouse.

Hall, C.J. (2012). *Millennial Hospitality V: The Greys*. AuthorHouse.

Hancock, G. (1996). *Fingerprints of the Gods.* Three Rivers Press.

Hardy, C. (2014). *DNA of the Gods: The Anunnaki Creation of Eve and the Battle for Humanity*. Bear & Co.

Harris, P. (2018, May 4). "Interview of the Month—Insider Charles Hall and the Tall Whites." The Paola Harris Report. http://paolaharris.com/english/paola-harris-interviews/interview-of-the-month-insider-charles-hall-and-the-tall-whites

Hellyer, P. (2018, February 3). "Paul Hellyer Earthshaking Confession 'Four Races of Aliens Are Here on Earth.'"

[Video]. YouTube. https://www.youtube.com/watch?v=EgrCQpWz6iI

Hesoid. (1987). *Hesoid's Theogony*. Richard S. Caldwell, translator. Focus Information Group, 1st edition.

Hopkins, B. (1987). *Intruders: The Incredible Visitations at Copley Woods.* New York, Random House.

Howe, L. M. (1989). *An Alien Harvest: Further Evidence Linking Animal Mutilations and Human Abductions to Alien Life Forms*. LMH Productions.

Hunt, S.J. (2012). *Bond of Secrecy: My Life with CIA Spy and Watergate Conspirator E. Howard Hunt.* Trine Day.

Icke, D. (1999). *The Biggest Secret.* Bertelsmann Industry Services, Inc.

Icke, D. "Arizona Wilder and the Shapeshifting Reptilians." [Video]. YouTube. https://duckduckgo.com/?q=arizona+wilder+and+the+shapeshifting+reptilians&va=z&t=hc&iax=videos&ia=videos&iai=https%3A%2F%2Fwww.youtube.com%2Fwatch%3Fv%3DU3LepJjegko

Jacobs, D. (1992). *Secret Life: Firsthand, Documented Accounts of UFO Abductions*. Atria Books.

Jacobs, D. (1998). *The Threat: Revealing the Secret Alien Agenda.* Simon & Schuster.

Jacobs, D. (2015) *Walking Among Us: The Alien Plan to Control Humanity*. MP3-CD.

Janney, P. (2012). *Mary's Mosaic: The CIA Conspiracy to Murder John F. Kennedy, Mary Pinchot Meyer, and Their Vision for World Peace.* Skyhorse Publishing.

Kasten, L. (2013). *Secret Journey to Planet Serpo: A True Story of Interplanetary Travel*. Bear & Co.

Kasten, L. "Secret Journey to Planet Serpo. Beyond 50 Radio. [Video]. YouTube. https://www.beyond50radio.com/Article-Secret_Journey_To_Planet_Serpo.html

Keller, R.A. (2016). *Venus Rising: A Concise History of the Second Planet.* Headline Books, Inc.

Keller, R.A. (2018). *The Final Countdown: Rockets to Venus: Book II of the Venus Rising Trilogy; A Concise History of the Second Planet.* Headline Books, Inc.

Keller, R.A. (2018). *Cosmic Ray's Excellent Venus Adventure: Book III of the Venus Rising Trilogy: A Concise History of the Second Planet.* Headline Books, Inc.

Kenyon, T. & Sion, J. (2013). *The Arcturian Anthology.* Orb Publishing.

Kitch, S. (2009). *The Specter of Sex: Gendered Foundations of Racial Formations in the United States.* SUNY Press.

Klotz, J. & Sala, R. (2005). *Faded Giant.* BookSurge Publishing.

Lamb, B. (2015). *Meet the Hybrids: The Lives and Missions of ET Ambassadors on Earth.* CreateSpace Independent Publishing Platform.

Lovelace, T. (2018). *Incident at Devils Den: A True Story.*

Mack, J. (1994). *Abduction: Human Encounters with Aliens*. New York, NY: Scribner's Sons.

Mack, J. (2002). *Passport to the Cosmos: Human Transformation and Alien Encounters*. Crown Publications.

MacLaine, S. (1986). *Out on a Limb.* Bantam.

Majestic 12 Group "Special Operations Manual SOM1-01 – Extraterrestrial Entities and Technology, Recovery and Disposal," April, 1954 Part 2.

Murphy, Col. John G. (1949, May–June). "Activities of The Ninth Army AAA – L.A.
'Attacked'" (PDF). *Antiaircraft Journal, the United States Coast Artillery Association*. **LXXXII** (3): 5. Retrieved 3 March 2016.

Newton, M. (2004). *Life Between Lives: Hypnotherapy for Spiritual Regression.* Llewellyn Publications.

O'Brien, B.J. & O'Brien, C. (2001). *The Shining Ones: An Account of the Development of Early Civilizations Through the Direct Assistance of Powers Incarnated on Earth.* Patrick Foundation Golden Age Project: UK. Dianthus Publishing Limited.

O'Brien, C. & Phillips, M. (2005). *TRANCE Formation of America: True life story of a mind control slave.* Revised Edition. Reality Marketing, Inc.

"Operation Cattle Mutilation," section 4, FBI report on cattle mutilations.

Priest, K., & Royal, L. (2011). *The Prism of Lyra: An Exploration of Human Galactic Heritage.* Light Technology Publishing, LLC.

Ryan, J. (2014). *The Missing Pill: The Rise of Energy Based Healing & Conscious Bio-spiritual Transformation.*

Ryan, J. (2018). *Unity Field Healing.*

Salas, R. "Zeuge #9. Captain Robert Salas US-Luftwaffe." [Video]. YouTube. *The Disclosure Project.* https://www.youtube.com/watch?v=OaeIO5aEEWI&feature=youtu.be

Salla, M. (2004). *Exopolitics: Political Implications of Extraterrestrial Presence.* Dandelion Books.

Salla, M. "Eisenhower's 1954 Meeting with Extraterrestrials: The 50th Anniversary of Contact?" Research Study #8. February 12, 2004. www.exopolitics.org.

Salla, M. (2013). *Kennedy's Last Stand: Eisenhower, UFOs, MJ-12 & JFK's Assassination.* Exopolitics Institute.

Salla, M. (2015). *Insiders Reveal Secret Space Programs and Extraterrestrial Alliances.* Exopolitics Institute.

Salla, M. (2016, December 19). "Charles Hall, the Tall Whites, and Richard Boylan."

https://www.exopolitics.org/charles-hall-the-tall-whites-and-richard-boylan/

Salla, M. (2017). *The US Navy's Secret Space Program and Nordic Extraterrestrial Alliance. (Secret Space Programs Book 2).* Exopolitics Consultants.

Salla, M. (2018). *Antarctica's Hidden History: Corporate Foundations of Secret Space Programs.* Exopolitics Consultants.

Salla, M. (2018, March 1). "Human Cloning About to Be Unleashed Upon the World." Exopolitics.org. https://exopolitics.org/human-cloning-about-to-be-unleashed-upon-the-world/

Salla, M. (2019). *US Air Force Secret Space Program: Shifting Extraterrestrial Alliances & Space Force.* Exopolitics Consultants.

Salla, M. (2018, October 4.) "Dr. Michael Salla- Exopolitics and Extraterrestrial Life Civilizations." Conscious Spirit Media. [Video]. YouTube. https://www.youtube.com/watch?v=TYTR6gatZZE.

Salla, M. (2020). *Rise of the Red Dragon: Origins and threat of China's secret space program*. Exopolitics Consultants.

Sepehr, R. (2015). *Occult Secrets of Vril*. Atlantean Gardens.

Sitchin, Z. (1976). *The Twelfth Planet: Book 1 of Earth Chronicles.* Harper, reprint edition 2007.

Sitchin, Z. (1985). *The Wars of Gods and Men: Book III of the Earth Chronicles*. Harper.

Sitchin, Z. (2002). *The Lost Book of Enki: Memoirs and Prophecies of an Extraterrestrial God.* Bear & Co.

Sphere Being Alliance Episode 83 Journey to Truth. [Video]. YouTube. https://www.youtube.com/watch?v=DK7SQA6vJrs&feature=youtu.be (clone topic from 1:19:25 to 1:21:50).

Sprinkle, L. (1999.) *Soul Samples: Personal Explorations in Reincarnation and UFO Experiences.* Granite Publishing.

Stone, B. (2012). *Transforming Fear into Gold: How Facing What Frightens You the Most Can Heal and Light Up Your Heart.* The Indigo Connection.

Stone, B. (2015). "Swimming with Humpback Whales 2015." [Video]. YouTube. https://www.youtube.com/watch?v=2DgLy2bWoOM&feature=youtu.be

Stranges, F.E. and Thor, V. (2001). *The Stranger at the Pentagon.* CreateSpace Publishing.

Stranges, F. "About Commander Valiant Thor (Part 1)." http://www.nextagemission.com/OSF/ST_AboutValiantThor1.html

Stranges, F. "About Commander Valiant Thor (Part 2)." http://www.nextagemission.com/OSF/ST_AboutValiantThor2.html

Strassman, R. (2000). *DMT: The Spirit Molecule: A Doctor's Revolutionary Research into the Biology of Near-Death and Mystical Experiences.* Park Street Press.

Tellinger, M. (2005). *Slave Species of god: Story of humankind from the cradle of humankind.* Music Masters Close Corporation.

Tellinger, M. (2009). *African Temples of the Anunnaki: The Lost Technologies of the Gold Mines of Enki*. Bear & Co.

"The Echo and Oscar Flight Incidents: UFOs Disabled American ICBMs." (2012, November 11). UFOs & Nukes website: https://www.ufohastings.com/articles/the-echo-and-oscar-flight-incidents

Tompkins, W. M. (2015). *Selected by Extraterrestrials: My life in the top-secret world of UFOs, Think Tanks, and Nordic secretaries. Volume 1.* Create Space Public Publishing Platform.

Tompkins, W. M. (2020). *Selected by Extraterrestrials: My life in the top-secret world of UFOs, Think Tanks, and Nordic secretaries, Volume 2.* Kindle Direct Publishing.

Watson, P. (2014, August 28). "The Cetacean Brain and Hominid Perceptions of Cetacean Intelligence." https://knowledgeutopia.

Wolf, M. (1996). *The Catchers of Heaven: A Trilogy*. Dorrance Publishing Co.

Wolfe, D. (2012). *The Last Days of Marilyn Monroe.* William Morrow Paperback.

About the Author

Dr. Barbara Stone is a spiritual coach and mentor, teacher, and author. Her passion is finding and resolving the spiritual disturbances behind mental and emotional problems. She developed Soul Detective Protocols to guide healing professionals to be able to work in these invisible spiritual realms safely and effectively, using win-win solutions.

Website: www.SoulDetective.net

Dr. Stone is an international teacher of Soul Detective Work and holds a Doctorate in Clinical Psychology from Pacifica Graduate Institute in Carpinteria, California.

She loves gardening, swimming, boating, and her family! She lives in central Ohio with her husband Robert Alcorn, MD, author of *Healing Stories: My Journey from Mainstream Psychiatry Toward Spiritual Healing* (2011).